Masters of Deception

The Rise of the Council on Foreign Relations

By G. Vance Smith
and Tom Gow

The people never give up their liberties but under some delusion.
— Edmund Burke (1784)

Freedom First Society
Colorado Springs, Colorado

Published by
Freedom First Society
P.O. Box 15099
Colorado Springs, CO 80935
(888) 347-7809
www.freedomfirstsociety.org

Printed in the United States of America

Library of Congress Control Number:
2012931216

ISBN 978-0-9816161-1-7

Dedicated to

Wayne Rickert, Tom & Nancy Dunn
Walt Ruckel, Keith Van Buskirk
W. Rusty Barlow, Don & Jean Fotheringham
Roger & Ann Vergo, and Lloyd Ward

In recognition of their devotion to correct principles, the cause
of freedom, and Freedom First Society.

Contents

IV: Controlling the People

V: The Executive Branch in the 21st Century

Acknowledgments

This exposé updates and summarizes the work of many others.

In particular, we wish to recognize the trailblazing work of the late former FBI agent Dan Smoot — his classic 1962 book, *The Invisible Government*, and his *Dan Smoot Report*.

However, much more of our story rests on the pioneering achievements of the research and journalistic team that the late Robert Welch assembled over 55 years ago to oppose the forces described herein.

That team kept its eyes focused on exposing the Conspiracy for more than 45 years. The body of its published material, supported by a strong culture of responsible and careful research, has been invaluable in developing this summary. Unfortunately, many traps await readers and careless authors seeking the truth in published news, history, and analysis.

Robert Welch took a huge step further than anyone else. He founded, and personally led for more than 25 years, an organization whose ambitious mission was to change the course of history. In particular, his organization was designed to inform and mobilize a segment of the American people to challenge the grip of a conspiracy on government and our opinion-forming institutions.

Among the many individuals Mr. Welch's organization woke up was the late Gary Allen. In 1972, Gary Allen published his blockbuster *None Dare Call It Conspiracy*, a superbly readable handbook on the Conspiracy. Thanks largely to distribution by Mr. Welch's organization, Allen's pocket exposé exceeded 5 million copies in print and had significant impact.

Gary Allen also wrote numerous articles for Robert Welch's magazine *American Opinion*. Many of Allen's groundbreaking articles were consulted in preparing this update.

Another tremendous contribution, visited frequently by your authors, was *Shadows of Power: The Council on Foreign Relations and the American Decline* by James Perloff. Perloff's unique 1988 exposé had nowhere near the circulation of Allen's earlier work. But it documented, from extensive research of Establishment sources and Council publications, the underreported impact of the internationalist Establishment of the United States on the tragic history of the previous century.

Introduction

Today, many Americans, having previously regarded the American dream as their birthright, are shocked to discover that the dream may be dying.

Many of these same Americans also recognize that much of what's wrong in our nation is coming from the federal government — all three branches. They recall the promises of political leader after political leader, from both major parties, to put America back on track. And they realize that, despite these promises, our nation's problems — economic, social, and political — have steadily become worse.

Most responsible Americans, however, are frustrated because they have no clear understanding of how America got into trouble, and therefore they have no realistic idea of what to do about it.

One of the earliest explanations to really hit the mark appeared in a groundbreaking 1962 book, *The Invisible Government*, authored by the late Dan Smoot.[1] Dan Smoot was a courageous former FBI agent, who undoubtedly became the first outsider to raise widespread alarm over the influence of a then little known organization — the Council on Foreign Relations. In addition to writing *The Invisible Government*, Smoot carried his warnings to an American audience via the *Dan Smoot Report* — a syndicated 15-minute weekly television broadcast (also a newsletter).

But Smoot was ahead of his time, and times were good. Too few Americans took his warning of well entrenched subversion seriously. Yet with the passing of almost half a century, the damage to our system from the invisible government Smoot described has neared the breaking point.

In the intervening years, several researcher-authors tried to carry the story to the American public (Robert Welch went so far as to build an organization to do so). Some of those sounding the alarm, such as Admiral Chester Ward (see Chapter 1) and former U.S. Ambassador and Assistant Secretary of State Spruille Braden, could even speak from first-hand inside experience. Yet again, too few Americans heard the evidence directly, and fewer still were willing to give the message serious attention and do what was necessary to stop the subversion.

Today, however, as our nation's health visibly evaporates, a great number of concerned Americans are willing to seek answers outside of television news and network documentaries. Our plan with this book is to bring the story of America's "missteps" up to date and show concerned Americans what must be done to avert disaster.

Our Message, in Short

In the pages that follow, we expect to demonstrate that most of America's serious woes stem from the designs of a very influential, very powerful Conspiracy. That Conspiracy has a grip on our government and many of our opinion-forming institutions. Indeed, the evidence supporting such a conclusion is overwhelming, although the Conspiracy's allies in the media manage to keep the evidence off the public's radar screen.

The Council on Foreign Relations (CFR) is a creation of this Conspiracy, but not it's heart. The CFR is simply the Conspiracy's most influential and useful "front group" in the United States. By virtue of its semi-public nature, its function, and the prominence of its members, the CFR offers an especially convenient window into the operations of the Conspiracy it represents.

For several decades, the CFR managed to keep a very low profile. However, following strong criticism in the sixties and seventies, the CFR adopted a more public image. The CFR often characterizes itself as merely a foreign policy study group, taking no official positions. But this effort to downplay its influence and agenda is misleading, as even many of its admirers admit.

A surprising October 30, 1993 column in the *Washington Post* entitled "Ruling Class Journalists" described the CFR as "the nearest thing we have to a ruling establishment in the United States." The column was authored by former *Post* ombudsman and deputy managing editor Richard Harwood.

Harwood identified the CFR members in top positions in the news publishing world — at the *New York Times*, the *Wall Street Journal*, *Time* magazine, and major daily newspapers, including the *Post* itself — and in network television news. Harwood claimed that these individuals "do not merely analyze and interpret foreign policy for the United States, they help make it."

Harwood also pointed to the CFR's influence in government, listing the prominent CFR members in the Clinton administration:

The president is a member. So is his secretary of state, the deputy secretary of state, all five of the undersecretaries, several of the assistant secretaries and the department's legal adviser. The president's national security adviser and his deputy are members. The director of Central Intelligence (like all previous directors) and the chairman of the Foreign Intelligence Advisory Board are members. The secretary of defense, three undersecretaries and at least four assistant secretaries are members. The secretaries of the departments of housing and urban development, interior, health and human services and the chief White House public relations man ... along with the speaker of the House [are members]....

According to the CFR's 1994 *Annual Report*, 463 of its members were serving as U.S. government officials.

The "Conspiracy" Claim

We have used the term "Conspiracy" several times, and we need to clarify what we mean and equally what we *do not* mean. A variety of evidence confirms the existence of a powerful Conspiracy, similar to many conspiracies throughout history. The modern version differs primarily in that it is much better organized and planned, based on long revolutionary experience. Our view of this group fits the dictionary definition of conspiracy — a secret plan among more than one to carry out an arguably evil end.

Any effective conspiracy must keep its designs secret or at least not allow the public at large to view them undisguised. This necessarily dictates that the innermost circle of the conspiracy be kept small. Outside this inner circle, many others may serve its designs, knowingly or unknowingly, for a variety of motivations. The most powerful means the present Master Conspiracy has for enlisting others in its cause is its ability to provide ladders (career, social, and financial) to the ambitious.

Those who wish to keep the public unaware of the massive evidence for a conspiracy have adopted a number of tactics. A primary tactic is to pretend as though no hard evidence exists — dismissing alarmists as simply unschooled minds embracing a simplistic explanation and speculative "theory" for complex events.

Another tactic seeks to make the conspiracy claim sound ridiculous through exaggeration and distortion or by highlighting the wild charges of "convenient" strawmen. Contrary to such spins, the Conspiracy is not a large, pervasive, disciplined army.

As with any front group, the CFR is designed to influence and *capture the influence* of those members outside the controlling inner core. Indeed, some of its members may not embrace or even be aware of all its subversive designs. Dan Smoot put it this way in *The Invisible Government*:

> I don't mean to imply that all of these people are controlled by the Council on Foreign Relations, or that they uniformly support the total program of international socialism which the Council wants. The Council does not *own* its members, it just has varying degrees of influence on each. [2]

However, the CFR does have an inner core of leaders. Moreover, those of its members *recommended* by CFR leaders for government positions have presumably shown themselves willing to carry the CFR ball.

How about the general membership? Although its members are not under organizational discipline, it is well to remember that membership is by invitation only. This would suggest that *most* members have a strong affiliation with the organization's agenda.

As a front group for the internationalist Establishment, the CFR serves a conspiratorial purpose. Even though many of the CFR's operations are conducted in public view, membership cannot be likened to mere information gathering by professional foreign policy elites.

Another tactic used to hide the evidence is to enforce an unwritten code for "respectable" public debate. Those Establishment forces that dominate the major media have been very successful in intimidating any who might consider speaking out of school. According to the code, it is "politically correct" to talk about ideological differences and sincere differences of opinion, but not to expose organized deception or hidden agendas.

In short, it is okay to discuss fires, building codes, and fire prevention, but those who would expose arson are to be, in the words of Nikita Khrushchev "subjected to the torments of hell." Today's politicians are well aware of how the late Senator Joseph McCarthy has been continuously vilified, and they get the message — don't go there, unless you wish to commit political suicide.

One Who Spoke Out

The purpose of this introduction is not to build a case for these claims. However, to give them some credibility, we point to remarks by the late Senator William Jenner from Indiana. Jenner was senate majority leader (1939–1941) at one point in his career. But what gave him particular authority to warn of organized subversion was his position in the early fifties as chairman of the Senate Internal Security Subcommittee.

The Senate Internal Security Subcommittee (killed by the Left in 1977) had been investigating subversive influences (most notably Soviet-allied Communist) that had gained a foothold in our government and political system, particularly while we were allies of the Soviets during World War II. On February 23, 1954, Senator Jenner addressed the Senate with a warning:

> Today the path to total dictatorship in the United States can be laid by strictly legal means, unseen and unheard by the Congress, the President, or the people.... Outwardly we have a Constitutional government. We have operating *within* our government and political system, *another* body representing another form of government, a bureaucratic elite which believes our Constitution is outmoded and is sure that it is the winning side.... All the strange developments in foreign policy agreements may be traced to this group who are going to make us over to suit their pleasure.... This political action group has its own local political support organizations, its own pressure groups, its own vested interests, its foothold within our government, and its own propaganda apparatus. [3]

The Council on Foreign Relations is not the only front group serving this Conspiracy. But it is arguably the most important. Indeed, the CFR sits at the hub of a network of organizations and powerful tax-exempt foundations supporting the same agenda. We will point to other members of the team as our story unfolds.

Our aim with this book is to show that the influence of the CFR is a deadly force working to destroy a free and independent United States. The CFR (and the Conspiracy it represents) must be exposed and its influence routed to prevent it from achieving that objective.

Those who earnestly want to be part of a realistic solution should know that the authors are also providing essential organizational leadership, following in the footsteps of Robert Welch.

Organization of Book

We present our story in loose chronological order. The first five chapters (**Part I**) introduce the CFR and take its development up through the Great Depression, World War II, and the founding of the United Nations.

The subsequent three Chapters (**Part II**) examine the major pretexts and deceptions used to expand post-World War II "international" authority on the path to world government.

Chapters 9, 10, and 11 (**Part III**) document CFR dominance in the post-war presidential administrations of the Twentieth Century (Truman to Clinton) and what that dominance achieved or sought to achieve.

Chapters 12 and 13 (**Part IV**) interrupt the presidential administration thread to examine Establishment dominance of opinion-forming institutions (such as the media and education), Establishment support for ostensibly anti-Establishment revolutionary organizations, and their reinforcing strategies.

Chapters 14 and 15 (**Part V**) conclude the executive branch story with the CFR dominance of the GOP (George W. Bush) and Democratic (Barak Obama) administrations in the 21st Century.

And finally, Chapter 16, **"What Can and *Must* Be Done!,"** summarizes the threat, projects the lines, and, most importantly, explains what responsible, freedom-loving Americans must do to change our nation's course — while there's still time.

Part I

The World Gets the United Nations

Chapter 1

The CFR's War *on* U.S. Independence

In the wake of World War I, Insiders closely associated with the international banking firm of J.P. Morgan sought to entangle the U.S. in the newly formed League of Nations. The League had been created largely through their influence in the Wilson White House.

But their plans suffered an unexpected setback. The U.S. Senate wisely refused to approve America's involvement in their scheme. And without America's participation, their infant League was doomed to irrelevance. It could never grow to adulthood and become a true world authority.

However, the internationalists did not give up on their objective. They regrouped and launched long-term plans to prepare America to give up her sovereignty in stages to a future world body.

In short, they sought to build "a new world order," in which a central authority, controlled by them from behind the scenes, would dominate all nations. A cornerstone of those plans was the creation of the Council on Foreign Relations. (For more on the events leading up to the Council's formation, see Chapters 2 & 3.)

Of course, the Council does not acknowledge that subversive purpose. Instead, it portrays itself as a public-spirited study group examining a variety of foreign policy options but taking no official positions. However, the circumstances of its formation alone (as described in the next two chapters) put the lie to that image.

The CFR's track record of promoting internationalism provides even stronger evidence of its subversive purpose. Indeed, the Council's war on the sovereignty of independent nations now spans close to a century.

Council Publications Reveal Attitude

Despite the CFR's repeated claim of taking no official position, from time to time Council publications have openly championed its true agenda (undoubtedly relying on the likelihood that no one with wide access to the public would connect the dots). For example, the second issue (December 1922) of the CFR's journal *Foreign Affairs* insisted:

> Obviously there is going to be no peace or prosperity for mankind so long as it remains divided into fifty or sixty independent states.... Equally obviously there is going to be no steady progress in civilization or self-government among the more backward peoples until some kind of international system is created which will put an end to the diplomatic struggles incident to the attempt of every nation to make itself secure.... The real problem today is that of world government.[1]

In 1944, another Council publication, "American Public Opinion and Postwar Security Commitments," asserted:

> The sovereignty fetish is still so strong in the public mind, that there would appear to be little chance of winning popular assent to American membership in anything approaching a super-state organization. Much will depend on the kind of approach which is used in further popular education.[2]

Three decades later, *Foreign Affairs* published a strategy of gradual international entanglements as a workable means for bringing nations to submit to a world authority. "The Hard Road to World Order," authored by Columbia University professor and State Department veteran Richard N. Gardner, spelled out a multi-point strategy of deceptive encroachment. In that April 1974 article, Gardner blatantly insisted:

> In short, the "house of world order" will have to be built from the bottom up rather than from the top down. It will look like a great "booming, buzzing confusion," to use William James' famous description of reality, but an end run around national sovereignty, eroding it piece by piece, will accomplish much more than the old-fashioned frontal assault.

Articles in *Foreign Affairs* would often foretell events years in advance and help form the attitudes and arguments of the

Establishment media toward those events. *Time* magazine once referred to *Foreign Affairs* as "the most influential periodical in print." This was certainly not because *Foreign Affairs* was widely read by the general public, but because it could count among its loyal readers those involved in formulating foreign policy and many of those in the media who "analyze" foreign policy for the public.

The CFR's Men of Affairs

However, the Council's war on national sovereignty has extended far beyond articles in obscure journals. Much more significant in this war are the members it recruits, influences, and helps to promote into leadership positions, particularly in government.

Joseph Kraft, in the July 1958 issue of *Harper's*, described the Council as a "School for Statesmen." [3] *The Christian Science Monitor* (September 1, 1961) noted that "there is a constant flow of its members from private life to public service. Almost half of the council members have been invited to assume official government positions or to act as consultants at one time-or another." [4] Indeed, Professor Richard Gardner (above) would be tapped to serve in the administration of President Clinton (CFR) as ambassador to Spain.

This was not always so. As we shall see, the ability of the Council to place its trusted members in government grew enormously with the outbreak of World War II. Indeed, Anthony Lukas, writing about the Council in the *New York Times* magazine for November 21, 1971, observed:

> When Henry Stimson — the group's quintessential member — went to Washington in 1940 as Secretary of War, he took with him John McCloy, who was to become Assistant Secretary in charge of personnel. McCloy has recalled: "Whenever we needed a man we thumbed through the roll of the Council members and put through a call to New York."
>
> And over the years, the men McCloy called in turn called other Council members. [5]

"Chairman of the American Establishment"

During the span of five decades, the Council's John J. McCloy would play a major role in shaping world history toward internationalist goals, earning the unofficial title of "chairman of the American Establishment." After the war, McCloy moved from assistant secretary of war to head up the UN's World Bank. Two years later he served as U.S. High Commissioner for Germany, boosting the movement for European merger with Marshall Aid funds.

In 1950, McCloy became chairman of the board of the Council on Foreign Relations, a post he held until 1973. In addition, he would head up the Chase National Bank and later the CFR-interlocked Ford Foundation. Writing in *Harper's*, Alan Brinkley observed that, as CFR chairman, McCloy "was able not only to organize members of his own generation to influence policy, but to help determine which members of the next generation would rise to prominence." [6] In 1956, McCloy decided to boost the career of a little known Harvard professor named Henry Kissinger. [7]

Eight presidents would seek out McCloy for advice. The final agreement ending the 1962 Cuban Missile Crisis was worked out in McCloy's Connecticut home, where he hosted Soviet Deputy Foreign Minister Vasily Kuznetsov. A year earlier, McCloy was photographed swimming with Nikita Khrushchev at Khrushchev's dacha on the Black Sea.

Anti-Sovereignty Influence

One CFR member who refused to embrace the CFR objectives was Admiral Chester Ward. Ward had accepted an invitation to join the CFR in 1959, when he was judge advocate general of the U.S. Navy. 16 years later, while still a member, Admiral Ward denounced the CFR for "promoting disarmament and submergence of U.S. sovereignty and national independence into an all-powerful one-world government...." [8]

Admiral Ward further charged that "this lust to surrender the sovereignty and independence of the United States is pervasive throughout most of the membership.... The majority visualize the utopian submergence of the United States as a subsidiary administrative unit of a global government...." [9]

Ward also clarified the CFR's role as an organization:

[The] vast influence attributed to CFR is *not exercised* through

or by the Council on Foreign Relations as an organization....
CFR, *as such*, does not write the platforms of both political
parties or select their respective presidential candidates, or
control U.S. defense and foreign policies. But CFR members, as
individuals, acting in concert with other individual CFR
members, do. [10]

Consider the career of Strobe Talbott. Talbott and future president
Bill Clinton were fellow Rhodes Scholars and roommates at Oxford.
Both would later be invited to join the CFR and the closely affiliated
Trilateral Commission (TC) (created much later, see the Carter
administration in Chapter 10). (Note: The Rhodes Scholar program
serves the same Insider objectives as the CFR and has related
origins.)

In the early 1990s, Talbot was an editor-at-large for *Time*
magazine. In its July 20, 1992 issue, Talbot authored a propaganda
piece, "America Abroad: The Birth of the Global Nation," in which
he asserted that "it has taken the events in our own wondrous and
terrible century to clinch the case for world government."

In recognition for this "leadership," the World Federalist
Association (WFA) presented Talbott with its Norman Cousins
Global Governance Award. President Clinton (CFR, TC) wrote the
WFA a letter of approval, which was read at the award ceremony by
WFA President John Anderson (CFR, TC). Incredibly, the
President's letter acknowledged approvingly that "Norman Cousins
[had] worked for world peace and *world government*." [Emphasis
ours.]

The following year (1994), President Clinton would bring Talbott
into his administration as deputy secretary of state. More recently,
Talbott has served as a "foreign policy analyst" associated with Yale
University and the CFR-interlocked Brookings Institution.

Admiral Ward also explained how the CFR leadership core
supported its representatives in government:

> Once the ruling members of CFR have decided that the U.S.
> Government should adopt a particular policy, the very
> substantial research facilities of CFR are put to work to develop
> arguments, intellectual and emotional, to support the new policy,

and to confound and discredit, intellectually and politically, any opposition. The most articulate theoreticians and ideologists prepare related articles, aided by the research, to sell the new policy and to make it appear inevitable and irresistible.... If a certain proposition is repeated often enough in [*Foreign Affairs*], then the U.S. Administration in power — be it Republican or Democratic — begins to *act as if* that proposition or assumption were an established fact. [11]

Deception Is Routine

Those supporting the sovereignty surrender regularly disguise their objective to minimize public resistance. One thinly disguised admission of the deception appeared in a "Special Davos Edition" of the international edition of *Newsweek* (edited at the time by CFR-member Fareed Zakaria). The Special Edition was intended for the movers and shakers attending an annual meeting of the World Economic Forum in Davos, Switzerland (2001–2002). In that special issue, Michael Hirsh (CFR) expressed pride in the internationalists' track record of deception:

[T]he internationalists were always hard at work in quiet places making plans for a more perfect global community. In the end the internationalists have always dominated national policy. Even so, they haven't bragged about their globe-building for fear of reawakening the other half of the American psyche, our berserker nativism. And so they have always done it in the most out-of-the-way places and with little ado. [12]

Mr. Hirsh then provided examples, beginning with a December 1917 secret meeting in New York of the Inquiry (see Chapters 3 and 13) — "a group of eager reformers who included a young Walter Lippmann," which drew up President Wilson's Fourteen Points, (the last of which was the proposal for a League of Nations). Hirsh's examples continued up through 1945, when the "United Nations came to life at a secluded Georgetown estate of Dumbarton Oaks.... So what emerged took us more or less by surprise. We had built a global order without quite realizing it, bit by bit, era by era...."

Although quite an admission, Hirsh's statement also contains its share of deception. The idea that the internationalists didn't realize what they were building is certainly poppycock. And the implication that the American people should take ownership of the subversion practiced by some of their leaders is nothing short of audacious. (We will comment shortly regarding the suggestion that the internationalists are generously serving the general interest and have to deceive us for our own good.)

An even more forthright and authoritative admission of the deception can be found in a speech delivered to fellow internationalists meeting in Copenhagen in 1931. In that speech, British historian Arnold J. Toynbee stated:

> I will merely repeat that we are at present working, discreetly but with all our might, to wrest this mysterious political force called sovereignty out of the clutches of the local national states of our world. And all the time we are denying with our lips what we are doing with our hands.... [13]

Although not so well known in this country, Arnold Toynbee was a prominent "historian" of the last century and propagandist for world government. From 1925 until 1955 he served as director of studies at the Royal Institute for International Affairs, a sister organization of the Council on Foreign Relations. In fact, Toynbee was at the conference in Versailles (see Chapter 3) at which both organizations were conceived, and for several decades was involved with many other international conferences. He knows whereof he speaks.

The above Toynbee statement was no passing comment. In discussing the trend in international affairs, he elaborated: "If we are frank with ourselves we shall admit that we are engaged on a deliberate and sustained and concentrated effort to impose limitations upon the sovereignty and independence of the fifty or sixty local sovereign independent States which at present partition the habitable surface of the earth and divide the political allegiance of mankind."

While being frank with his fellow internationalists, he emphasized the need to deceive the general public:

It is just because we are really attacking the principle of local sovereignty that we keep on protesting our loyalty to it so loudly. The harder we press our attack upon the idol, the more pains we take to keep its priests and devotees in a fool's paradise — lapped in a false sense of security which will inhibit them from taking up arms in their idol's defense. [14]

Understandably, the internationalists are not so frank when propagandizing the public in the mass media. For example, they often disguise their advocacy by implying that the trends are natural and inevitable. In more targeted publications, they communicate their world government schemes in high sounding terms so as not to alarm outsiders who might stumble across their words.

For Our Own Good?
The determination of the internationalists to deceive the world to achieve their aims reveals their character. And it provides a stark warning of what to expect should they ever attain *unrestrained* power over the planet.

Another window into their character is the track record of the CFR elites during the previous century in supporting totalitarian states. As we shall show in Chapter 3, the Insiders of the intended new world order actually nurtured and sustained the Communist menace.

During the 20th Century, Insider-supported totalitarian states carried out crimes against humanity that defy description. University of Hawaii Professor R.J. Rummel devoted most of a decade to researching the genocide and mass murder perpetrated by these regimes. Rummel defined a new term, "democide," as the systematic murder of human beings by governments:

In total, during the first eighty-eight years of this [20th] century, almost 170 million men, women, and children have been shot, beaten, tortured, knifed, burned, starved, frozen, crushed, or worked to death; buried alive, drowned, hung, bombed, or killed in any other of the myriad ways governments have inflicted death on unarmed, helpless citizens and foreigners. The dead could conceivably be nearly 360 million people. [15]

10

There is no reason to expect the death toll to be any less from unrestrained *world* government. Remember that the orchestrators of the world-government drive insist we must merge with the perpetrators of these crimes in order to promote world peace. And they tell us not to worry about forfeiting constitutional protections against the abuse of power.

Another important discovery is that the totalitarian dictatorships of the previous century did not spring up independently. They were the offspring of the revolutions promoted by the Conspiracy as steppingstones to its world government. So it is the Conspiracy, not just its bad children, who really turned the 20th Century into the bloodiest in recorded history.

Chapter 2

The Great Federal Reserve Deception

To appreciate the destructive designs of the Council on Foreign Relations, it will be helpful to examine some prior deeds of the cabal that founded it.

An unusual source for much of this history was the late Carroll Quigley. Quigley earned his reputation as a professor of history at the Foreign Service School of Georgetown University (1941–1976). Among the many students Quigley influenced was a bright young Bill Clinton.

In 1992, Bill Clinton received the Democratic nomination for president at the party's convention in Madison Square Garden. In his televised acceptance speech, Clinton took time to pay homage to his professor: "As a teenager, I heard John Kennedy's summons to citizenship. And then, as a student, I heard that call clarified by a professor I had named Carroll Quigley...."

In 1966, Quigley published a monumental 1,348 page work entitled *Tragedy and Hope: A History of the World in Our Time*. A portion of *Tragedy and Hope* described the secret maneuvers of a network of international banking families seeking to control the finances and affairs of governments:

> There does exist, and has existed for a generation, an international Anglophile network.... I know of the operations of this network because I have studied it for twenty years and was permitted for two years, in the early 1960's, to examine its papers and secret records. I have no aversion to it or to most of its aims and have, for much of my life, been close to it and to many of its instruments. I have objected, both in the past and recently, to a few of its policies ... but in general my chief difference of opinion is that it wishes to remain unknown, and I believe its role in history is significant enough to be known. [1]

The core of the international network Quigley described was a secret society established in 1891 by Cecil Rhodes, the South

African diamond and gold mogul, whose legacy created the Rhodes Scholarships.

To launch his South African financial empire, Rhodes relied on early financial support from Lord Rothschild and Alfred Beit (a German financier and Rhodes partner).[2] Lord Rothschild represented one of several "international banking" dynasties. According to Quigley:

> The greatest of these dynasties, of course, were the descendants of Meyer Amschel Rothschild (1743–1812) of Frankfort, whose male descendants, for at least two generations, generally married first cousins or even nieces. Rothschild's five sons, established at branches in Vienna, London, Naples, and Paris, as well as Frankfort, cooperated together in ways which other international banking dynasties copied but rarely excelled.[3]

Quigley goes on to describe the function of a special class of bankers:

> The names of some of these banking families are familiar to all of us and should be more so. They include Baring, Lazard, Erlanger, Warburg, Schröder, Seligman, the Speyers, Mirabaud, Mallet, Fould, and above all Rothschild and Morgan.... [T]hey remained different from ordinary bankers in distinctive ways: (1) they were cosmopolitan and international; (2) they were close to governments and were particularly concerned with questions of government debts, including foreign government debts.... These bankers came to be called "international bankers"....[4]

For centuries, the international bankers prospered by financing governments and encouraging government debt. Moreover, they recognized that nothing drives a nation into debt like war. The most unscrupulous were known to finance both sides of terribly tragic conflicts, as with our own Civil War: The Rothschilds financed the North through their American agent August Belmont, and the Erlangers, Rothschild relatives, financed the American South.[5]

As collateral for their loans, the international bankers would insist on a voice in government. The most sought after privilege from government was the grant of a monopoly over the issuance of the nation's money and credit, i.e., control of a national central bank. Profits were not the only goal of such a monopoly; even more important was control.

In January 1924, Reginald Mckenna, former Chancellor of the Exchequer, admitted the power of the Bank of England: "I am afraid the ordinary citizen will not like to be told that the banks can, and do, create money.... And they who control the credit of the nation direct the policy of Governments and hold in the hollow of their hands the destiny of the people." [6]

According to Quigley:

> In addition to [restoring the pre-World War I financial system], the powers of financial capitalism had another far-reaching aim, nothing less than to create a world system of financial control in private hands able to dominate the political system of each country and the economy of the world as a whole. The system was to be controlled in a feudalist fashion by the central banks of the world acting in concert, by secret agreements arrived at in frequent private meetings and conferences. [7]

Could the international bankers achieve such control in America? They could and did — long ago. In a 1968 newsletter to constituents, Congressman Wright Patman of Texas, chairman of the House Committee on Banking and Currency (1965–1975) wrote:

> In the United States today we have in effect two governments.... We have the duly constituted Government.... Then we have an independent, uncontrolled and uncoordinated government in the Federal Reserve System, operating the money powers which are reserved to Congress by the Constitution. [8]

Central Banking in America

As far back as the earliest days of our Republic, the Founding Fathers were aware of forces seeking to control our nation by controlling its money. In a letter to John Adams, Thomas Jefferson wrote: "I sincerely believe, with you, that banking establishments are more dangerous than standing armies...." [9]

Law records show that the Rothschilds were powers in the (Second) Bank of the United States, which was abolished by President Andrew Jackson in 1836. [10]

At the beginning of the Twentieth Century, the top agent of the English Rothschilds in America was John Pierpont Morgan. J. P. Morgan was American born, but his education included a private school in Switzerland and over a year at the University of Goettingen in Germany. [11] J. P. took control of the family's banking business in 1879 when his father, Junius, retired.

By the early 1900s, under Morgan's aggressive leadership, J. P. Morgan & Company had become the most powerful investment-banking firm in America, surpassing even the power of the Rothschilds in Europe. (In the next chapter, we will see the Council on Foreign Relations formed as a front for "J.P. Morgan and Company in association with the very small American Round Table Group." [12])

In those years, the Morgans, Whitneys, and Rockefellers dominated the American Establishment. They were tied together through family as well as financial alliances, and J.P. Morgan was the ringleader of the combine. According to Quigley:

> At the center [of financial capitalism] were a group of less than a dozen investment banks, which were, at the height of their powers, still unincorporated private partnerships. These included J.P. Morgan; the Rockefeller family; Kuhn, Loeb & Company; Dillon, Read & Company; Brown Brothers and Harriman; and others....
>
> J.P. Morgan worked in close relationship to a group of banks and insurance companies.... The whole nexus dominated a network of business firms which included at least one-sixth of the two hundred largest nonfinancial corporations in American business. Among these were twelve utility companies, five or more railroad systems, thirteen industrial firms, and at least five of the fifty largest banks in the country. [13]

One reason why Morgan was so successful was that he had learned to control both sides of negotiations. Carroll Quigley cites one example of Morgan shrewdness: "To [J.P.] Morgan all political parties were simply organizations to be used, and the firm always was careful to keep a foot in all camps."

According to Quigley, one Morgan colleague allied with the Democrats, Morgan himself and other partners supported the Republicans, and still other Morgan associates had connections with the "extreme Right" and the Left. [14]

Despite Morgan's success, by the opening of the 20th Century, the big New York banks saw their dominance eroding as the nation's commerce expanded westward and the American economy became more competitive. In response, the New York monopolists would seek again to establish a central bank in the United States under their control.

Yet ever since President Andrew Jackson had called the Bank of the United States a conspiracy against the people, Americans were properly suspicious of central banking. So the international bankers adopted a clever deception to reintroduce their scheme.

They decided to inflame public opinion against the "Money Trust" and then propose a new banking cartel, the Federal Reserve System, ostensibly to protect the economy by regulating the big banks. In fact, however, the plan would do just the opposite, providing the "Money Trust" with enormous new power.

To create demand for legislation to bring banking under control, J. P. Morgan seized an opportunity in 1907 to precipitate a banking panic. (He also designed the panic to eliminate some of his competition.) And when he was ready, Morgan brought the panic to an end. Historian Frederick Lewis Allen explained: "The lesson of the Panic of 1907 was clear, though not for some six years was it destined to be embodied in legislation: the United States gravely needed a central banking system...." [15]

Paul Warburg

The leading figure in the drive to fasten a central bank on America was Paul Warburg.

Paul Warburg and his brother Felix had immigrated to the United States from Germany in 1902. A third brother, Max Warburg, stayed behind to run the family bank, M.N. Warburg & Company. The top banking families were tightly intertwined. Paul Warburg would become a partner in Kuhn, Loeb and Company and marry Nina

Loeb, daughter of Solomon Loeb. (Brother Felix married Jacob Schiff's daughter, Frieda.)

In addition to his role in establishing the Federal Reserve System, Paul Warburg would play a further part in our story as a member of "Colonel" E. M. House's "Inquiry" (see next chapter) and become a founding member of the Council on Foreign Relations.

In 1907, the year J.P. Morgan staged the panic, Paul Warburg began a full-time crusade for a central bank, writing and lecturing on behalf of "bank reform." Kuehn, Loeb, and Company paid Warburg a $500,000 per year salary while he championed "the public good." Joining Warburg in this crusade was Senator Nelson Aldrich of Rhode Island.

Senator Nelson Aldrich

Senator Aldrich was closely identified with the international bankers, even referred to by some as "[J.P.] Morgan's floor broker in the Senate."[16] Aldrich's daughter Abby would marry John D. Rockefeller Jr. and their son (Senator Aldrich's grandson) Nelson Aldrich Rockefeller would become governor of New York and vice president of the United States under Gerald Ford.

Another son, David, would become one of the world's most powerful bankers and chairman of the Council on Foreign Relations.

The year following the "Panic of 1907," Congress established the National Monetary Commission to study banking issues and make recommendations. Senator Nelson Aldrich maneuvered to get himself appointed chairman.

For almost two years, Aldrich, in his role as chairman, led a team on a tour of the capitals of Europe to "study" central banking in Europe. The Commission and its reports (tightly controlled by Aldrich) would provide the camouflage for an enormous deception and power grab by the international bankers.

Jekyll Island Hunt Club

Near the close of 1910, Aldrich and Warburg arranged with several other international bankers to hold a secret meeting at the Jekyll Island [Georgia] Hunt Club owned by J.P. Morgan. The purpose of the meeting was to formulate the plan that would be presented to

Congress as the final recommendations of the National Monetary Commission.

Among those Aldrich invited (in addition to Paul Warburg of Kuhn, Loeb) were Henry P. Davison of J.P. Morgan & Company; Benjamin Strong of Morgan's Bankers Trust, A. Piatt Andrew, assistant secretary of the Treasury; Charles D. Norton, president of J.P. Morgan's First National Bank of New York; and Frank A. Vanderlip, president of the Rockefeller-owned National City Bank.

In his memoirs, published decades later, Vanderlip revealed:

Despite my views about the value to society of greater publicity for the affairs of corporations, there was an occasion, near the close of 1910, when I was as secretive — indeed as furtive — as any conspirator.... I do not feel it is any exaggeration to speak of our secret expedition to Jekyll Island as the occasion of the actual conception of what eventually became the Federal Reserve System....[17]

We were instructed to come one at a time and as unobtrusively as possible to the railroad terminal on the N.J. littoral of the Hudson, where Sen. Aldrich's private car would be in readiness, attached to the rear end of a train for the South....

Once aboard the private car we began to observe the taboo that had been fixed on last names. We addressed one another as "Ben," "Paul," "Nelson," "Abe." Davison [Morgan's emissary] and I adopted even deeper disguises, abandoning our own first names. On the theory that we were always right, he became Wilbur and I became Orville, after those two aviation pioneers the Wright brothers.

The servants and the train crew may have known the identities of one or two of us, but they did not know all, and it was the names of all printed together that would have made our mysterious journey significant in Washington, in Wall Street, even in London. Discovery, we knew, simply must not happen, or else all our time and effort would be wasted.[18]

The prize these men were seeking was control over the monetary system of the United States and thereby the entire economy. And they could not afford to have the legislation they proposed identified as Wall Street's bill.

Paul Warburg astutely recognized that the term "central bank" must not be attached to their scheme. Instead, they designed a "regional reserve" system with four (later twelve) branches spread across the nation. Although the bankers intended for the New York branch to dominate the rest, the several branches provided useful camouflage disguising the essence of a central bank.

Warburg wanted the bill to be known as the "Federal Reserve System," but Aldrich insisted that a banking reform bill not bearing his name would arouse public suspicion. Unfortunately for the schemers, the Aldrich Bill was immediately recognized as a project of the international bankers.

Aldrich Bill Defeated

The most tenacious opponent of the machinations of the international bankers was Congressman Charles A. Lindbergh (R-Minn.), father of the famous aviator. In a speech before Congress on June 13, 1911, Lindbergh warned that the Aldrich Bill would hand Wall Street insiders unprecedented new power:

> Wall Street, backed by Morgan, Rockefeller, and others, would control the Reserve Association, and those again, backed by all the deposits and disbursements of the United States, and also backed by the deposits of the national banks holding the private funds of the people, which is provided in the Aldrich plan, would be the most wonderful financial machinery that finite beings could invent *to take control of the world*. [Emphasis added.] [19]

At Lindbergh's behest, Congress authorized a subcommittee of the House Committee on Banking and Currency to probe Wall Street's power. The subcommittee, chaired by Representative Arsène Pujo of Louisiana, found evidence that there was a conspiracy it called the "Money Trust."

Another opponent helping to doom the Aldrich bill was Republican President William Howard Taft, who promised a veto. So when the Aldrich bill was defeated in 1911, the would-be central bankers hatched a plan to defeat Taft the following year and put their man in the White House.

Moreover, they decided to have a new bill introduced, masqueraded as a "reform" measure to strip Wall Street of its power, and have the Democrats champion the "reform."

1912 Presidential Election

In order to defeat Taft and elect a submissive Woodrow Wilson, the international bankers behind the Aldrich Bill decided to support a third-party candidate, former President Theodore Roosevelt. In *America's 60 Families*, Ferdinand Lundberg describes the Morgan influence on the campaign:

> As soon as Roosevelt signified that he would again challenge Taft [on the ticket of the Progressive "Bull Moose" Party] the President's defeat was inevitable. Throughout the three-cornered fight [Taft-Roosevelt-Wilson] Roosevelt had [Morgan agents] Munsey and Perkins constantly at his heels, supplying money, going over his speeches, bringing people from Wall Street in to help, and, in general, carrying the entire burden of the campaign against Taft.... Perkins and J.P. Morgan and Company were the substance of the Progressive Party; everything else was trimming....
>
> In short, most of Roosevelt's campaign fund was supplied by the two Morgan hatchet men who were seeking Taft's scalp. [20]

While Morgan interests supported Roosevelt, they also championed Woodrow Wilson. Lundberg identifies the forces behind Wilson: "For nearly twenty years before his nomination Woodrow Wilson had moved in the shadow of Wall Street." [21] In 1906, George Harvey, president of the Morgan controlled *Harper's Weekly*, began promoting Wilson for President. [22] Lundberg further asserts:

> The financial genius behind Woodrow Wilson was Cleveland H. Dodge, of the [Rockefeller] National City Bank....
>
> Sitting with Dodge as co-directors of the National City Bank at the time were the younger J.P. Morgan, now head of the firm, Jacob Schiff, William Rockefeller, J. Ogden Armour, and James Stillman. In short, except for George F. Baker, everyone whom

the Pujo [Congressional investigating] Committee had termed rulers of the "Money Trust" was in this bank. [23]

During their campaigns, both Woodrow Wilson and Teddy Roosevelt regularly denounced the Wall Street "Money Trust," which in fact was financing each. The voters would be betrayed.

Deception Upon Deception

Professor Gabriel Kolko argued that, at the beginning of 1912, banking reform "seemed a dead issue.... The banking reform movement had neatly isolated itself." [24] But the Wilson campaign brought the issue back to life. Wilson promised reforms that would give the country a money system free from domination by the New York bankers. Moreover, the Democratic platform stated: "We are opposed to the Aldrich plan for a central bank." [25]

The banker Insiders also organized the appearance of independent support. Professor Kolko explains:

> It was especially crucial to remove the stigma of its [banking reform] having been originated by Wall Street interests and Nelson Aldrich. During the spring of 1911 the backers of the plan moved to create the National Citizens' League for the Promotion of a Sound Banking System to accomplish the task. Warburg and the other New York bankers behind the Aldrich plan arranged to have the league centered in Chicago.... [26]

Once Woodrow Wilson was ensconced in the White House, the essential points of the Aldrich Bill were repackaged and reintroduced as the Glass Act (named for Senator Carter Glass, a critic of the Aldrich Bill).

In order to convince the public and Congress that the Federal Reserve Act was really "a people's bill," the central bankers staged a show of opposition. Senator Aldrich and Frank Vanderlip denounced what was, in essence, their own bill. In his memoirs, Vanderlip admitted: "Now although the Aldrich Federal Reserve Plan was defeated when it bore the name Aldrich, nevertheless its essential points were all contained in the plan that finally was adopted." [27]

A Congress, anxious to recess for the Christmas holidays,

approved the Federal Reserve Act on December 22, 1913 — the House by a vote of 298 to 60, the Senate by 43 to 25. Paul Warburg commented to fellow Insider "Colonel" E.M. House (see next chapter): "Well, it hasn't got quite everything we want, but the lack can be adjusted later by administrative process." [28]

Following the vote, Congressman Charles A. Lindbergh admonished his colleagues:

> This act establishes the most gigantic trust on earth.... When the President signs this act the invisible government by the money power, proven to exist by the Money Trust investigation, will be legalized....
> This is the Aldrich Bill in disguise....
> The new law will create inflation whenever the trusts want inflation....
> From now on depressions will be scientifically created. [29]

Five days before the bill was enacted, Senator Henry Cabot Lodge Sr. (R-Mass.) objected:

> The bill as it stands seems to me to open the way to a vast inflation of currency.... I do not like to think that any law can be passed which will make it possible to submerge the gold standard in a flood of irredeemable currency. [30]

The following year, with the deception consummated, Senator Aldrich would acknowledge: "[B]efore the passage of this Act the New York bankers could only dominate the reserves of New York. Now we are able to dominate the bank reserves of the entire country." [31]

The Nature of the Beast

The question of who really *owns* the Federal Reserve banks is not nearly as important as *control*. Although the president appoints the members of the Federal Reserve Board to fourteen-year terms, no president has risked making an appointment contrary to the wishes of the New York banking lobby.

President Wilson pretty much left the selection of the original

Federal Reserve Board to his "alter ego," "Colonel" House, who had been in constant contact with Warburg while the Act was being developed and driven through Congress. [32] (House's biographer Charles Seymour would refer to House as the "unseen guardian angel" of the Federal Reserve Act.) Among those selected for the Board was Paul Warburg.

According to Lundberg:

In practice the Federal Reserve Bank of New York became the fountainhead of the system of twelve regional banks, for New York was the money market of the nation. The other eleven banks were so many expensive mausoleums erected to salve the local pride and quell the Jacksonian fears of the hinterland. Benjamin Strong, ... president of the [Morgan] Bankers Trust Company, was selected as the first Governor of the New York Reserve Bank. An adept in high finance, Strong for many years manipulated the country's monetary system at the discretion of directors representing the leading New York banks. Under Strong the Reserve System, unsuspected by the nation, was brought into interlocking relations with the Bank of England and the Bank of France.... [33]

Concerning this domination of the system, Professor Kolko informs us:

Until the passage of the Federal Reserve Act the relative power of New York in national banking was declining, but from 1914 to 1935 it dominated American banking as it had only in the 1890's. And throughout this period Strong became at least as powerful as Morgan had been in his best years. [34]

Few Americans realize how many of our problems today can be traced to the adoption of the Federal Reserve Act in 1913. By authorizing a central bank to control our money supply (and the value of the dollar), Congress enabled federal spending to explode, transforming the very nature of our government in Washington.

Politicians could henceforth spend well beyond their revenue, which had just received a boost through the institution of the income tax (see next). Indeed, the Federal Reserve simply purchases "excess" government debt using fabricated checking account "money" [monetizing the debt], thereby inflating the money supply.

Seduced by the new federal "deep pockets," our state governments, lacking such a mechanism for financing debt, would become dependent on Washington for resources, reversing their relationship. And taxpayers would still bear the brunt of government spending, whether financed directly through taxes or the hidden tax of inflation.

In 1913, Americans were told that establishment of the Federal Reserve System would end inflation and deflation, boom and bust, forever. However, in the years since, America has experienced recurring recessions, a disastrous depression, and unparalleled inflation.

Americans are now supposed to believe one of the biggest ruses of all — that a modern economy simply cannot function without a mastermind economist at the helm managing the money supply.

In 2009, with the Fed "fighting" to bring America out of a deep "recession," CNNMoney.com examined the Fed's challenge in weaning "the economy off the $1 trillion of new money created by the Fed when disaster loomed last fall. 'Your timing has to be perfect,' said David Jones, former Fed economist and president and CEO of DMJ Advisors LLC in Denver. 'If you do it too soon [i.e., stop inflating the money supply], you keep us in recession. And if you do it too late, you get inflation.'" [35]

What the Establishment media will not mention is that in the process of spreading new money all over town, the Fed dilutes the value of all money, just as does a counterfeiter. And in the process it confiscates and redistributes wealth. The new money enriches some Americans [the earlier recipients] at the expense of those on fixed incomes and later recipients of the new money. And the value of all savings is eroded.

Although it is often productive to "follow the money," we don't want to leave the impression, as does Quigley, that the Conspiracy [our term] is driven entirely by ambitious banking families. International banking is just one branch, although an absolutely essential branch, of the Conspiracy.

"A Heavy Progressive ... Income Tax"

In its 1908 platform, the Democratic Party advocated a tax on incomes. However, as a result of an earlier Supreme Court decision, it was widely understood that a constitutional amendment would be required to allow such a tax.

When the new Congress convened in 1909, Senate Majority Leader Nelson Aldrich surprised opposition Democrats by introducing a constitutional amendment to allow for an income tax. A decade earlier, Aldrich had labeled a similar measure "communistic."

Indeed, "[a] heavy progressive or graduated income tax" is one of the ten planks Karl Marx advocated for communizing a nation in his *Communist Manifesto*. Nevertheless, the Aldrich reversal is not that contradictory. What most "genuine" liberals refuse to recognize is that the Left actually serves and is controlled by its alleged enemy.

Radical movements have never been successful without sufficient outside support that "allowed" them to succeed. The great 20th Century historian Oswald Spengler had it figured out when he wrote in his classic *Decline of the West*:

> There is no proletarian, not even a Communist, movement, that has not operated in the interest of money, in the directions indicated by money, and for the time being permitted by money — and that, without the idealist amongst its leaders having the slightest suspicion of the fact.[36]

Karl Marx was no exception. He was commissioned to write the *Manifesto* by the well-off leaders (no starving workers) of the "League of the Just" (later the "Communist League") as a guideline for unifying the "proletarian" socialist movements. In fact, the very flawed ideology of socialism serves the interest of the wealthy seeking power, while posturing convincingly as a bottom-up humanitarian movement to help the poor.

Marx would include a graduated income tax and a central bank as two of his ten planks for communizing a nation. However, rather than soaking the rich and establishing banking "democracy," these two planks were designed respectively to wipe out the middle class (but, not the sheltered rich) and provide a powerful elite with complete control of a nation's economy.

As the "soak the rich" drive for an income tax was proceeding, Andrew Carnegie, John D. Rockefeller, and other managers of the great family fortunes were busy shifting major portions of their assets to "charitable" foundations. Nelson Aldrich was at the center of efforts to ensure that income from these foundations would be exempt from the taxes planned for the rest of us.

On July 12, 1909, with "bipartisan" support and lopsided majorities (a two-thirds vote in each house was required), Congress sent the proposed 16th amendment to the states for ratification — the Senate without any opposition (77 to 0). The House went along 318 to 14.

Richard R. Byrd, Speaker of the Virginia House of Delegates, warned prophetically in 1910, while the proposed Sixteenth Amendment was before the states, that the income tax:

> ... will extend the federal power so as to reach the citizen in the ordinary business of life. A hand from Washington will be stretched out and placed upon every man's business; the eye of a federal inspector will be in every man's counting house....
>
> An army of federal inspectors, spies, and detectives will descend upon the state. They will compel men of business to show their books and disclose the secrets of their affairs.... They will require statements and affidavits....
>
> When the federal government gets a stranglehold on the individual businessman, state lines will exist nowhere but on the maps. Its agents will everywhere supervise the commercial life of the states. [37]

On February 3, 1913, Delaware, New Mexico, and Wyoming became the 36th, 37th, and 38th states to ratify, supplying the minimum 36 states (3/4) required to add the 16th Amendment to the Constitution. Before the year was out, Congress would enact the first graduated income tax law.

Initially, only four-tenths of one percent of the population had to file returns, with most paying no more than a one percent tax. The rate for the top bracket was seven percent. But the Insiders had their foot in the door, and the burden would soon escalate.

America's adoption of two planks of the *Communist Manifesto* in 1913 — the progressive income tax and the Federal Reserve Act — enabled the Woodrow Wilson administration to spend almost twice as much during Wilson's eight years in office as all the American Presidents before him had spent in 125 years. [38]

In particular, these twin revolutionary changes allowed America to throw her weight into one of most unnecessary conflicts in European history — World War I. [39] The victors would subsequently force a "peace" that set the stage for the rise of Hitler and another great tragedy.

Chapter 3

The "First Try" at "World Order"

Wilson's Puppeteer

The international bankers who put Wilson in the White House did not have to rely on Wilson's leadership to advance their agenda. Throughout most of Wilson's eight years as president, they had their trusted representative — Edward Mandell House — at Wilson's elbow.

"Colonel" Edward Mandell House was the son of a wealthy Texas merchant banker and landowner. House developed a reputation as a "Kingmaker" in Texas politics, helping four governors get elected, beginning with James S. Hogg (1892). [1] Hogg gave House the title "Colonel" in promoting House to his staff.

But "Colonel" House was only getting started. He relocated to New York City around 1902 and placed his talent for intrigue and manipulation at the service of the New York Establishment. In late 1911, House befriended the governor of New Jersey, former Princeton University President Woodrow Wilson. House helped Wilson in his successful campaign for the presidency the following year.

A strange relationship developed between Wilson and House, described by George Viereck in his 1932 book, *The Strangest Friendship in History*. [2] Wilson would refer to House as "my alter ego," further declaring: "Mr. House is my second personality. He is my independent self. His thoughts and mine are one." [3]

House was actually provided living quarters in the White House for a time. In his memoirs, Colonel Edmund Starling, who commanded the Secret Service detail in the White House, observed that "Colonel" House was "[t]he only man whose company [Wilson] seemed to relish...." [4]

House held no official position and preferred to remain in the background. Yet some historians considered House to be the real president during most of the Wilson years (not until late 1919, following Wilson's stroke, did the friendship begin to fall apart).

Indeed, House would develop much of Wilson's legislative

agenda, as well as Wilson's famous 14 Points and the first draft of the Covenant of the League of Nations (see Chapter 13 for more of that story).

Philip Dru: Administrator

Even though House preferred to remain in the background, he had revealed his agenda in a boring novel, published in the fall of 1912, just as Wilson was elected president. In *Philip Dru: Administrator*, House mapped out a subversive plan for socialist revolution in America. Through his fictional Philip Dru, House would champion "Socialism as dreamed of by Karl Marx" with a "spiritual leavening."[5]

Because of the novel's political dynamite, B.W. Huebsch published the book anonymously. But in private letters to friends, House admitted that he was the author.[6]

House had started writing *Philip Dru* right about the time he met Woodrow Wilson, who enthusiastically embraced House's vision of socialism. Much of the *Philip Dru* plan was implemented during the Wilson administration. For example, House has his fictional Dru establish "a new banking law affording a flexible [paper] currency."

In 1937, Thomas W. Phelps, Washington bureau chief for the *Wall Street Journal*, provided an updated assessment of Colonel House's impact:

> As Congress puts the finishing touches on the legislative program for the first four years of the [Franklin] Roosevelt Administration, Col. E.M. House, confidant of President Roosevelt, emerges as the prophet, if not the real brain trust of the New Deal. Almost 25 years ago, House wrote of a revolution led by a young West Pointer, who triumphed in one brief but bloody battle; became a benevolent dictator and proceeded to reshape the American Government. In its large outlines, almost the entire revolutionary program has been put through or is in process of being realized under two Democratic Presidents who have served since House turned novelist for a few weeks.[7]

The following year (1938), House told his biographer Charles Seymour, by then president of Yale University, how his political influence had continued into the post-Wilson years:

> During the last fifteen years I have been close to the center of things, although few people suspect it. No important foreigner has come to America without talking to me. I was close to the movement that nominated [Franklin Delano] Roosevelt.... He has given me free hand in advising [Secretary of State Cordell] Hull. All the Ambassadors have reported to me frequently.[8]

In many respects, with *Philip Dru* House could claim to have invented Fascism, years before Mussolini came along. However, when the United States went to war with Naziism and Fascism, *Philip Dru* (now recognized as written by House) became an embarrassment to the Establishment, which sought to cast the book into the memory hole.

The blackout of *Philip Dru,* however, was challenged by columnist Westbrook Pegler, a determined opponent of collectivism. Pegler understood that *Dru* provided powerful evidence of conspiracy in high places:

> [E]ven today few citizens have heard of [Philip Dru] and hardly one in a million has read it.... And, of course, the press will still ignore it diligently.... Practically all our historians and our teaching professors either know nothing about all this or refuse to teach this historical information to their students. One of the most important political documents of our age has been blacked out.[9]

Note: The text of *Philip Dru Administrator* is available on the Internet, complete with explanatory appendices and introduction, at www.robertwelchuniversity.org/ PhilipDru-Final.pdf

"He kept us out of war."

During the summer of 1914 war broke out in Europe, expanding to involve virtually all of the world's great powers. It would become known as the Great War or First World War. While campaigning for a second term, a year and a half later (1916), Woodrow Wilson would achieve a narrow victory aided by the slogan, "he kept us out of war."

However, Wilson's public opposition to American involvement appears to have been just another deception. From the onset of the war in Europe, the Wilson government had been neutral in name only. And certainly the J.P. Morgan Company had never been neutral, serving as Britain's greatest financial ally.

Arms financed by J.P. Morgan & Company were being shipped on "passenger ships" to Great Britain. The firm was heavily at risk should Britain default on its loans, and the Company was eager for the U.S. to side formally with Britain in the war. Newspapers owned by the Morgan empire worked steadily to whip up war hysteria.

Despite his campaign slogan, only a few months into his second term Wilson would lead America into a "war to end all wars" (a term Wilson borrowed from British Fabian Socialist H.G. Wells). On April 6, 1917, Congress complied with Wilson's request for a declaration of war on Germany.

Once war was declared, the U.S. extended one billion dollars in credit to the "Allies" out of which England immediately repaid J.P. Morgan & Company $400 million. [10]

When the U.S. entered the war, Colonel House asked his brother-in-law, Sidney Mezes, president of the City College of New York, to head up a study committee (later known as The Inquiry). The Committee would work in secret to develop proposals for the post-war Paris Peace Conference (see below).

The *Lusitania*

Prior to America's entry, the war in Europe had developed into a stalemate of trench warfare (with huge losses on both sides attacking the fixed lines of the other). The First World War also saw Germany pioneer the development of submarine warfare, in an attempt to cut off British supply lines and starve Britain into submission.

On May 7, 1915, a German submarine torpedoed the ocean liner *Lusitania* sending 1,198 persons, including 128 Americans to their deaths. This brutal act against a peaceful "passenger ship" turned world opinion against Germany and set the stage for America's entry into the war on the side of Britain. However, there was much more to the story of the *Lusitania*, most of which has been kept buried.

In 1972, *London Times* correspondent Colin Simpson published a shocking piece of revisionist history regarding the sinking. In the course of his extensive research, he was able to access many previously classified records from the British Admiralty, the U.S. Treasury, and the Cunard Company (owner of the *Lusitania*).

In his resulting book, *The Lusitania*, Simpson showed that the *Lusitania*, though nominally a passenger ship, was actually an armed auxiliary cruiser of the Royal Navy carrying munitions for the Allies. Simpson's research further revealed that the *Lusitania* had likely been set up by the British Admiralty, with high American complicity, to provoke a successful German attack and bring America into the war.

A sample of the evidence Simpson uncovered included the following:

- Two days before the attack, as the *Lusitania* sailed eastward, First Lord of the Admiralty Winston Churchill conferred with top British naval officials in the Admiralty's map room. They estimated that the *Lusitania* would cross into an area off the coast of Ireland where a German submarine had been reported. The British Admiralty then ordered the patrol cruiser Juno, which had been assigned to escort the *Lusitania*, to abandon its mission. The Captain of the *Lusitania* was not informed. [11]

- One of the officials present at the meeting, Commander Joseph Kenworthy, left the meeting in disgust. In his 1927 book, *The Freedom of the Seas*, Kenworthy wrote that the *Lusitania* "was sent at considerably reduced speed into an area where a U-boat was known to be waiting and with her escorts withdrawn." [12]

- As a member of the political section of British Intelligence, Kenworthy had, on a prior occasion, prepared a paper for Churchill (at Churchill's request) estimating the American reaction should the Germans sink an ocean liner with Americans on board. [13]

- Although President Wilson had access to a copy of the Lusitania's manifest, he nevertheless accused Germany of attacking an *unarmed* passenger ship. Earlier, Wilson's secretary of state, William Jennings Bryan, had written the president pointing out the continuing dangers of allowing American citizens to travel on munitions ships.[14] Fearing that the President's position on the *Lusitania* would involve the U.S. in the war, Bryan resigned on June 8, 1915. [15]

- President Wilson sealed the *Lusitania* manifest "in an envelope, marked it 'Only to be opened by the President of the United States,' and consigned it to the Treasury archives...." [16] There it sat until January 1940 when President Franklin Roosevelt, who had been under secretary of the Navy in 1918 during a *Lusitania* inquiry, retrieved the packet. FDR had the manifest bound in a leather case and placed in his own personal collection of naval manuscripts. Simpson discovered the manifest while examining that collection. [17]

- Decades later, divers examined the wreckage of the *Lusitania* and reported that her bow had been blasted open by a massive *internal* explosion. [18] After being hit by a single torpedo, the *Lusitania* sank within 18 minutes.

Carnegie Minutes

More evidence of a sinister Establishment agenda to involve America in a war was discovered during the Reece Committee investigations of Tax-Exempt Foundations (see next chapter). In 1954, the Committee's research staff was permitted to examine the minutes of the Carnegie Endowment for International Peace, founded in 1910.

In the minutes circa 1911, legal analyst Kathryn Casey was shocked to find discussions among the Carnegie trustees over the question: "Is there any means known to man more effective than war, assuming you wish to alter the life of an entire people?" The trustees concluded that there was not and that war would also help set the stage for world government. They resolved to influence the U.S. diplomatic machinery toward that end by controlling the State Department. [19]

Once America was in the war, the Carnegie trustees dispatched a telegram to President Wilson urging him not to end the war too soon.[20] The president of the Carnegie Endowment during that time was former Secretary of State Elihu Root. Root became an honorary member of the Council on Foreign Relations in 1922 and would serve as its first honorary president until his death in 1937.

Even Wilson's biographer, Jennings C. Wise, acknowledged concerns that the war had been escalated to lay the groundwork for world government: "Whether or not [British Ambassador Sir Cecil] Spring-Rice was correct in his belief that [Theodore] Marburg [the force behind the League to Enforce Peace, supported by Andrew Carnegie] and the Internationalists had brought on the war, certain it is they proposed to 'make hay' out of it." [21]

Gearing Up for War

Two years before Congress declared war on Germany, President Wilson invited Wall Street financier Bernard Baruch to design a plan for a defense mobilization committee. When America entered the war, the Baruch plan became the War Industries Board and Wilson appointed Baruch as its chairman. According to Professor Antony Sutton:

By March 1918 President Wilson, acting without congressional authority, had endowed Baruch with more power than any other individual had been granted in the history of the United States. The War Industries Board, with Baruch as its chairman, became responsible for building all factories, and for the supply of all raw material, all products, and all transportation, and all its final decisions rested with chairman Bernard Baruch. In brief, Bernard Baruch became economic dictator of the United States.... [22]

While placing government contracts worth billions of dollars, Baruch made lots of friends and, according to Wall Street rumors increased his own net worth by $200 million. [23] Bernard's Baruch's influence grew proportionately and would become even greater in the F.D.R. administration.

The League of Nations

Fighting in Europe came to an end in November 1918 with a series of armistices and the capitulation of the Central Powers. The Paris Peace Conference opened in January to begin work on the terms for the war's aftermath. The conference ran for a full year and involved diplomats from more than 29 countries. Defeated Germany and the newly formed communist Russia were not invited to attend.

The Paris Peace Conference resulted in a series of treaties that reshaped the map of Europe. The Treaty of Versailles formally ended war with Germany, but forced Germany to pay harsh reparations, which devastated the German economy and created the opportunity for Adolph Hitler's rise to power.

President Wilson personally headed up the American delegation to the Conference. He was accompanied by Colonel E. M. House and members of House's Inquiry, including Walter Lippmann, Isaiah Bowman, Ph.D., future secretary of State Christian Herter, future Secretary of State John Foster Dulles, and John Foster's brother and future CIA head, Allen W. Dulles. House, Bowman, Lippmann, and John Foster Dulles would become founding members of the CFR. Allen Dulles would later become president of the CFR.

A year earlier, President Wilson had addressed Congress and the world with "his" Fourteen Points for establishing "a just and lasting peace." Point number 14 was the proposal for a League of Nations. Although the proposal for a League was adopted at the Paris Conference (the League went into operation in January 1920), President Wilson returned home in June of 1919 to find a Republican-controlled Senate unwilling to ratify the treaty.

A severe stroke suffered in October of 1919 would prevent Wilson from seeking the Democratic nomination for a third term. Nevertheless, the 1920 Democratic platform favored "the League of Nations as the surest, if not the only, practicable means of maintaining the permanent peace of the world and terminating the insufferable burden of great military and naval establishments."

The platform also charged: "We reject as utterly vain, if not vicious, the Republican assumption that ratification of the treaty and membership in the League of Nations would in any wise impair the integrity or independence of our country." [24]

By contrast the Republican platform stated: "the Republican Party stands for agreement among the nations to preserve the peace of the world.... We believe that ... this can be done without depriving the people of the United States in advance of the right to determine for themselves what is just and fair ... and without involving them as participants and not as peacemakers in a multitude of quarrels, the merits of which they are unable to judge."

And the Republican platform blasted the covenant establishing the League as "not only intolerable for an independent people, but certain to produce the injustice, hostility and controversy among nations which it proposed to prevent." [25]

The Internationalists Regroup

News of the U.S. Senate's resistance to the League of Nations reached Colonel House and members of the Inquiry, while they were still in Paris. They understood that without American participation, the first try at what the internationalists like to refer to as "world order" was doomed to irrelevance.

Clearly American public opinion would have to be altered before America could be brought into the early stages of world government. So Colonel House arranged a series of meetings between members of the American delegation and his British (mostly Milner group) counterparts to map out a strategy for so altering public attitudes. On May 30, 1919 over dinner at the Majestic Hotel, the group decided to form an "Institute for International Affairs," with two branches — one in England, the other in the United States.

The American founders would incorporate their branch in New York on July 29, 1921 as the Council on Foreign Relations. Behind the Council on Foreign Relations was the secret society established in 1891 by Cecil Rhodes. Following Rhodes' death in 1902, his successors carried on his conspiratorial aims by establishing semisecret "Round Table" groups in the chief British dependencies and the United States.

Each Round Table would then expand its influence by creating a public front group with itself as a nucleus. In England, the public front was the Royal Institute of International Affairs. According to Professor Quigley: "In New York it was known as the Council on Foreign Relations, and was a front for J.P. Morgan and Company in association with the very small American Round Table Group." [26]

The founding members were pretty much Wall Street bankers or attorneys closely associated with them. In 1927, the various Rockefeller family foundations began providing financial assistance, soon followed by the Carnegie and Ford foundations. (In later years control of the Council would shift to the Rockefellers.)

Still, it would be some years before the prestige of Council membership was established. The Council would then afford the internationalists with the opportunity to indoctrinate America's academic, media, business, political, and foreign policy elite in the necessity for their new world order.

One of those present at the meeting at the Majestic Hotel in 1919 was Whitney H. Shepardson, an aide to Colonel House. Shepardson would become a founding member and a director of the CFR. In 1960, Shepardson published a small booklet entitled *Early History of the Council on Foreign Relations*. Therein, Shepardson identifies the meetings leading up to the CFR as "a preliminary meeting" on May 30, 1919, another "informal meeting" on June 9th for "preparing the scheme," and "a constituent meeting" on June 17th that "voted the new organization into being."

In his history, Shepardson reproduces a "Committee Report and Resolutions" from the June 17th meeting. The preface to the eight organizational resolutions endorsed a new internationalism:

> Until recent years, it was usual to assume that in foreign affairs each government must think mainly, if not entirely, of the interest of its own people. In founding the League of Nations, the Allied Powers have now recognized that national policies ought to be framed with an eye to the welfare of Society at large. The proceedings at Paris have shown how necessary it is to create some organization for studying the relation of this principle to practical questions as they arise.

So here we have an admission by the CFR founders that they are not looking to advance American interests, but instead advance their vision of the interests of the world as a whole. However, even that ostensibly noble aim did not reflect their real agenda, which has supported some of the worst excesses of government in history.

CFR Founders Support Russian Revolution

If more evidence were needed that the internationalists should not be trusted with power, their persistent support for totalitarianism should clinch the case. Indeed, the roster of founding members of the

Council on Foreign Relations reads like a "Who's Who?" list of Bolshevik supporters.

A syndicate of international bankers actually bankrolled the Bolsheviks. Rockefeller and Morgan interests contributed in the U.S. and Alfred Milner in England. [27] Jacob Schiff, Paul Warburg's brother-in-law and partner at Kuehn Loeb and Company, provided the chief U.S. financial support. As the *New York Journal-American* noted on February 3, 1949:

> Today it is estimated even by Jacob's grandson, John Schiff, a prominent member of New York Society, that the old man sank about 20,000,000 dollars for the final triumph of Bolshevism in Russia.

Paul Warburg's brother Max, who was running the family bank in Frankfurt (M.N. Warburg & Company), supplied the chief European funding for the Revolution. (When the American press got wind of brother Max's financing, Paul Warburg resigned his post at the Federal Reserve.)

The international bankers didn't just throw money at the Revolution from afar. They had representatives on the ground providing material and technical aid while manipulating events. In July 1917, William Boyce Thompson led a delegation of Wall Street financiers to Petrograd, using the cover of a phony American Red Cross Mission.

Thompson was a director of the Federal Reserve Bank of New York and a large stockholder in the Chase National Bank. In December of 1917, Thompson cabled the J.P. Morgan Company from Petrograd to wire him $1 million, which Thompson subsequently donated to the Bolsheviks.

Thompson returned home via London, where he teamed up with Morgan partner Thomas Lamont, who had been in Paris with Colonel House. Together they persuaded Prime Minister David Lloyd George to support the new Soviet regime. [28] Thompson and Lamont would both become founding members of the CFR.

Contrary to popular history, the Communists didn't lead the downtrodden Russian masses to overthrow the Czar. The Czar abdicated under pressure in March of 1917. Since Lenin and Trotsky had been exiled, they were not even in Russia at the time.

With the abdication of the Czar, power passed to a combination of liberal and social revolutionaries. First Prince Lvov headed up a provisional government, but that regime soon gave way to a coalition led by Alexander Kerensky, a social democrat.

Up to that time, Russia had been supporting the Allies in World War I. However, the Communists had promised to pull Russia out of the war if they came to power, which would enable the Germans to shift more resources to the Western front.

Nevertheless, the Woodrow Wilson administration helped Trotsky, who was living in the U.S., to return to Russia. Jennings C. Wise, in *Woodrow Wilson: Disciple of Revolution*, writes: "Historians must never forget that Woodrow Wilson, despite the efforts of the British police, made it possible for Leon Trotsky to enter Russia with an American passport."[29]

When Trotsky's ship pulled into Halifax, Nova Scotia in April of 1917, the Canadians arrested Trotsky. Yet Trotsky was soon released under pressure from Washington, in particular through the intervention of Colonel Edward Mandell House.[30]

Lenin was able to return in April, Trotsky in May. Together, and with outside aid, they organized the Bolsheviks to overthrow the Kerensky government in November.[31]

Initially, Lenin's hold on power was very fragile. Moreover, the emerging Soviet Union was inherently unstable. However, at every critical juncture, when the Soviet regime got into serious trouble, U.S. policymakers moved to bail the Soviets out. The consequences of this internationalist support have been disastrous.

In short order, Russia would begin to gobble up its neighbors and commit genocide on its own and neighboring peoples. Professor R. J. Rummel of the University of Hawaii estimates that the Soviets, during six decades, murdered nearly 62 million human beings.[32]

This enormous crime did not prevent the CFR from supporting the Soviets. The Council on Foreign Relations opened up the pages of *Foreign Affairs* to Red leaders and invited them as guest speakers at Council events. *Foreign Affairs* would even eulogize Trotsky: "He gave us, in a time when our race is woefully in need of such restoratives, the vision of a man. Of that there is no more doubt than of his great place in history."[33]

Incredibly, at a time when the Federal Reserve was intensifying the Great Depression by contracting the domestic money supply, it was secretly making loans to the Soviet regime, which the U.S. had not yet recognized. Congressman Louis T. McFadden, chairman of the House Banking and Currency Committee for more than 10 years, revealed:

> The Soviet government has been given United States Treasury funds by the Federal Reserve Board and the Federal Reserve Banks acting through the Chase Bank and the Guaranty Trust Company and other banks in New York City. England, no less than Germany, has drawn money from us through the Federal Reserve banks and has re-lent it at high rates of interest to the Soviet government or has used it to finance its sales to Soviet Russia and engineering works within the Russian boundaries. The Dnieperstroy Dam was built with funds unlawfully taken from the United States Treasury by the corrupt and dishonest Federal Reserve Board and the Federal Reserve banks....[34]

The Communist revolution served the Conspiracy by consolidating control in many areas of the world. When Soviet militancy became more obvious following World War II, the conflict also helped high-level internationalists advance their revolutionary goals in the West. The Cold-War conflict became the pretext to persuade nations, most notably the United States, to submit to new international authority controlled by the internationalists from behind the scenes.

So in the previous century, these internationalist schemers worked privately to *help* the Communists, while *publicly* denouncing them.

CFR Founders Support Nazi Germany

The Treaty of Versailles (1919) forced Germany to accept blame for the war. Article 231, the so-called "War Guilt Clause," was the brainchild of CFR founder (and future Secretary of State) John Foster Dulles.

The clause ostensibly provided legal justification for the reparations demanded of Germany (eventually paid off 92 years later). But the clause also aided Hitler's rise to power. The harsh reparation payments would drive Germany to despair and set the stage for another war.

41

To escape the heavy burden of reparations, Germany inflated its currency, leading to the 1923 hyperinflation, which decimated the German middle class. Even so, that same year Germany defaulted on part of its agreement to supply coal and steel to the victors. In response, French and Belgium troops occupied the Ruhr River Valley.

The Allies then set up a committee headed by American banker (and future Vice President) Charles G. Dawes to propose a solution. The Dawes Plan (1924) scaled back Germany's annual payments and provided massive loans from the United States to help stabilize the German economy.

Dawes would receive the Nobel Peace Price in 1925 for his work on the plan (he joined the CFR in 1929). Behind the scenes, the J. P. Morgan firm had its hand in developing the plan. According to Quigley:

> It is worthy of note that this system was set up by the international bankers and that the subsequent lending of other people's money to Germany was very profitable to these bankers.[35]

David Lloyd George, who had been British Prime Minister during the Paris Peace Conference while the Treaty of Versailles was "negotiated," blasted the real forces pulling the strings:

> The international bankers dictated the Dawes reparation settlement.... They swept statesmen, politicians and journalists to one side and issued their orders with the imperiousness of absolute monarchs who knew that there was no appeal from their ruthless decrees.[36]

But the Dawes Plan would have much more significance than just money in the pockets of the international bankers. The Plan aided three German cartels that became the industrial backbone of the Nazi war machine and provided the financing for Adolph Hitler's rise to power.

The most significant of the three cartels was I.G. Farben, which became the largest chemical firm in the world. An investigation by the U.S. War Department after World War II concluded: "Without

I.G.'s immense productive facilities, its intense research, and vast international affiliations, Germany's prosecution of the war would have been unthinkable and impossible...." [37]

I.G. Farben also supplied forty-five percent of the campaign funds that allowed the Nazi party to dominate the March 1933 elections and enabled Adolph Hitler to consolidate power. [38]

The I.G. Farben cartel not only received funding under the Dawes Plan, but the Rockefellers' National City Bank floated a $30 million loan. Even greater evidence of complicity of Wall Street (and its CFR compatriots) in the development of the Nazi war machine were the American firms doing business with Germany right up to Hitler's blitzkrieg and extending even into the war itself.

For example, I.G. Farben had an American branch — American I.G. (A.I.G.). On the board of directors of A.I.G. were CFR founders Paul Warburg and Herman A. Metz. Another director, Charles E. Mitchell, joined the CFR in 1923, shortly after its founding. In addition to his A.I.G. role, Metz sat on the board of directors of the New York branch of the Federal Reserve and was a director of National City Bank.

The Establishment has carefully ignored this history. Perhaps the most authoritative, non-Establishment study, among several, is Professor Antony Sutton's *Wall Street and the Rise of Hitler*. The Sutton study is unique in demonstrating that much more than greed was at work. Indeed Wall Street's build-up of Germany was part of a plan to use socialism to cartelize the world. Sutton summarizes part of his findings as follows:

> In brief, American companies associated with the Morgan-Rockefeller international investment bankers — not, it should be noted, the vast bulk of independent American industrialists — were intimately related to the growth of Nazi industry. [39]

Chapter 4

Resetting the Stage for Revolution

"A Return to Normalcy"
Aided by their influence in the Wilson White House, the Insiders had made enormous progress in undermining America's restraints on unaccountable power — despite their failure to entangle the U.S. in their League of Nations. But their Wilson/House inside track would not last.

In the 1920 presidential campaign, a nation weary of Wilson, war, and taxes embraced Republican candidate Warren G. Harding's pledge of a "return to normalcy," electing him with more than sixty percent of the popular vote.

Harding strongly opposed the League of Nations and reportedly had no sympathy for Russian Bolshevism. Harding would die while in office, but his conservative vice president, Calvin Coolidge, finished off the Harding term and gained reelection in 1924. (Coolidge was the last President not to add to the national debt during his term of office, 1923–1929.)

Of course, what made sense to the public did not sit well with the international bankers. The Insiders desperately wanted to regain control of the White House, and they would a need new crisis (or crises) as a pretext to sell their revolutionary agenda.

The election of Herbert Hoover in 1928 represented some progress for the Insiders at the CFR. Hoover had served as Food Administrator under Wilson during the war, and following the war he directed life-saving relief to the Bolshevik regime through the American Relief Administration.

Contrary to the conservative image crafted for Hoover by liberal "historians," as president Hoover supported a "progressive" agenda including government management of the economy (see, for example, Joan Hoff Wilson, *Herbert Hoover: Forgotten Progressive*, Boston: Little, Brown, *1975*).

Hoover would lose much of his Insider financial support for reelection when he refused to support the National Industrial Recovery Act (NRA) (subsequently implemented by FDR).[1]

Nevertheless, Hoover had provided an immense service to the Insiders by helping to launch the Great Depression.

The Fed "Sparks" the Great Depression

The Great Depression provided the pretext for a grand expansion of federal power. After the passage of the Federal Reserve Act in 1913, Congressman Charles Lindbergh had ominously predicted: "From now on, depressions will be scientifically created."

Indeed, between 1923 and 1929 the Fed fueled enormous speculation in the stock market with easy credit policies and by expanding the money supply sixty-two percent. Then at the right moment a planned shortage of call money in the New York money market triggered the crash. One syndicate manager for Lehman Brothers described it as "a calculated 'shearing' of the public by the World-Money powers...."[2]

The unexpected drop in stock prices ruined numerous investors, but a small group of top money barons were tipped off in advance and prospered from the crash. Through timely withdrawal from the market they preserved the financial means to return later and buy up whole companies at bargain-basement prices. As an example, Joseph P. Kennedy's worth reportedly grew from $4 million in 1929 to $100 million in 1935.

Yet despite the crash's tragic effect on some, the majority of Americans were not seriously affected. However, the crash provided the pretext for President Hoover to institute unprecedented unconstitutional programs and controls — including a series of wage and price controls, bailouts of failing firms, and public works projects.

The combined effect of these measures caused the economy to stagnate and prevented recovery. Louis McFadden, chairman of the House Banking Committee, would insist: "[The depression] was not accidental. It was a carefully contrived occurrence."[3]

Of concern regarding the Fed's actions today, in 1931 the Fed responded by injecting more money into the economy. However, the economy was carrying an additional burden of billions in new federal "relief" spending and could not revive.

Led by the media, the people blamed Hoover. This enabled FDR, with strong Wall Street financial support, to become president. (With great audacity, Roosevelt, himself a creature of Wall Street, would publicly disparage Wall Street interests thus cultivating the phony image of "a man of the little people.")

Once in office, FDR would use the dying economy as the excuse permanently to enlarge the role of the federal government, giving the country more of the Hoover "medicine" and accelerating the economy's collapse.

The "People's Choice"

One way potential presidential candidates have signaled their willingness to carry the Establishment's ball is to champion the Insider agenda with an article in *Foreign Affairs*.

In 1967, presidential candidate Richard Nixon wrote "Asia After Vietnam" for *Foreign Affairs*, in which he advocated opening diplomatic relations with Communist China. After his election victory the following year, Nixon tapped numerous CFR members to fill key positions in his administration — including Henry Kissinger, who would implement this next step in the continuing Insider betrayal of the Chinese people.

Similarly, in the July 1928 issue Franklin Delano Roosevelt argued in favor of an internationalist foreign policy:

> The United States has taken two negative steps. It has declined to have anything to do with either the League of Nations or the World Court....
>
> Even without full membership we Americans can be generous and sporting enough to give the League a far greater share of sympathetic approval and definite official help than we have hitherto accorded....
>
> The time has come when we must accept not only certain facts but many new principles of a higher law, a newer and better standard in international relations.

Shortly after the article appeared, Roosevelt was tapped to campaign for the governorship of New York, a useful steppingstone to the presidency. Four years later he would run successfully for president with Wall Street support.

As president-elect, Roosevelt drew on CFR rolls for several key appointments, including Edward Stettinius (former board chairman of U.S. Steel and the son of a J.P. Morgan partner) as secretary of state, Sumner Welles as assistant secretary of state, and Henry Stimson as secretary of war.

James P. Warburg (CFR) became a member of FDR's original "brain trust." James was the son of Federal Reserve architect, international banker, and Rothschild agent Paul Warburg. And FDR's close friend Norman H. Davis (CFR), who became president of the CFR during Roosevelt's second term, would travel abroad on special presidential missions.

Following his nomination at the 1932 Democratic convention, FDR travelled to Massachusetts to pay respects to one of his campaign contributors — Colonel Edward Mandell House, a leader in founding the CFR. House had supported Roosevelt going back to FDR's days as assistant secretary of the Navy during the Wilson Administration.[4] In the January 1933 issue of *Foreign Affairs*, House would lay out an agenda for the new administration.

FDR's son-in-law, Curtis Dahl, the aforementioned "syndicate manager for Lehman Brothers," was a regular visitor at the Roosevelt home. Dahl would later register some unwelcome conclusions about FDR:

> For a long time I felt that FDR had developed many thoughts and ideas that were his own to benefit this country, the U.S.A. But, he didn't. Most of his thoughts, his political "ammunition," as it were, — was carefully manufactured for him in advance by the CFR-One World Money group. Brilliantly, with great gusto, like a fine piece of artillery, he exploded that prepared "ammunition" in the middle of an unsuspecting target, the American people — and thus paid off and retained his internationalist political support.[5]

Roosevelt in the White House

By June of 1933, President Roosevelt had obtained authority from Congress to establish the National Recovery Administration (NRA), greatly desired by corporate socialists who wished to use their political clout to escape the competition of the free market.

Just as President Wilson had appointed Wall Street financier

Bernard Baruch to head up the War Industries Board, Roosevelt would appoint several titans of industry as administrators for the NRA: General Electric president Gerard Swope, General Motors vice president John Raskob, Wall Street banker Otto Kahn, Standard Oil Company of New Jersey president Walter C. Teagle, and International Harvester Company president Alexander Legge.

The actual plan for the NRA had been drawn up by G.E. president Gerard Swope (CFR). The plan's tight regulation of every aspect of American business paralleled Mussolini's fascism in Italy. Each industry would be organized into a federally supervised trade association, known as a Code Authority, which "could regulate production, quantities, qualities, prices, distribution methods, etc., under the supervision of the NRA." [6]

Fortunately, a then more faithful U.S. Supreme Court would rule that the NRA and the Roosevelt-created Agricultural Adjustment Administration (AAA) were unconstitutional. In response, Roosevelt tried unsuccessfully to have Congress authorize him to appoint additional justices — the infamous "court packing" scheme.

During his first year in office, Roosevelt also rewarded his CFR backers by granting diplomatic recognition to the Soviet regime, quite likely saving it from collapse. The Soviet Union was virtually bankrupt at the time, staying alive by the equivalent of kiting checks. U.S. recognition opened up financial markets in New York and abroad for the struggling dictatorship.

Even during the so-called Cold War, future administrations would push for American aid to the Soviet Union, particularly when it faced critical shortages. The CFR-controlled media never allowed the American people to discover how fragile the Soviet hold on its territories was at those times.

Soviet Agents

A side effect of diplomatic recognition was that it allowed the Soviet Union, through its official diplomatic corps, to create and manage a worldwide network of secret agents. This led to an extensive Communist penetration of our government during World War II, when we were allied with the Soviets.

Most Americans today no longer recall that in the aftermath of the war Soviet agents, such as Assistant Secretary of the Treasury Harry

Dexter White, were found in government, along with Communist cells, such as the Harold Ware cell, the Nathan Silvermaster cell, and the Victor Perlo cell. In fact, White's assistant (and first secretary of the IMF) Virginius Frank Coe was identified as a member of the Silvermaster spy ring, moved to China in the 1950s, and became an economic advisor to the Red Chinese.

In the 1990s, the NSA released a batch of the decoded "Venona" intercepts — secret Soviet radio traffic collected in the 1940s — confirming that Soviet penetration of our government was even greater than had been previously disclosed. The Establishment has never apologized for its attack on those who were trying to clean house.

However, our security problems were not totally due to a wartime alliance with the Soviets. Significantly, the Insider love affair with Communism started long *before* the outbreak of World War II (see previous chapter).

Moreover, this "love affair" with Communism was not confined to outright Communists — open or secret. FDR's secretary of the interior, Harold L. Ickes claimed in his "secret diary" for July 16, 1935 that the "Roosevelt Brain Trust" had been "working toward a society of modified Communism."[7]

Takeover of State Department

In September 1939, Germany and the Soviet Union invaded Poland triggering World War II in Europe. Since Britain and France had committed their nations to the defense of Poland, they immediately declared war on Germany. (Although both Germany and the Soviet Union would annex portions of Poland, the involvement of the Soviet Union, later invaded by Hitler, is largely ignored in the Establishment's history of the war.)

Within two weeks of the outbreak of war in Europe, the Council on Foreign Relations seized the opportunity to gain a foothold within the U.S. State Department. Hamilton Fish Armstrong, editor of *Foreign Affairs*, and Walter Mallory, the CFR's executive director, met in Washington with Assistant Secretary of State George Messersmith (CFR). Armstrong and Mallory offered the CFR's help in developing wartime policy and postwar planning for the State Department. Out of their offer grew the War and Peace Studies project, with financing by the Rockefeller Foundation.

The group worked in secret. Keep in mind that this "study group" was formed a full two years before the United States was brought officially into the war by the Japanese attack on Pearl Harbor. The CFR's "temporary" project and personnel were gradually absorbed into the State Department, and their influence expanded into permanent domination.

In 1954, a special House committee chaired by Representative B. Carroll Reece of Tennessee began investigating America's tax-exempt foundations and the causes they supported. The Committee followed the trail to the Council on Foreign Relations.

In its report, the Reece Committee noted the "interlock between the Carnegie Endowment for International Peace, and some of its associated organizations, such as the Council on Foreign Relations and other foundations, with the State Department." It then summarized the nature of this relationship:

> They have undertaken vital research projects for the [State] Department; virtually created minor departments or groups within the Department for it; supplied advisors and executives from their ranks; fed a constant stream of personnel into the State Department trained by themselves or under programs which they have financed; and have had much to do with the formulation of foreign policy both in principle and detail.
>
> They have, to a marked degree, acted as direct agents of the State Department. And they have engaged actively, and with the expenditure of enormous sums, in propagandizing public opinion in support of the policies which they have helped to formulate. [8]

The Reece Committee also concluded that the CFR had become "in essence an agency of the United States government" and that its "productions [books, periodicals, study guides, reports, etc.] are not objective but are directed overwhelmingly at promoting the globalist concept." [9]

America Enters the War
The Insiders who had founded the CFR to alter American attitudes toward international entanglements undoubtedly realized that

America would have to suffer another war before it could be persuaded to surrender its independence to a world authority.

Indeed, as we have seen, beginning with the Treaty of Versailles, these Insiders, as well as their British counterparts, had laid the groundwork for another war. Now that Europe was at war, the challenge was to involve a reluctant America.

In a reelection speech on October 30, 1940, President Roosevelt promised: "I have said this before, but I shall say it again and again and again: Your boys are not going to be sent into any foreign wars." But secret dispatches between Churchill and FDR revealed that FDR was already planning to get America into the war. (See John Toland, *Infamy: Pearl Harbor and Its Aftermath*. Also, John Howland Snow, *The Case of Tyler Kent*.) [10]

Winston Churchill provided further confirmation of FDR's intent in his published history of the war. According to Churchill, Roosevelt's top advisor Harry Hopkins visited him in January 1941 with the following message: "The President is determined that we shall win the war together. Make no mistake about it. He has sent me here to tell you that at all costs and by all means he will carry you through, no matter what happens to him — there is nothing he will not do so far as he has human power." [11]

In the winter of 1940, FDR's biographer Robert Sherwood commented to William Stephenson, Churchill's secret envoy in New York: "If the isolationists had known the full extent of the secret alliance between the United States and Britain, their demands for the President's impeachment would have rumbled like thunder through the land." [12]

Just prior to Pearl Harbor, *Foreign Affairs* openly revealed the Council's priorities:

[H]ope for the world's future — the only hope — lies in the continued collaboration of the oceanic Commonwealth of Free Nations.

To the overwhelming majority of Englishmen, and to very many thousands of Americans, this recognition by both nations of their common needs and common responsibilities is the great good that is coming out of the war, just as for their fathers (and the thought is a warning) the League of Nations was the offset that could be made against the misery of the last war.

Without suggesting any sympathy for the Axis powers, we note that FDR undertook several specific steps to compromise American neutrality and, particularly, to provoke the Japanese to attack. [13] Secretary of War Henry Stimson wrote in his diary following discussions with FDR: "We face the delicate question of the diplomatic fencing to be done so as to be sure Japan is put into the wrong and makes the first bad move—overt move." [14] And following still more discussions, he noted: "The question was how we should maneuver them [the Japanese] into the position of firing the first shot." [15]

Fruits of the War
In exchange for the millions of dead and wounded, what did the war accomplish? On the plus side we can certainly count the defeat of the despicable Hitler/Nazi regime and the militarists in Japan. But there were other not-so-admirable "accomplishments," many engineered with the influence of CFR members.

Through our lend-lease aid to the Soviets and the concessions made to Stalin at the "Big Three" conferences (Tehran, Yalta, and Potsdam) we helped build a post-war Soviet threat. In the Pacific, strategic territory was ceded to the Soviets. Roosevelt's top advisor Harry Hopkins even saw to it that the Soviets were sent the materials to make an atomic bomb. [16]

The Soviets gobbled up Eastern Europe and Poland. The war had started over a commitment to the defense of Poland against Nazi aggression. However, in the war's aftermath, Poland was still in chains and forgotten by its allies.

And significantly for our story, the U.S. and the world got the United Nations.

Chapter 5

The "Second Try" at "World Order"

The world has been led to believe that the UN is a democracy of nations. However, the UN is actually the creation of a small clique who wish to use it, or rather an expanded version, to rule the world. But before we examine the UN structure and how it is really dominated, let's first look at what we know about the origins of the UN.

Of course, we know that the CFR was formed as a result of the refusal of the U.S. Senate to allow the U.S. to enter the League of Nations. Although the League continued for several years, it was a forgone conclusion that without U.S. participation, the League was almost meaningless. Against that background, it should not be surprising to discover that the UN was conceived by the CFR brain trust.

The UN — a CFR Creation

The term United Nations was actually introduced *during* the War (1942) to refer to the Allies. The reference would dispose Americans to regard a body formed by "the United Nations" as an extension of the war effort, designed to provide collective security and prevent future wars. Indeed the UN was advertised for years, particularly in view of the advent of the nuclear age, as "mankind's last, best hope for peace" — powerful propaganda directed at war-weary peoples.

The original proposal for a *specific* United Nations was developed under the leadership of Secretary of State Cordell Hull. In January 1943, Hull formed a "secret steering committee," later known as the Informal Agenda Group, to come up with a specific proposal. In addition to Hull, the steering committee included Leo Pasvolsky, Isaiah Bowman, Sumner Welles, Norman Davis, and Myron Taylor — all but Hull CFR members. A draft of the American proposal was shown to FDR on June 15, 1944. FDR gave his consent and publicly endorsed the proposal that afternoon.

Dumbarton Oaks Conference

A few months later, an initial draft of the UN Charter came out of a secret conference held at the Dumbarton Oaks mansion in Washington, D.C. from August 21 thru October 7, 1944. Although U.S. Secretary of State Edward Stettinious officially chaired the conference, the U.S. side was represented in practice by secret Soviet agent Alger Hiss (CFR), who served as the "executive secretary" for the conference. (The UN has often been referred to by those aware of the Hiss perfidy as the "The House that Hiss Built.")

Working with Hiss from the official Soviet "diplomatic" side were V. M. Molotov, Andrei Vyshinsky, and Andrei Gromyko. Hiss drew support from 15 other U.S. officials named by the State Department as working on the UN Charter who were subsequently identified in official investigations as Soviet agents. (Prominent among the 15 were Lauchlin Curie, Noel Field, Victor Perlo, and Nathan Silvermaster.) [1]

During February of the following year (1945), Hiss served as a top advisor to President Roosevelt at the Yalta Conference with Stalin and Churchill. William C. Bullitt, former U.S. ambassador to the Soviet Union, would say of the Yalta agreement: "No more unnecessary, disgraceful and potentially disastrous document has ever been signed by a President of the United States." [2] At Yalta, Hiss helped Stalin obtain concessions regarding the UN.

In April of 1945, the founding conference for the UN began in San Francisco, lasting into June (Japan did not surrender until August). Alger Hiss served as the acting secretary-general of the conference, helping to finalize the UN Charter. *Time* magazine commented in advance of the conference: "As secretary-general, managing the agenda, [Hiss] will have a lot to say behind the scenes as to who gets the breaks." [3]

At the conclusion of the conference, Hiss personally transported the Charter in a small safe to Washington for Senate ratification. The CFR had done its propaganda work well. The debate lasted a mere six days before the Senate voted overwhelmingly to embrace the new superstate.

Alger Hiss became a member of the CFR in 1945. After the UN began to function, Hiss left the State Department to become president of the Carnegie Endowment for International Peace. He was recommended to the position by CFR founder and future Secretary of State John Foster Dulles, who at the time was chairman of the Endowment. In 1950, Hiss was convicted of perjury for lying about his Communist Party membership and sent to prison.

We do not mean to suggest that the CFR leaders were in any way snookered, or even surprised, by the Soviet agents in their midst. The San Francisco conference was almost entirely a CFR show. More than 40 of the American delegates to the San Francisco conference were or would later become CFR members, only a portion of whom would subsequently be identified as Communists. Among the Establishment CFR members present were Isaiah Bowman (founding CFR member); Nelson Rockefeller; future Secretary of State John Foster Dulles (founding CFR member); and John J. McCloy (future chairman of the CFR).

The UN purchased land for its headquarters in New York with a $8.5 million gift from John D. Rockefeller, Jr.

Deceptive Architecture
At first glance the United Nations General Assembly appears to represent the nations of the world. However, the organization's main power is vested in the Security Council.

Nevertheless, characterizing even the UN's showpiece General Assembly as representing the peoples of the world is a fraud. Most of the member nations are dictatorships of one sort or another and really do not represent the interests of their people. Few of the member nations are genuine constitutional republics like the U.S.

Although the opening words of the preamble to the UN Charter mimic those of the U.S. Constitution (calculated to win American support), the analogy to our federation of states with similar ideals fails. It's a bit like expecting a coalition of organized crime, religious leaders, and the KGB to work together in the best interests of humanity.

Given the origins of the UN, it is not surprising that the UN Charter, spelling out the world body's authority and organization, has many serious defects compared to the U.S. Constitution. The U.S. Constitution limits the federal government to a few appropriate functions, with the vast majority of functions reserved to the states and/or the people. By contrast the UN Charter provides an open-ended grant of authority, which the CFR architects planned to use once they could entangle the U.S. in their creation.

The three principal UN structures — the Security Council, the General Assembly, and the Economic and Social Council (ECOSOC) — have already created a mind-boggling multitude of agencies and programs involved in every conceivable area of human activity. Absent from the UN Charter are the checks and balances that the U.S. founders knew were necessary to prevent the accumulation and improper exercise of power by even the most well intentioned and respectful of political leaders.

Within the Security Council, any of the five permanent members (the United States, the United Kingdom, France, Russia, and now the People's Republic of China, having replaced the pro-Western Nationalist government on Taiwan) can exercise a veto over "decisions." And the governments of each of the permanent members are all committed to the globalist concept of expanding UN power (as fast as the peoples of the Western three can be deceived into going along).

While regular abdication of our Security Council veto authority may constitute a sin of *omission*, the greater UN subversive agenda is implemented through sins of *commission*.

The CFR Controls Its Creation

The UN's trappings of democracy are merely a sham to deceive the public. In reality, the UN is controlled by a hidden oligarchy relying heavily on the CFR.

The hierarchical structure of the UN facilitates that control. The UN and its agencies are structured so that controlling a number of key spots at the top is sufficient to control the entire beast. And the CFR and its Communist children have made sure that their agents occupy key posts in the apparatus.

For example, during the negotiations leading up to the founding of the UN, U.S. Secretary of State Edward Stettinius agreed that the top UN military post — the strategic Under-Secretary for Political and Security Council Affairs — would go to a Soviet national. The post remained in Communist hands until 1992, when the position was reorganized. When Americans fought in the UN-authorized Korean War, a "police action" in UN parlance, the Soviet occupying this strategic post was Konstantin Zinchenko.

At the UN founding conference in San Francisco, Alger Hiss filled a number of key posts with Americans who were secret Soviet agents, not to mention the many Soviet bloc nationals who found their way into the UN bureaucracy. In 1952, Senate Judiciary Committee Chairman James O. Eastland stated that extensive evidence indicates "there is today in the UN among the American employees there, the greatest concentration of Communists that this Committee has ever encountered." [4]

The prominent position of UN secretary-general is filled by a nominee of the Security Council (subject to veto, of course, by Russia or Red China) following approval by the General Assembly.

Although the direct power of the secretary-general is limited, it is instructive to look at those who serve as his advisers. The chief speechwriter for the current UN Secretary-General Ban Ki-moon is Michael Ryder Meyer (CFR). Jeffrey Sachs (CFR) also serves as a special advisor. The official residence of the secretary general is a five-story townhouse in Manhattan built by the daughter of J.P. Morgan and donated to the UN in 1972.

Another illustration of CFR dominance is the leadership of UNICEF, the United Nation's Children's Fund. The first five executive directors of UNICEF were: Maurice Pate (1947–1965); Henry R. Labouisse (1965–1979) (CFR); James P. Grant (1980–1995) (CFR); Carol Bellamy (1995–2005) (CFR); and Ann Margaret Veneman (2005–2010) (CFR and former U.S. secretary of agriculture).

The current executive director of UNICEF, W. Anthony Lake, was appointed to the post by UN Secretary-General Ban Ki-moon in March of 2010, following Lake's nomination by President Barak Obama. Lake, a former member of the CFR, has advised several presidents on foreign policy. (In 1966, President Clinton nominated Lake, a blatant security risk, to become director of the Central Intelligence Agency, but Lake withdrew his name under pressure.)

One of the most effective ways Establishment Insiders maintain a grip on the United Nations is through their control of the massive international aid dispensing institutions — the World Bank and the IMF, as well as the U.S. Agency for International Development (USAID), the U.S. department that manages foreign aid. These institutions wield enormous leverage over many governments, whose nations are in debt to these institutions.

By convention, the president of the World Bank has always been an American internationalist (see Table 5.1), nominated by the U.S. (the president) and approved by the World Bank's Board of Governors. Representation on the Board of Governors is proportional to contributions — the U.S. is the only country able to block a supermajority on its own. The U.S. representative on the board is Secretary of the Treasury Timothy Geithner (CFR), the alternate — Fed Chairman Ben Bernanke.

Whereas the IMF managing director has traditionally been a European, the second in command, the first deputy managing director, has been (and is today) an American (internationalist, of course). John Lipsky (CFR), former vice president of J.P. Morgan, held the post from September 2006 through August 2011. Over at USAID, the administrator is Rajiv Shah (CFR), who replaced acting chief Alonzo Fulgham (CFR) at the end of 2009.

Bretton Woods

The IMF and World Bank are part of the UN-affiliated post-war financial system, another CFR creation. The planning for these institutions originated within a subgroup of the CFR's War and Peace Studies Project during 1941–42. The final plan was established in July 1944 at an international conference in the Mount Washington Hotel and Resort, situated in Bretton Woods, New Hampshire.

Heading up the U.S. delegation and dominating the three-week conference was secret Soviet agent and Assistant Secretary of the Treasury Harry Dexter White (CFR). White would also initially head up the IMF after it was formed. Supporting White at Bretton Woods was his assistant at Treasury, fellow Soviet agent Virginius Frank Coe, as well as British Fabian Socialist John Maynard Keynes.

The IMF was established ostensibly to help stabilize currencies at the end of World War II and to control international exchange rates. However, it was purposefully designed to evolve at an opportune time into a world central bank, issuing an international currency. At the Bretton Woods conference, Federal Reserve Board governor Mariner Eccles was moved to point out: "An international currency is synonymous with international government."[5]

More recently, world financial ministers have sought to use the

World Bank Presidents

Eugene Meyer	1946	CFR & Former Fed Chairman
John J. McCloy	1947-1949	CFR Chairman (1953-1970)
Eugene R. Black Sr.	1949-1963	CFR
George Woods	1963-1968	
Robert McNamara	1968-1981	CFR & Trilateralist
Alden W. Clauson	1981-1986	
Barber Conable	1986-1991	CFR
Lewis T. Preston	1991-1995	CFR Director (1981-1988)
James Wolfensohn	1995-2005	CFR
Paul Wolfowitz	2005-2007	CFR
Robert B. Zoellick	2007-present	CFR Director (1994-2001)

Table 5.1

IMF First Deputy Managing Director

Stanley Fischer	1994-2001	CFR
Anne Osborn Krueger	2001-2006	CFR
John Lipsky	2006-2011	CFR
David Lipton	2011 forward	

Table 5.2

2009 global financial crisis to strengthen both the IMF and World Bank, in the guise of reform. In March of that year, the IMF announced that both Russia and China would be investing in the first-ever notes to be issued by the fund.

The IMF's sister agency, the World Bank, was ostensibly created to provide loans to member nations for the purpose of reconstruction and development after World War II. The U.S. taxpayer has been the primary contributor.

World Bank loans to socialist governments have often helped to plunge their unfortunate nations further into debt and bring them more under internationalist control. The New York banks have also profited from this sovereign debt. The banks are apparently convinced that international bailouts (and the American taxpayer) will prevent default.

In his February 14, 1979 *Dan Smoot Report*, the outspoken former FBI agent cut through all of the propaganda supporting the two agencies. Smoot charged that the policies set at the Bretton Woods conference and adhered to relentlessly by our government "were intended to accomplish four major objectives:

(1) Strip the United States of its monetary gold reserve by giving the gold to other nations;

(2) Build the industrial capacity of other nations, at our expense, to eliminate American productive superiority;

(3) Take world markets — and much of the American domestic market — away from American producers to stop American domination of world trade;

(4) Entwine American affairs with those of other nations until the United States could not have an independent policy, but would become an interdependent link in a worldwide socialist chain."

A Foot in the Door

Those seeking world government (controlled by a few) viewed American acceptance of the United Nations as merely a foot in the door. Accordingly, the CFR has continued to lobby for more authority to be given to its creation.

As one example, in 1959 the Council published "Study Number 7, Basic Aims of U.S. Foreign Policy." Listed prominently in the section titled "The Foreign Policy Tasks Which Lie Ahead," we find point number 3: "Maintain and gradually increase the authority of the UN."

The Insider domination of both major parties is confirmed by the fact that every president since Truman has supported U.S. membership in the UN.

MASTERS OF DECEPTION

Part II

Strategies for a
New World Order

Chapter 6

The "Third Try" at "World Order"

The UN founders always regarded their UN system as a work in progress. That work would not be completed until all nations had been forced to give up their independence and submit to world authority. However, American enthusiasm for the UN waned quickly after the UN Charter was accepted, making it more difficult for the UN architects to complete their task.

The Korean War (a "police action" in UN parlance), in which Americans could die but were not allowed to win, further eroded public support for UN "peacekeeping." Congressional investigations revealing communist involvement in the UN founding and staffing, as well as a massive grassroots anti-UN educational campaign added to the world body's declining image.

And to top if off, scandals rocked the UN, and Americans became aware of rampant anti-Americanism within the General Assembly and at UN conferences. Many Americans would wholeheartedly agree with U.S. Senator Robert Taft of Ohio, who had originally voted in favor of U.S. participation, when he said: "The U.N. has become a trap. Let's go it alone." [1]

However, all too often anti-UN sentiment was deflected in Washington with calls for UN reform, which UN architects knew could easily serve to strengthen the UN. The CFR-dominated U.S. executive branch could criticize the UN, but bottom-line U.S. support never wavered.

Multiple Strategies

World order architects knew they had a long path ahead before they could reach their goal of world government. Rather than put all of their eggs in one basket, they would pursue several different approaches toward their goal, each with its own milestones.

One major milestone is to equip the UN with its own standing army, accustoming the world to an independent UN police force. Another is to provide the UN with an independent source of revenue (e.g., some form of global taxation), so it would no longer have to beg national governments for an "allowance." UN enforcement could then take on a new edge.

Numerous proposals, conferences, and reports have advocated those two objectives (under suitable pretexts, of course), but the direct approach has so far failed to win the acceptance of the America public and its Congress. Nevertheless, the enemies of national sovereignty have made enormous progress following other approaches.

Arms Control and Disarmament

With the dawn of the nuclear age at the end of World War II, the most promising pretext for expanding UN power appeared to be the threat of nuclear annihilation and the parallel promise of providing "collective security." Even so, the immediate goal of arming the UN had to be camouflaged.

The idea was to make it appear that the world would be safer if nations would halt the arms race and disarm. Rarely mentioned was the fact that modern arms were the great equalizer for industrial societies when confronting aggressive, backward tyrannies capable of deploying huge expendable armies.

But more significantly, the term universal disarmament masked a clever deception. In reality, the Insiders controlling our State Department and much of the media sought to *transfer* sufficient arms to the UN (including even *nuclear weapons*) so that the UN could force all nations to comply with its decisions. And they called that "universal" or "general" disarmament.

The New World Army

In 1961, John J. McCloy, chairman of the CFR and chief disarmament advisor at the time to President Kennedy, wrote the statute establishing the U.S. Arms Control and Disarmament Agency. He was assisted in this work by Arthur H. Dean (a director of the CFR). Together, McCloy and Dean drafted an incredibly subversive proposal for the transfer of America's military might, in stages, to the United Nations.

A document boldly describing the long-range program was issued by the Dean Rusk (CFR) State Department as Department of State

Publication 7277. It carried the title *Freedom From War: The United States Program for General and Complete Disarmament in a Peaceful World*. Confirming that *Freedom From War* had become official U.S. policy, President Kennedy presented it personally before the UN General Assembly on September 25th of that year (1961).

According to *Freedom from War*, the transfer of arms to the UN is to occur in three stages:

> In Stage III progressive controlled disarmament ... would proceed to a point where *no state would have the military power to challenge the progressively strengthened U.N. Peace Force*. [Emphasis added.]

When Stage III was fully implemented, the United States would no longer be able to stand up to the "friendly, benevolent" world authority and would have to comply fully with UN decisions, (i.e., decisions of the CFR oligarchy). As the text for *Freedom From War* makes clear, the term "General Disarmament" in its full title seriously misrepresents the plan. While *nations* would disarm, a new superpower would be armed:

> The progressive steps to be taken during the final phase of the disarmament program would be directed toward the attainment of a world in which:
> (a) States would retain only those forces, non-nuclear armaments, and establishments required for the purpose of maintaining internal order; they would also support and *provide agreed manpower for a U.N. Peace Force....* [Emphasis added.]
> (d) The peace-keeping capabilities of the United Nations *would be sufficiently strong* and the obligations of all states under such arrangements sufficiently far-reaching as to assure peace and the just settlement of differences in a disarmed world. [Emphasis added.]

During that same period, the Kennedy State Department also contracted with the private Institute for Defense Analysis to prepare a classified study. In support of the study, a memorandum entitled *A World Effectively Controlled By the United Nations* candidly discussed the best strategy for establishing world government (for the complete text, see the "Conspiracy" archives at www.freedomfirstsociety.org).

The memorandum's author was MIT professor Lincoln P. Bloomfield. A member of the Council on Foreign Relations, Bloomfield served 11 years in the State Department and just prior to the aforementioned study was attached to the State Department's disarmament staff. The opening paragraph of the Bloomfield contribution reads:

> A world effectively controlled by the United Nations is one in which "world government" would come about through the establishment of supranational institutions, characterized by mandatory universal membership and some ability to employ physical force. Effective control would thus entail a preponderance of political power in the hands of a supranational organization.... [T]he present UN Charter could theoretically be revised in order to erect such an organization equal to the task envisaged, thereby codifying a radical rearrangement of power in the world.

The classified report was clearly intended for a select, trusted audience, so Bloomfield dropped much of the deceptive verbiage internationalists regularly use to camouflage their designs. Indeed, Bloomfield emphasized: "[I]t is world government we are discussing here — inescapable." And under "Definitions" he notes: "Finally, to avoid endless euphemism and evasive verbiage, *the contemplated regime will occasionally be referred to unblushingly as a 'world government.'*" [Emphasis added.]

Bloomfield's report also clarified the U.S. "disarmament" agenda:

> National disarmament is a condition sine qua non for effective UN control....
>
> The essential point is the transfer of the most vital element of sovereign power from the states to a supranational government....
>
> The overwhelming central fact would still be the loss of

control of their military power by individual nations.

But perhaps the most shocking is the claim that the UN would need nuclear weapons to ensure world "peace":

> The appropriate degree of relative force would, we conclude, involve total disarmament down to police and internal security levels for the constituent units, as against a significant conventional capability at the center backed by a marginally significant *nuclear* capability. [Emphasis added.]

A Persistent Agenda

Building this permanent UN military force has been the fixed policy of the U.S. government, regardless of the administration and party in control. But the right moment and much deception have been needed to prepare the public for such a step. Even with CFR media support, it has been a tough sell.

In 1992, the final year of the George H. W. Bush (Sr.) administration, the Establishment gave it a strong try:

- On January 31, 1992, the UN Security Council convened for the first time ever at the level of heads of state. At that meeting the Security Council directed UN Secretary General Boutros Boutros-Ghali to report back with recommendations for strengthening the UN's peacekeeping capabilities.

- In June, Boutros-Ghali delivered the requested recommendations in *An Agenda for Peace*. His report called for UN members to designate troops to be kept on standby for use by the Security Council and for "permanent" arming of the UN.

- In August, presidential candidate Bill Clinton voiced his support for "a new voluntary U.N. rapid deployment force."[2]

- In his September 21, 1992 address to the United Nations, President Bush pledged U.S. support for expanded UN peacekeeping operations and applauded Boutros-Ghali's call "for a new agenda to strengthen the United Nations' ability to prevent, contain, and resolve conflict across the globe."

- Articles and editorials in the Establishment's *New York Times* greeted these proposals with great enthusiasm. (See, for example, these 1992 *Times* editorials: "The New World Army," "The Unsung New World Army," and "Help the U.N. Arm for Peace.")[3]

Presidential Decision Directive 13

Once in office, President Clinton issued a secret presidential decree (PDD-13) concerning U.S. involvement in UN military operations. When portions of PDD-13 were leaked to the press, they created a storm of controversy.

The news that Americans might have to "serve under a foreign commander on a regular basis" prompted immediate opposition from both the public and Congress. Initially, President Clinton remained steadfast. In his September 27, 1993 speech to the United Nations, the president argued:

> The United Nations must also have the technical means to run a modern world-class peacekeeping operation. We support the creation of a genuine UN peacekeeping headquarters with a planning staff, with access to timely intelligence, with a logistics unit that can be deployed on a moment's notice, and a modern operations center with global communications.

A few days later, Senator Trent Lott (R-Miss.) addressed the controversy on the floor of the Senate:

> The Clinton administration appears dedicated to sending the U.S. military into the dangerous seas of multinational peacekeeping in an effort to elevate the status of the United Nations into the guardian arbiter of the new world order.
>
> Key to this new vision of the world is creation of a new world army whose singular purpose is to enforce the whims of the arcane United Nations Security Council. The administration's effort to create a new vision for the U.S. military is embodied, I fear, in a new Presidential Decision Directive, called PDD-13. Under PDD-13, the United States becomes the trainer and bill-

payer of an effort to create a military command structure for the Secretary General of the United Nations. [4]

Responding to the controversy, President Clinton eventually issued another Presidential Decision Directive, PDD-25, with an "unclassified" summary reassuring the public and Congress that the U.S. would not forfeit its authority over the use of its troops.

Efforts to arm the UN, piecemeal, continued below the surface of public attention. In October 1996, Secretary of State Warren Christopher instituted the "African Crisis Response Initiative" (ACRI) — a five-year program to enhance the peacekeeping capabilities of African nations.

The "Brahimi Report"

In August 2000, the UN released the *Report of the Panel on United Nations Peace Operations*, also known as the Brahimi Report. The Brahimi Report argued that the UN needs more resources if it is to meet the peacekeeping demands of its member states. One example of where the UN (or rather its CFR masters) wants to go is this recommendation:

126. Summary of key recommendations on civilian police personnel:

(a) Member States are encouraged to each establish a national pool of civilian police officers that would be ready for deployment to United Nations peace operations on short notice, within the context of the United Nations standby arrangements system....

At the UN Millennium Summit in September 2000, Secretary-General Kofi Annan urged the world's leaders to consider "very seriously" the Brahimi Report's recommendations. When he took the podium, President Clinton showed he was on board with the Insider agenda:

[In East Timor and Sierra Leone], the U.N. did not have the tools to finish the job. We must provide those tools — with peacekeepers that can be rapidly deployed with the right training and equipment, missions well-defined and well-led, with the necessary civilian police.[5]

Global Peace Operations Initiative (GPOI)

The subsequent George W. Bush administration also picked up the internationalist ball, developing its own plans to equip the UN with an army for "peacekeeping." Initially, the administration would absorb, rename, and expand the Clinton administration's African Crisis Response Initiative.

However, in April 2004, the Pentagon announced: "The Bush administration is planning a new drive to boost the supply of foreign troops available for peacekeeping missions worldwide." The Global Peace Operations Initiative (GPOI) would be launched as a five-year joint venture of the Defense and State Departments. President Bush introduced the plan himself in a September 21, 2004 speech to the UN General Assembly:

> Because we believe in human dignity, the world must have more effective means to stabilize regions in turmoil, and to halt religious violence and ethnic cleansing. We must create permanent capabilities to respond to future crises. The United States and Italy have proposed a Global Peace Operations Initiative. G-8 countries will train 75,000 peacekeepers — initially from Africa — so they can conduct operations on that continent and elsewhere. The countries of the G-8 will help this peacekeeping force with deployment and logistical needs.

A year later, the GPOI scope was expanded to include selected countries in Central America, Europe, and Asia. According to a Congressional Research Service Report: "As of the end of January 2009, GPOI funds have supported the training of 54,245 military troops as peacekeepers," most of whom "were deployed to 18 peacekeeping operations...." Of the 18, ten were UN operations.

The GPOI was renewed for another five years, and the Obama administration has continued to support and budget for the program.

In a 1984 CFR supported self-history, *The Wise Men of Foreign Affairs: The History of the Council on Foreign Relations*, Professor Robert D. Schulzinger informs us that to "curtail excesses of sovereignty," the CFR architects knew that the "United States would have to participate in years of conferences to create the new world order. Disarmament would be a slow process...."

The Gradualism Route

In 1976, Harlan Cleveland (CFR) wrote *The Third Try at World Order: U.S. Policy for an Interdependent World*, published by the CFR-interlocked Aspen Institute for Humanistic Studies (since renamed as just the Aspen Institute.) A Rhodes Scholar, Cleveland was a prolific author of books and articles advocating world governance. Before examining his book, let's take a look at the author.

Cleveland's career is instructive. In 1961, President Kennedy appointed Cleveland assistant secretary of state for International Affairs. Initially, however, State Department security officials refused to grant Cleveland even a temporary security clearance.

Cleveland had a long list of pro-communist exploits. For example, he wrote articles for the Institute of Pacific Relations, described by a Senate Committee as "an instrument of Communist policy, propaganda and military intelligence." He worked with several prominent Communists on the staff of the LaFollette Civil Liberties Committee. And he had served as deputy to Soviet agent Harold Glasser within the United Nations Relief and Rehabilitation Administration.[6]

The Cleveland appointment was only allowed because Secretary of State Dean Rusk (CFR) personally intervened to waive the clearance. Keep in mind, however, Dean Rusk's Establishment history. In the 1950's, as president of the Rockefeller Foundation, Rusk had fought the Reece Committee investigation of the tax-exempt foundations.

Once in office, Cleveland attempted to staff a committee he chaired with other security risks, including three who had served on the staff of Alger Hiss. He even inquired about the possibility of employing Hiss again after his release from prison.

When Cleveland's selections were met with security objections, he hired them as consultants. It was Cleveland who brought fellow Rhodes Scholar Richard N. Gardner into the State Department.

Given that background, many Americans would be amazed to learn that President Johnson would appoint Harlan Cleveland as U.S. ambassador to NATO and that President Nixon would continue the appointment.

The Third Try at World Order

According to Cleveland's book, the first try at world order failed when the U.S. Senate refused to allow America into the League of Nations. Of course, the second try was the establishment of the United Nations. In Cleveland's view, that attempt failed when the founders were unable to provide the United Nations with sufficient authority to enforce its decisions.

"The third try at world order," wrote Cleveland, "stems from the growing awareness of the interdependence of peoples, problems, and policies." [7] The only practical way to achieve world governance, Cleveland argues, is to build it step by step.

A new spirit of cooperation, Cleveland predicts, will permit the forging of new bargains and institutions to address individual problems [presumably under the overall umbrella of an upgraded UN]:

Somehow the community of nations — or at least of those most concerned — will need to create a food reserve, assure energy supplies, depress fertility rates, stabilize commodity markets, protect the global environment, manage the ocean and its seabed, ... rewrite the rules of trade and investment, reform the monetary system, mediate disputes....

It is this impressive agenda, taken as a whole, that will amount to a third try at world order.... [T]here is no consensus to entrust any nation or race or group with general responsibility for world governance, yet there is an urgent need to tackle problems which will yield only to world-scale solutions. [8]

What Harlan avoids saying is that his "world scale-solutions" require the development of world-scale government force. Moreover, his claim that there is "no consensus to entrust any ... group" ignores the behind-the-scenes work of the CFR to orchestrate the evolution of its world control, while creating the appearance, at least in the next stages, that its decisions are the democratic consensus of independent nations.

The claim that global problems have created a demand for global governance is also deceptive, because it inverts cause and effect. Instead, the CFR's goal of world governance demands credible pretexts — hence the CFR's propaganda creates global challenges that supposedly can only be addressed through global governance.

A more subtle deception is the pervasive presumption that the constructive interaction of the peoples of the world requires *the interdependence of their governments*. The 19th Century British political leader, Richard Cobden, saw the danger and drew a huge distinction: "Peace will come to this earth when her peoples have as much as possible to do with each other; their governments the least possible." [9]

Cobden was not advocating isolationism. However, proponents of international *government* entanglements have disingenuously characterized their opponents as isolationists, hoping the epithet would stick.

"The Hard Road to World Order"

Cleveland's "Third Try" arguments were not new — they were just a new attempt to reinforce support for a long-standing Insider agenda. The gradualist strategy Cleveland was advocating had actually been taking place ever since the UN was founded.

The true object of these efforts has rarely been spelled out with greater candor than in Richard Gardner's previously quoted April 1974 essay for *Foreign Affairs* entitled "The Hard Road to World Order." The following longer excerpt clarifies the Insider strategy for overcoming resistance:

> The hope for the foreseeable future lies, not in building up a few ambitious central institutions of universal membership and general jurisdiction, as was envisaged at the end of the last war, but rather in the much more decentralized, disorderly, and pragmatic process of inventing or adapting institutions of limited jurisdiction and selected membership to deal with specific problems on a case-by-case basis, as the necessity for cooperation is perceived by the relevant nations....

In short, the "house of world order" will have to be built from the bottom up rather than from the top down. It will look like a great *"booming, buzzing confusion,"* to use William James's famous description of reality, but an end-run around national sovereignty, eroding it piece by piece, will accomplish much more than the old-fashioned frontal assault. [Emphasis added.]

For his piecemeal approach, Gardner recommended focus on ten programs already underway. Here is a sample:

- "[R]eform of the international monetary system...." Specifically, Gardner called for strengthening the International Monetary Fund with "power to back its decisions by meaningful multilateral sanctions, such as ... the withholding of multilateral and bilateral credits and reserve facilities from recalcitrant deficit countries."

Note: In May 2011, Reuters described the IMF as "the institution that manages the world's economy." [10]

- "[A] parallel effort to rewrite the ground rules for the conduct of international trade. Among other things, we will be seeking new rules in the General Agreement on Tariffs and Trade to cover a whole range of hitherto unregulated nontariff barriers. These will subject countries to an unprecedented degree of international surveillance over up to now sacrosanct 'domestic' policies...."

Note: Congress approved America's entry into the World Trade Organization in 1994.

- "[C]ontinued strengthening of the new global and regional agencies charged with protecting the world's environment." (See Chapter 8 Post-Cold War Pretexts.)

- "We are entering a wholly new phase of international concern and international action on the population problem.... By the end of this decade, a majority of nations are likely to have explicit population policies, many of them designed to achieve zero population growth by a specific target date."

- "In the 1974 Law of the Sea Conference and beyond — in what may be several years of very difficult negotiations — there should eventually emerge a new international regime governing the world's oceans. New law is, all agree, urgently needed on such crucial matters as ... the exploitation of the mineral resources of the seabed.... To make these new rules of law meaningful, there will have to be tough provisions to assure compliance as well as to provide for the compulsory settlement of disputes."

Internationalists are very eager for the UN to gain control of the huge mineral resources of the ocean's seabeds. The potential revenue is enormous. Several presidents have endorsed the plan, which is part of the UN's Law of the Sea Treaty. But thus far ratification of the treaty has been narrowly blocked in the Senate.

In 2004, J. William Middendorf, former secretary of the Navy during the Nixon-Ford administrations, testified that ratification of the treaty would constitute "a potential turning point for the U.S. in the history of international relations." Middendorf warned that the treaty would be "a step in the direction of international taxing authority" and posed "unnecessary risks to national security." [11]

A "Booming, Buzzing Confusion."

The UN system long ago became a "booming, buzzing confusion." In a 1970s speech, UN "philosopher" Robert Muller, who has held many of the UN's top posts, identified the following UN activities:

> Yes, the UN is concerned with our globe's climate....
>
> Yes, the UN is concerned with the total biosphere through project Earthwatch, the Global Environment Program of UNEP and UNESCO's program, "Man and the Biosphere."
>
> Yes, the UN is dealing with our planet's seas and oceans....
>
> Yes, the UN is dealing with the world's deserts....
>
> Yes, the UN is dealing with the human person, that alpha and omega of our efforts.... The person's basic rights, justice, health, progress and peace are being dealt with from the fetus to the time of death.
>
> Yes, the UN is dealing with the atom in the International Atomic Energy Agency....

Yes, the UN is dealing with art, folklore, nature, the preservation of species, germ banks, labor, handicrafts, literature, industry, trade, tourism, energy, finance, birth defects, sicknesses, pollution, politics, the prevention of accidents, of war and conflicts, the building of peace, the eradication of armaments, atomic radiation, the settlement of disputes, the development of worldwide cooperation, the aspirations of East and West, North and South, black and white, rich and poor, etc.[12]

Later, Muller would lament the "gaps" in the UN program:

[Th]ere was no worldwide cooperation for the globe's cold zones, the mountains, our topsoil, standardization, world safety ... the family, morality, spirituality, world psychology and sociology, the world of senses, the inner realm of the individual, his needs, values, perceptions, love and happiness ... on consumer protection ... on the world's elderly, on world law, on the ultimate meaning of human life and its objectives.[13]

UN treaties are addressing many of Muller's "gaps." With Establishment support for such unchecked UN "responsibility," is it any wonder that America has lost its *own* vision of a limited *federal* government?

Global Taxation

Various schemes for funding the United Nations outside of government contributions have been floated in recent decades. Internationalists are seeking the right climate to implement one or more of the plans.

In 1995, Harlan Cleveland wrote the lead essay for a special UN anniversary issue of *Futures*, a UN-connected publication from England. The issue, consisting of the first report of the Global Commission to Fund the United Nations, proposed several plans for global taxation. In his essay, "The United Nations: Its Future is its Funding," Cleveland declared:

Financing the UN is no longer an issue to be ignored, bypassed, or swept aside.... It is high time we looked hard at how best to finance a widening range of international functions that grows more obviously necessary with every passing year. [14]

Cleveland drew support from an earlier 1975 Aspen Institute report that argued the UN should not be dependent on "the worn-out policy of year-to-year decisions by individual governments" for its funding. Instead, "what's needed is a flow of funds for development which are generated *automatically* under *international control*...." [15] [Emphasis in original.] Regarding potential opportunities for UN taxation, Cleveland concluded that "the list is limited only by the human imagination." [16]

Chapter 7

Progressive Regionalization

"In short, the house of world order will have to be built from the bottom up rather than from the top down.... Of course, for political as well as administrative reasons, some of these specialized arrangements should be brought into an appropriate relationship with the central institutions of the U.N. system...."
— Richard N. Gardner, "The Hard Road to World Order,"
Foreign Affairs, April 1974

Among the paths to world government conceived by world-order architects, "regionalism" has been one of their most effective. The idea is to persuade nations to give up some of their sovereignty piecemeal to regional alliances, such as the European Union, having open-ended authority.

Similar to the UN model, these regional alliances are designed with the outward trappings of democracy, but in reality the internationalists in the background exercise control. As these regional alliances develop and the nations lose the ability to control their own destiny, the regions can be absorbed into a revamped world authority.

Top Insider Zbigniew Brzezinski, Jimmy Carter's national security advisor and architect with David Rockefeller of the Trilateral Commission, explained the regionalism strategy at Gorbachev's 1995 State of the World Forum:

> We cannot leap into world government in one quick step.... In brief, the precondition for eventual globalization — genuine globalization — is progressive regionalization, because thereby we move toward larger, more stable, more cooperative units. [1]

Of course, these regional governments are naturally "more cooperative units," because the CFR Insiders set them up as their babies.

The CFR planners — experts in psychology — long ago recognized the advantage of the regionalization approach over persuading all nations to accept the same master authority in one fell swoop. That advantage was the natural tendency to regard nearby nations as family when pitted (particularly economically) against distant nations on other continents.

Even so, nations are reluctant to merge with their neighbors. To accomplish their goal the Insiders had to move in steps ("progressive regionalization" in Brzezinski's words), while vehemently denying the destination of those steps. In Europe, they would offer elaborate pretexts to camouflage their intentions — until the nations of Europe were caught in the trap.

The European Model

Europe is in an advanced stage of Insider regionalization. Indeed, the internationalist drive for a united Europe actually predates the UN.

Everyone today is familiar with the European Union. But few Americans are aware of the role that American money, guided by members of the CFR, played in trampling the sovereignty of Europe's long-established nations.

Moreover, most Americans are unaware of the deception that was used to create the EU. Certainly, our Establishment media is trying to keep it that way. Yet Americans need to know the truth about these events, because the plan and deceptions have been imported successfully into this hemisphere and are in motion today.

The Marshall Plan

At the end of World War II, Congress approved the European Recovery Program (ERP) — a program of massive aid to Europe, popularly known as the Marshall Plan. The Marshall Plan was actually developed by a CFR study group — headed by Charles M. Spofford with David Rockefeller as secretary.[2] Marshall's name was used to elicit bipartisan support.

In his June 5, 1947 Harvard University speech proposing the plan, Secretary of State George C. Marshall insisted: "Our policy is directed not against any country or doctrine, but against hunger, poverty, desperation, and chaos." Recognizing American political sentiments, however, President Truman cleverly sold the foreign aid as a means to help stop the spread of Communism.

In general, American Insiders have used foreign aid to saddle recipient nations with socialist policies and governments. The ERP certainly followed that pattern. But in Europe the aid was also used to promote European unification.

The most prominent public figure in this plan was millionaire-socialist Jean Monnet, who would earn the title "Father of Europe" for his "leadership" in the drive to build a united Europe. Monnet would subsequently acknowledge that Marshall funds were "used with the intention of encouraging European unity." [3]

However, the orchestration by American elites went far deeper than mere "encouragement." Indeed, the political careers of European politicians were made to depend on support for European merger. And those inclined to sound an alarm found little opportunity to do so.

The CFR Hidden Hand

Although the Frenchman Jean Monnet gave the European movement the outward appearance of a purely European initiative, he had strong ties to the American Establishment.

During the Second World War, Monnet fled to America where he ingratiated himself with American Insiders and developed a friendship with David Bruce — a rising star on the staff of President Roosevelt. After the war, Bruce (CFR 1945–1977) would serve as U.S. ambassador to France (1949–1952) in the Truman administration. Bruce's wife, Evangeline, wrote of that period:

> A great deal of the making of Europe was between Dean Acheson, Jean Monnet and Robert Schuman, who would meet at the American embassy in Paris when my husband was ambassador there.... One could actually see the idea crystallizing. The talks went on daily and in the end they beat out what was really the original plan for the Common Market [the precursor of the EU]. [4]

When David Rockefeller founded the Trilateral Commission in 1973, he chose Georges Berthoin to chair the European Branch. Berthoin was the president of Jean Monnet's European Movement and a former aide to Monnet.[5]

In his May 28, 1997 speech celebrating the 50th anniversary of the Marshall Plan, President Clinton (CFR, TC) acknowledged that American aid had "planted the seeds of institutions that evolved to bind Western Europe together, from the OECD [the Paris-based Organization for Economic Cooperation and Development], the European Union, and NATO."

In September 2000, Ambrose Evans-Pritchard, the (London) *Telegraph's* Europe correspondent, reported on new evidence of American orchestration of the United Europe movement. According to Evans-Pritchard, recently declassified American government documents disclosed "that the US intelligence community ran a campaign in the Fifties and Sixties to build momentum for a united Europe. It funded and directed the European federalist movement." In particular, he noted:

> Washington's main tool for shaping the European agenda was the American Committee for a United Europe [ACUE], created in 1948. The chairman was [William J.] Donovan [who had headed the American wartime OSS — precursor to the CIA], ostensibly a private lawyer by then.
>
> The vice-chairman was Allen Dulles, the CIA director in the Fifties. The board included Walter Bedell Smith, the CIA's first director, and a roster of ex-OSS figures and officials who moved in and out of the CIA. The documents show that ACUE financed the European Movement, the most important federalist organization in the post-war years. In 1958, for example, it provided 53.5 per cent of the movement's funds.
>
> The European Youth Campaign, an arm of the European Movement, was wholly funded and controlled by Washington. The Belgian director, Baron Boel, received monthly payments into a special account. When the head of the European Movement, Polish-born Joseph Retinger, bridled at this degree of American control and tried to raise money in Europe, he was quickly reprimanded.[6]

All three of the U.S. officials mentioned above — Allen Dulles, Walter Bedell Smith, and William J. Donovan — were trusted members of the CFR. Allen Dulles and his brother John Foster Dulles were members of Colonel Edward Mandell House's brain trust, the Inquiry. In that capacity, they attended the Paris Peace Conference after World War I and the parallel meetings at which the CFR was conceived. Allen Dulles served as a director of the CFR from 1927 until his death in 1969 and president of the CFR from 1946 to 1950.

General Walter Bedell Smith would serve on the Bilderberger Advisory Committee — a select inner circle of the internationalist Bilderbergers — along with such CFR heavyweights as Joseph E. Johnson (a CFR director) and Arthur H. Dean (a CFR director).

Ernst H. van der Beugel, honorary secretary-general of the Bilderberger Group revealed more of the inner workings of the EU conspiracy in his 1966 book, *From Marshall Aid to Atlantic Partnership*, which contains a foreword by "my friend Henry Kissinger." Van der Beugel had impeccable Insider credentials. He was vice-chairman of the Netherlands Institute for Foreign Affairs (a CFR affiliate) and a member of the Trilateral Commission.

Van der Beugel's book told how Monnet's Action Committee, "supported by funds from United States foundations," used strong arm tactics in the negotiations for the Treaties of Rome [which established the Common Market, see below]:

> Monnet and his Action Committee were unofficially supervising the negotiations and as soon as obstacles appeared, the United States diplomatic machinery was alerted, mostly through Ambassador Bruce ... who had immediate access to the top echelon of the State Department....[7]

And since war-ravaged Europe was very dependent on U.S. aid in the immediate postwar years, our diplomats carried enormous clout.

In 1947, John J. McCloy (future chairman of the board of the CFR) was appointed American High Commissioner to Germany. McCloy arranged financial support for Paul Henri Spaak, known in Europe as "Mr. Socialist," to lobby for European merger. The source of the support was the reserve of European currencies called "counterpart funds," which had built up through American (Marshall Plan) aid.

In 1987, Ohio State University Professor Michael J. Hogan published a detailed history of Marshall Plan Aid, which documented the CFR hand in shaping the plan. [8]

Of course, our internationalist "leaders" never told the American people that they were using taxpayer dollars to restructure a dependent Europe into a regional government run by top Insiders from behind the scenes. Although the story of American involvement was largely blacked out in Europe, too, a few voices there tried to bring the conspiracy to public attention. [9]

A Monstrous "Bait and Switch"

Concealing CFR leadership and American funding was only part of the deception driving European integration. The crucial part was deceiving the peoples of Europe by denying that political unification was in the works.

To that end, the path to full integration was broken into several intermediate steps, each presented under false colors to disguise its intended destination: In 1951, the Treaty of Paris launched the European Coal and Steel Community with six nations; followed by the Treaties of Rome (1957) creating the European Economic Community (the Common Market), originally with six members; and then evolving into the European Community (EC) in 1967 with 15 nations.

In 1992 the Treaty of Maastrict was signed leading to the European Union a year later (now 27 member states), which is still expanding its authority over member nations (e.g., the Treaty of Nice went into force in 2003 and the Lisbon Treaty in 2009). The EU now has its own central bank, and the euro has replaced the currencies of 17 of its member states.

In its initial stages, the architects of European unity vehemently denied that member nations would need to relinquish significant sovereignty to a regional body. Looking back in 1991, British journalist Sir Peregrine Worsthorne declared: "Twenty years ago, when the process began, there was no question of losing sovereignty. That was a lie, or at any rate, a dishonest obfuscation." Worsthorne further charged:

For the past twenty years or so anybody wanting to have a

career in the public service, in the higher reaches of the city, or the media has had to be pro-European. In the privacy of the closet or among close friends, even many federalists would admit as much. But such is the momentum behind the European movement that none of these individual doubts, expressed separately, will be remotely sufficient to stop the juggernaut. [10]

A glimpse into the perfidy committed by British politicians came to light in 2000 with the release of documents associated with Britain's 1970 application to join the Common Market. British journalist Christopher Booker and Dr. Richard North (a former research director for an agency of the European Parliament) summarized the revelations in their excellent 2003 book, *The Great Deception: A Secret History of the European Union*:

> [Prime Minister Edward] Heath's own bid to join the Common Market began what for the British people was to be the greatest deception of all.... Heath persistently misrepresented Britain's membership of the Common Market as no more than a trading issue....
>
> Only 30 years later would it come to light from the Foreign Office's confidential papers just how conscious were its officials of the extent to which Britain was about to surrender its powers of self-government. None of this was publicly admitted at the time, although the author of the FCO's internal memorandum on "Sovereignty" justified the concealment by suggesting that the British people would not notice what was happening until the end of the century, by which time it would be too late to protest because the process would have become irreversible. [11]

Edward Heath was not alone, even among British politicians, in perpetrating the deception. "For 40 years," says Booker, "British politicians have consistently tried to portray it [the Common Market and EU] to their fellow-citizens as little more than an economic arrangement: a kind of free-trading area primarily concerned with creating jobs and prosperity, which incidentally can help preserve the peace." [12]

Although the architects of the Common Market denied that

political union was the object of economic union, the historical record reveals that from the beginning their intention was to create a European socialist superstate. At the 1948 Congress of Europe, chaired by Winston Churchill, Jean Monnet pushed through a resolution stating: "The creation of a United Europe must be regarded as an essential step towards the creation of a United World." [13]

A Totalitarian Future
The unification of Europe envisioned by Monnet has not reached its conclusion, not by a long shot. But glimpses of the future European superstate are already available:

• In 2000, the Establishment's *New York Times* applauded the demise of the nation-state in Europe:

> One area where the nation-state seems to be losing ground particularly fast to the idea of a united Europe is that of law. This was evident in recent days as European court verdicts obliged Germany and Britain to reconsider or revise basic military policy....
>
> For some time, treaties have enshrined the pre-eminence of European law over national legislation in many areas, including the environment, trade, human rights and working conditions. But it has taken a long time for this reality to reach ordinary citizens.... Now, however, the power of pan-European courts is being brought home....
>
> It was a ruling in September by the Court of Human Rights that led Britain this week to end its ban on openly gay men and women as members of the armed forces. [14]

• In a 1998 decision, the European Court of Human rights overturned British law. Parents could no longer use anything but their hands to spank their children. [15]

• The Summer 2001 issue of *Scottish Life* reported: "Beginning this spring, a show of national pride in the form of a Saltire affixed to a license plate can result in a £1,000 (approximately $1,600) fine. New

European Union (EU) legislation bans the display of any member's flag; only the EU's 12-star flag will be allowed."

• In 2002, the *Wall Street Journal* carried a front-page story — "Tough Tactics: European Regulators Spark Controversy With 'Dawn Raids'" — describing the increasingly "creative" actions of EU bureaucrats:

> European Union antitrust investigators showed up unannounced at Coca-Cola Co.'s London offices early one morning in 1999.... Even though they didn't have a search warrant, the investigators scoured desktop computers and searched e-mail servers. They sifted through hundreds of messages and left with copies of those that contained such key words as "confidential," "competition," and "discount." They also took copies of confidential legal documents prepared by Coke's in-house lawyers....
>
> There is no judicial review before what's known as a dawn raid.... In fact, judges don't have the authority to question, or even see, the justification for a raid. The only approval needed is from the EU's antitrust chief, Mario Monti.... [16]

A year earlier (2001), British journalist Christopher Booker prepared a detailed analysis of the evolution of Britain's subservience to the European Union and concluded:

> What in fact has been taking place has been a transfer of power from Westminster and Whitehall to Brussels on a scale amounting to the greatest constitutional revolution in our history. But much of this has remained buried from view because our politicians like to preserve the illusion that they are still in charge. The result is that remarkably few people now have any proper understanding of how the political system which rules our lives actually works. [17]

Booker's paper provides a serious wake-up call for Americans on what to expect if we allow our leaders to take us down a similar route.

NAFTA

Buoyed by their success in enticing the nations of Europe into their regional trap, the Insiders would apply similar tactics in Africa, Asia, and the Americas.

In November 1993, CFR elites accomplished their first major foot in the door in this hemisphere when Congress approved the North American Free Trade Agreement (NAFTA) between the U.S., Mexico, and Canada.

Although President George H. W. Bush (a former director of the CFR) had signed the agreement a year earlier, both Houses of Congress still had to approve implementing legislation before NAFTA could take effect. The battle for congressional approval in the face of strong public opposition provides important lessons.

When President Clinton assumed office at the beginning of 1993, it fell on his shoulders to carry the Insiders' ball and gain approval for NAFTA. This posed a challenge for the liberal president, since such a radical assault on sovereignty needed to be sold to the American people as a "conservative" measure.

Just as in Europe decades earlier, NAFTA was promoted as an effort to improve the economies of the member nations by lowering tariff barriers. And the words "Free Trade" in the title were calculated to win conservative support.

But, as in Europe, the alleged economic benefits were just bait for a treasonous attack on the sovereignty of all the nations in the Western Hemisphere. While proponents would ridicule any suggestion that NAFTA would undermine U.S. sovereignty, the NAFTA treaty, combined with side agreements, would set up more than 30 new international committees to decide issues previously the responsibility of the individual national legislatures.

The entire NAFTA document would comprise 1700 pages of government intervention in the affairs of the three member nations: Free trade or government bureaucracy?

Aiding the deception that NAFTA was a "conservative" measure, many liberals would oppose it. To offset the opposition in Congress within his own party, President Clinton hoped to get the support of three-quarters of the House GOP members and at least a third of the Democrats. Fortunately, he had the help of Republican congressional leaders — Minority Whip Newt Gingrich (CFR) in the House and

Minority Leader Bob Dole in the Senate.

The final vote in the House was 234 to 200, with 132 Republicans voting in favor, as against 43 opposed. (More House Democrats shunned the agreement: 102 voted in favor to 156 opposed. The lone Independent, Bernie Sanders, voted "No.") In the Senate, Republicans again could take credit for NAFTA with 34 voting in favor and only 10 opposed. (Democrats were almost evenly divided: 27 in favor, 28 opposed, 1 not voting.)

Several months later, an editorial in the *New York Times* would acknowledge Gingrich's role in delivering the crucial Republican vote. The Establishment *Times* was chastising Gingrich for hesitating to support the next goal of the Insiders — U.S. acceptance of the World Trade Organization and a stronger GATT:

> That is a bizarre turnabout for a man who almost single-handedly bailed out the Clinton Presidency by rounding up Republican votes for a similar accord — the North American Free Trade Agreement — over the opposition of House Democrats. [18]

Indeed, the yearlong battle for NAFTA approval was hard fought. Stories regularly surfaced suggesting that the White House raided the Treasury to buy the votes needed to push the measure over the top.

CFR Insiders Acknowledge Goal

Both David Rockefeller (former CFR chairman) and CFR heavyweight Henry Kissinger lobbied openly in the nation's press for NAFTA. But they tipped their hand by announcing that much more was involved than just lowering trade barriers.

In a 1993 column that appeared in the July 18 *Los Angeles Times*, former Secretary of State Henry Kissinger declared:

> It [NAFTA] will represent the most creative step toward a new world order taken by any group of countries since the end of the Cold War, and the first step toward an even larger vision of a free-trade zone for the entire Western Hemisphere.... [NAFTA] is not a conventional trade agreement, but the architecture of a new international system.... A Western Hemisphere-wide free-

trade system — with NAFTA as the first step — would give the Americas a commanding role no matter what happens.

A few months later, David Rockefeller championed the agreement in the *Wall Street Journal*: "Everything is in place — after 500 years — to build a true 'new world' in the Western Hemisphere," Rockefeller enthused, adding "I don't think that 'criminal' would be too strong a word to describe ... rejecting NAFTA." [19]

Well before the Bush administration negotiated the agreement, the Fall 1991 issue of *Foreign Affairs* revealed that the Insiders were well aware that NAFTA was following in the EU's footsteps:

> The creation of trinational dispute-resolution mechanisms and rule-making bodies on border and environmental issues may also be embryonic forms of more comprehensive structures. After all, international organizations and agreements like GATT and NAFTA by definition minimize assertions of sovereignty in favor of a joint rule-making authority....
>
> It may be useful to revisit the spirit of the Monnet Commission, which provided a blueprint for Europe at a moment of extraordinary opportunity. The three nations of North America, in more modest fashion, have also arrived at a defining moment. They may want to create a wiseman's North American commission to operate in the post-ratification period. [20]

World Trade Organization (WTO)

Of course, America's entry into NAFTA was only one step in the Insiders' game plan to submerge the United States in international government. The next major step was to pull America into the proposed World Trade Organization, designed to give the old General Agreement on Tariffs and Trade (GATT) real teeth.

Before the year (1994) was out, President Clinton with the help again of Bob Dole in the Senate and soon-to-be Speaker of the House Newt Gingrich would hand the Insiders this crucial victory.

Newt Gingrich is typical of many politicians who talk a conservative line, feigning concerns about yielding sovereignty, but in the end act to give the internationalists what they want. In testimony before the House Ways and Means Committee, Gingrich indicated clearly that he understood the implication of the WTO agreement he would effectively champion:

> I agree with you, this is very close to Maastricht [the treaty establishing the European Union], and 20 years from now we will look back on this as a very important defining moment. This is not just another trade agreement. This is adopting something which twice, once in the 1940s and once in the 1950s, the U.S. Congress rejected. I am not even saying we should reject it, I in fact lean toward it. But I think we have to be very careful, because it is a very big transfer of power. [21]

In November of 1994, the GOP, capitalizing on public disillusionment with President Clinton, won control of both Houses of Congress for the first time in 40 years. The new Congress would be sworn in in January. Gingrich would initially protest the suggestion that GATT/WTO be voted on in a lame duck December 1994 session of Congress. However, the president's fast track authority for negotiating the agreements was due to expire on December 15th, and the agreements faced the prospect of strong opposition in the new Congress.

In the end, both Gingrich and Dole agreed to the lame duck session for the purpose of taking up the WTO. And neither would protest that WTO was really a treaty disguised as a trade agreement (as was also the case with NAFTA before) and should accordingly require a two-thirds vote in the Senate. Although the accord amounted to some 26,000 pages, which no member of Congress had the time to read, both houses accepted the agreement.

Hemispheric Integration

A few months following his NAFTA victory, President Clinton announced a Summit of the Americas to be held later in the year (1994) in Miami.

The primary purpose of the Summit was to launch negotiations for a so-called Free Trade Area of the Americas (FTAA) — an expansion of NAFTA that would include all (34) of the countries of North and South America, with the exception of Cuba. The Summit pledged to complete the negotiations no later than 2005.

Like so many initiatives advertised as presidential leadership, however, the plan was really hatched elsewhere. Indeed, decades earlier, architects of world government, such as David Rockefeller, had developed the networks of Latin American allies needed to support the FTAA. The FTAA plan was merely revealed publicly in 1994 and embraced by President Clinton. Following the Miami event, one researcher-journalist observed that it was *completely* a Rockefeller show from start to finish:

> The summit and the FTAA were conceived, nurtured, and brought to fruition by the Council of the Americas (David Rockefeller, founder and honorary chairman), the Americas Society (David Rockefeller, chairman), the Forum of the Americas (David Rockefeller, founder), the U.S. Council of the Mexico–U.S. Business Committee (Rodman C. Rockefeller, chairman), the Council on Foreign Relations (David Rockefeller, former chairman), the Trilateral Commission (David Rockefeller, founder and honorary chairman), and the Chase Manhattan Bank (David Rockefeller, former chairman). [To the list, add the Institute for International Economics (David Rockefeller, financial backer and board member).] [22]

A revealing admission regarding the Summit came from Thomas F. "Mack" McLarty, President Clinton's chief of staff: "[T]his summit is much broader than [lowering tariffs], and that's how it should be looked at. This is not a trade summit, it is an overall summit. It will focus on economic integration and convergence." [23]

McLarty's characterization of the summit carries authority. McLarty also served as Clinton's special envoy to the Americas and was heavily involved in the negotiations for NAFTA, the FTAA, and other "trade" agreements. And he was a board member of David Rockefeller's Council of the Americas. In 2001, McLarty's globalist credentials would earn him a spot in the Council on Foreign Relations.

The goals and timeline for FTAA negotiations announced in Miami in 1994 were picked up by President Clinton's successor — Republican President George W. Bush. At the conclusion of the Quebec Summit of the Americas, staged April 20–22, 2001,

President Bush and the other heads of state issued a joint declaration:

> We, the democratically elected Heads of State and Government of the Americas, have met in Quebec City at our Third Summit, to renew our commitment to hemispheric integration....
>
> We reiterate our firm commitment and adherence to the principles and purposes of the Charters of the United Nations and of the Organization of American States (OAS)....
>
> We direct our Ministers to ensure that negotiations of the FTAA Agreement are concluded no later than January 2005 and to seek its entry into force as soon as possible thereafter, but in any case, no later than December 2005.** [** refers to a Venezuelan reservation.]
>
> The Agreement should be balanced, comprehensive and consistent with World Trade Organization (WTO) rules and disciplines....

Reporting on the conclusion of the Quebec Summit, the *New York Times* observed that "the leaders proposed an 'action plan' backed by billions of dollars in support from international financial institutions. The World Bank and the Inter-American Development Bank committed more than $20 billion to strengthen democratic foundations in the Americas and prepare for free trade despite disparate levels of development." [24]

The insistence that foreign aid is necessary to set up the foundations for free trade among nations should awaken suspicions. Actually, the aid was needed so the Insiders could grease the skids in Latin America to build their convergence "consensus." A similar path was followed in Europe leading to the desperate plight of Greece in 2011.

Speaking to representatives of the Organization of American States and the World Affairs Council in January of 2002, President Bush listed several steps his administration was taking to help create the FTAA by 2005 including:

> Today, I announce that the United States will explore a free trade agreement with the countries of Central America.... Our

purpose is to strengthen the economic ties we already have with these nations ... and to take another step toward completing the Free Trade Area of the Americas. [25]

The president also announced plans to expand U.S. funding of the World Bank for that purpose.

However, as 2005 grew closer, the Insiders' timetable for an FTAA agreement would prove unrealistic. Indeed, following a decade of actually living with NAFTA, NAFTA ghost towns and lost jobs were all too apparent on the U.S. landscape, and many Americans were strongly opposed to any enlargement.

The CAFTA Battle
Nevertheless, the Bush administration was determined to bring us closer to an FTAA, despite obvious political consequences. A big step was CAFTA, a so-called free trade agreement between the United States and Central America. (The Dominican Republic later joined the agreement, changing the name to DR-CAFTA.)

After negotiating the Central American Free Trade Agreement, the Bush administration waited for more than a year before submitting the agreement to Congress, because the plan simply did not have enough votes. On June 30, 2005, the United States Senate approved the DR-CAFTA by a vote of 54 to 45. But resistance in the House was still strong. Another month would elapse before supporters dared bring the measure to a vote.

On July 21, the *Washington Post* reported: "[A]dministration officials concede they still do not have the votes to pass CAFTA in the House.... The White House had hoped to win over blocs of undecideds.... But those blocs have barely budged. Now the administration is going vote by vote." According to the *Post*, Republican leaders have been authorized "to secure votes with whatever is at hand, from amendments to the highway and energy bills to the still incomplete appropriations bills." [26]

The internationalist pressure finally won out. On July 27, 2005, the House of Representatives approved the pact by an exceptionally narrow 2-vote margin 217–215, with two representatives not voting. Following the vote, the *New York Times* acknowledged the intense top-down pressure:

Whatever the economic merits, the vote on Wednesday night made it clear that the political appeal of the trade agreement was low. Only 15 Democrats supported the measure. And despite intense pressure from President Bush and House Republican leaders, 27 Republicans voted against the deal; many others badly wanted to do so. [27]

The March Goes On

An agreement encompassing the entire hemisphere has not been abandoned, just placed on the back burner, while a slower approach to hemispheric integration is pursued. Just as with Europe, full integration (and the unfolding hand of tyranny) is a drawn-out process. Because of resistance, Insider timetables are not always met, but the internationalists don't give up on their goal.

The Insiders have sought to encourage the immigration invasion as one step to deepen NAFTA (see, for example the Security and Prosperity Partnership proposal of the George W. Bush administration in Chapter 14). And despite its unpopularity, NAFTA is still in place, quietly waiting for the Insiders to preset the dials, so it can expand its authority in the name of convergence, as originally intended.

In the meantime, NAFTA is exercising the authority it already has. In April 2004, the *New York Times* reported how American jurists and politicians were surprised that Chapter 11 of the NAFTA agreement was already empowering NAFTA tribunals to override U.S. court decisions:

> Abner Mikva, a former chief judge of the federal appeals court in Washington and a former congressman, is one of the three Nafta judges considering the Mississippi case. He declined to discuss it but did offer his perspective on Chapter 11. "If Congress has known that there was anything like this in Nafta," he said, "they would never have voted for it." [28]

Meanwhile, Insider attacks on U.S. sovereignty are well underway on other fronts.

Chapter 8

Post-Cold War Pretexts

For several decades following World War II, the greatest pretext for empowering the UN was the purported danger of a nuclear holocaust. For example, the introduction to *Freedom From War* (the 1961 U.S. "disarmament" proposal — see Chapter 6) begins:

> The revolutionary development of modern weapons within a world divided by serious ideological differences has produced a crisis in human history. In order to overcome *the danger of nuclear war now confronting mankind*, the United States has introduced at the Sixteenth General Assembly of the United Nations a *Program for General and Complete Disarmament in a Peaceful World*. [Emphasis added.]

However, the threat of a nuclear confrontation with the Soviets failed to resolve what Lincoln Bloomfield, in his confidential 1962 study memorandum, termed the "central dilemma in world politics today":

> [G]iven a continuation unabated of communist dynamism, the subordination of states to a true world government appears impossible; but if the communist dynamic were greatly abated, the West might well lose whatever incentive it has for world government. [1]

In other words, for the West to accept world government the Soviets would need to be transformed and adopt a tamer image, but then "Bloomfield" saw a paradox — the driving pretext for nations to submit to a world authority would be gone.

Unless, Bloomfield postulated, there was "a crisis, a war, or a brink-of-war situation so grave or commonly menacing that deeply-rooted attitudes and practices are sufficiently shaken to open the possibility of a revolution in world political arrangements."

Bloomfield further argued that accelerated world government

"may be brought into existence as a result of a series of sudden, nasty, and traumatic shocks.... The transforming experience, whether evolutionary or revolutionary, must, to achieve the foundation of consensus requisite for community, be enough to reach and move great masses of people...." [2]

By the middle of the 1980s, the Insiders were ready to give the Soviets the desired facelift through *glasnost* and *perestroika*. Since the internationalists could no longer use a "Soviet threat" to drive the movement toward world government, they would have to rely on alternative threats. However, with its new face-lift, the former Soviet Union could henceforth be enlisted as *our partner* in combating these new threats.

So the Insiders modified their propaganda, claiming that several of their long-standing issues — such as drug trafficking, terrorism, and damage to the environment — had, with the end of the Cold War, become global crises, requiring international attention.

Internationalist politicians and the Establishment media would repeatedly insist that nations could no longer deal we these threats individually but would need to embrace global action. And slickly, we were told that meant investing new authority in the United Nations and agreeing to be bound by UN decisions.

We next examine how the CFR Insiders have capitalized on two of those threats — allegations of impending environmental catastrophe and terrorism — elevating them to major imperatives for empowering global government.

Saving the Planet

Revolutionary groups had exploited environmental concerns even prior to America's involvement in the Vietnam War. However, the 1969 Santa Barbara oil spill and Earth Day 1970 marked a major investment of the CFR-interlocked foundations in the environmental movement.

Earth Day 1970
On November 30, 1969, the Establishment's *New York Times* devoted a lengthy front-page story to the planning for the upcoming Earth Day:

Rising concern about the "environmental crisis" is sweeping the nation's campuses with an intensity that may be on its way to eclipsing student discontent over the war in Vietnam.... [A] national day of observance of environmental problems, analogous to the mass demonstrations on Vietnam, is being planned for next spring, when a nationwide environmental "teach-in" ... coordinated from the office of Senator Gaylord Nelson is planned....[3]

By some estimates, as many as 20 million Americans participated in the April 22, 1970 event.[4] On that day, *Saturday Review* editor Norman Cousins (CFR) brazenly unveiled the pre-programmed solution:

Humanity needs a world order. The fully sovereign nation is incapable of dealing with the poisoning of the environment.... The management of the planet, therefore — whether we are talking about the need to prevent war or the need to prevent ultimate change to the conditions of life — requires a world-government.[5]

Foundation Funding
To identify the forces that have built up the worldwide environmental movement, we need to follow the money. At the top of the money and control pyramid, the agenda has nothing to do with concern over the environment, but everything to do with building government power, particularly world government power, over our lives.

In following the money, we find ties between the leadership of the CFR and a network of organizations that provide research, funding, and public pressure. For example, both the Ford and Rockefeller Foundations provided substantial funding to help make Earth Day 1970 a success and catapult the environmental movement.[6] And as Gary Allen wrote in 1969:

Ford Foundation President McGeorge Bundy is a member of the C.F.R., and so are ten of its nineteen officers and trustees. Sixteen of twenty-three Rockefeller Foundation officers and trustees are members of the C.F.R., including

President J. George Harrar.[7]

That same year (1970), the Ford Foundation provided the seed money for a group of Yale Law School graduates together with several New York attorneys to found a "public interest" law firm — the National Resources Defense Council (NRDC). Over the next several years, Ford would provide the NRDC with additional millions in grants.

In his 2009 exposé *Green Hell*, scholar-columnist Steve Milloy identified the central role of the NRDC within the environmentalist network:

> The green workhorses are the Natural Resources Defense Council, boasting $88 million in annual revenue and $167 million in assets, according to *Forbes*, and the Environmental Defense Fund, enjoying $83 million in annual revenue and $108 million in assets.[8]

The Ford Foundation was also active in financing the early growth of the Environmental Defense Fund. Between 1971 and 1977, Ford grants totaled nearly $1 million. And in the intervening years, dozens of environmentalist organizations have regularly received grants from CFR-interlocked foundations.

Milloy also described the various components of this immense network that gave it so much clout:

> From the Earth Liberation Front, an FBI-labeled terrorist group, to "street theater" groups like Greenpeace and the Rainforest Action Network, to suit-and-tie "mainstream" activist organizations like the Natural Resources Defense Council and Environmental Defense Fund, to "old money" private foundations like the Rockefeller Foundation and the Pew Charitable Trusts, the greens can muster an array of forces — protestors, lawyers, scientists, journalists, and others — to get things done.[9]

Earth Day Fallout

Media exploitation of the 1969 Santa Barbara oil spill and the subsequent Earth Day event set the stage for major socialist power grabs in the name of protecting the environment. Environmental groups quickly seized upon the public concern to develop "pressure from below" for major federal legislation to control America's natural resources and economic life.

Three weeks following the Santa Barbara "ecological disaster," Senator Henry "Scoop" Jackson re-introduced his previously defeated bill to establish the Council on Environmental Quality (CEQ). Congress passed Jackson's National Environmental Policy Act of 1969 (NERA) in December, and President Nixon signed it into law on January 1st. The law, requiring federal environmental impact statements, was a dream come true for environmentalist attorneys. The law would be used to tie up construction of the Alaskan oil pipeline for five years.

On December 2, 1970, "Republican" President Nixon, through executive order, created the Environmental Protection Agency. Within five years of Earth Day, environmental pressure groups could list these major victories in new federal regulations: the Clean Air Amendments Act; the Clean Water Act; the Endangered Species Act of 1973; the Insecticide, Fungicide, and Rodenticide Act; the Water Pollution Control Act; the Forest and Rangelands Renewable Resources Planning Act; the Marine Protection, Research and Sanctuaries Act; and the Federal Land Policy and Management Act.

Environmental groups have succeeded with their legislative agenda not just because of well prepared lobbying in the halls of Congress, but more importantly because the groups were able to invest heavily in softening up the public. As one researcher summed up the strategy:

> Beginning with the first Earth Day in 1970, the foundation-fueled eco-lobby conducted an assault on the public mind. Propaganda promoting the Green Revolution was woven into the media, entertainment, and education. Millions of Americans were led to believe that the environmental movement sprang from authentic grass-roots concern for nature — rather than being built on a foundation of "AstroTurf" lobbies funded and organized by elitists seeking to control the human population. [10]

The Unfinished Agenda

In the decade following the first Earth Day, several foundation-funded studies bolstered the case for oppressive federal measures. One of the most significant was *The Unfinished Agenda: The Citizen's Policy Guide to Environmental Issues*, a 1977 report of a task force sponsored by the Rockefeller Brothers Fund.

The panel of "experts" preparing the report was staffed with leaders from foundation-funded groups, such as the National Resources Defense Council, the Environmental Defense Fund, and Friends of the Earth. The finished *Unfinished Agenda* summarized its message: "[T]his book is about a world transition from abundance to scarcity, a transition that is already well underway." [11]

Laurence Rockefeller had introduced the line the previous year in an article for *Reader's Digest*. Rockefeller warned that if we did not adopt a simpler lifestyle "voluntarily and democratically, it may be forced upon us." [12] The notion that rising consumption is no longer "sustainable" — requiring government action — would be heard over an over in the ensuing years.

The Unfinished Agenda called for many federal measures designed to restrict ostensibly environmentally damaging consumption and the American standard of living, such as a "progressively increasing gasoline tax, the proceeds of which should be used to begin reducing the ill effects of automobiles." [13] The task force report had an immediate impact on federal policy. The Jimmy Carter administration adopted *The Unfinished Agenda* as its blueprint for its energy and environmental policies.

One of the authors of the task-force report was Amory Lovins, a British spokesman for Friend of the Earth. The previous year, Lovins had authored a defining article for the CFR's *Foreign Affairs* entitled "Energy Strategy: The Road Not Taken." [14] His much quoted essay gave "scientific" standing to a clever campaign to stifle America's energy production by pushing for conversion to "soft" energy sources (e.g. solar, wind, and geothermal). The campaign has been in full swing during the Obama administration.

Following the money, we also find that the taxpayer has been tapped to feather the environmental nest. Both federal contracts and direct grants to "environmental" groups abound.[15]

Meanwhile, the CFR's creation, the United Nations, was preparing to accept the mantle of authority over *all* behavior affecting the "global" environment.

The International Front
In June 1972, the UN held its first major conference on environmental "threats" in Stockholm, Sweden. The secretary-general of the conference was a trustee of the Rockefeller Foundation — Canadian billionaire Maurice Strong.

One outcome of the conference was the establishment of the United Nations Environment Programme (UNEP), "to become the world's leading environmental agency," according to the UN's website. Maurice Strong was selected as the first executive director of the new agency.

Although environmental alarms were sounded throughout the seventies and eighties, the public had not yet been hammered with the notion that these problems had developed into global crises. With the end of the Cold War, that would change.

The UN's 1992 Earth Summit in Rio was the watershed event staged to bring about that change. Rio would provide the launching pad for a wave of new "disaster" propaganda and government programs to "save the planet." The CFR, its foundation allies, and their supported environmental groups would invest heavily in staging this major media event, orchestrated to make it appear as though a universal consensus was demanding action.

Run-up to Rio
Serious planning for the Rio conference got underway in 1987 with publication of the report of the United Nations World Commission on Environment and Development.[16]

The Commission was more commonly referred to as the Brundtland Commission, after its chair, Gro Harlem Brundtland, prime minister of Norway and future first vice president of the Socialist International.

The Brundtland Report would bring the term "sustainable development" into public discourse. Brundtland would serve as vice chairman of the Rio Conference. Maurice Strong, who would manage the Rio Conference as its secretary-general, was a member of the Brundtland Commission.

In the years immediately preceding the Rio conference, there were UN Preparatory Committee Meetings (PrepComs), declarations, and numerous op-eds underscoring the seriousness of the disaster confronting planet earth.

The CFR-led orchestra served several purposes: The illusion of consensus deceived the public, providing political cover for sympathetic politicians to advance the CFR agenda. The massive propaganda campaign also acted to silence other right-thinking politicians, who lacked the "ammunition" to go up against the media and their heavily "armed" opponents.

A *sample* of the CFR propaganda leading up to Rio is instructive:

• "Redefining Security," an article for the Spring 1989 issue of the CFR's *Foreign Affairs*, signaled the emerging internationalist line. Its author — Jessica Tuchman Mathews (CFR, later a CFR senior fellow) — was at the time vice president and director of research of the foundation-funded World Resources Institute (an environmentalist think tank). In her article, Mathews cleverly builds the case for planetary management:

> Global developments now suggest the need for ... broadening [the] definition of national security to include resource, environmental and demographic issues....
>
> Environmental strains that transcend national borders are already beginning to break down the sacred boundaries of national sovereignty....
>
> The traditional prerogatives of nation states are poorly matched with the needs for regional cooperation and global decision-making....

Mathews is currently the president of the Carnegie Endowment for International Peace, the post once held by Alger Hiss.

• Also in 1989, the Smithsonian Institution hosted a conference on the global environment. The conference was funded by the Carnegie, Ford, and Rockefeller Foundations. At the conference, biologist Thomas Lovejoy, who would join the CFR that year, paid his Establishment dues by sounding an alarm:

[U]nless there is a major shift in the rate in which policy is developed or changed, it's likely that we are simply not going to make it.... It's not very far off before the problems are so big that it's almost beyond our capacity to recover.... We are in a sense, or should be, at war with our life-styles and that is something we've never had to face with our species before. [17]

Dr. Lovejoy is a big name in the conservation world. He is credited with introducing the term "biodiversity." In 1998, Lovejoy would add the position of chief biodiversity advisor for the World Bank to his impressive resumé.

• In November 1989, George F. Kennan (CFR), who first enunciated the strategy of "containment" that became U.S. Cold War policy, signaled an important change in Insider strategy. In a syndicated article for the *Washington Post*, the CFR "wise man" stated that we now live "in an age where the great enemy is not the Soviet Union, but the rapid deterioration of our planet as a supporting structure for civilized life." [18]

• With the Rio summit less than a year away, its secretary general, Maurice Strong, set much of the tone for the upcoming conference in an (August 1991) UNCED report:

It is clear that current lifestyles and consumption patterns of the affluent middle-class ... involving high meat intake, consumption of large amounts of frozen and "convenience" foods, ownership of motor-vehicles, numerous electric household appliances, home and workplace airconditioning ... suburban housing ... are not sustainable.

Repeating a theme promoted 15 years earlier by Laurence Rockefeller, Strong argued that a shift is necessary "towards lifestyles ... less geared to ... environmentally damaging consumption patterns."

• A month prior to the Rio Summit, Mikhail Gorbachev visited the United States and spoke at Westminster College in Fulton Missouri.

Westminster College is where Winston Churchill made his famous "Iron Curtain" speech at the outbreak of the Cold War (1946). Following in Churchill's steps, Gorbachev would warn of a new enemy:

> The prospect of catastrophic climatic changes, more frequent droughts, floods, hunger, epidemics, national-ethnic conflicts, and other similar catastrophes compels governments to adopt a world perspective and seek generally applicable solutions. [19]

Gorbachev emphasized that those solutions would require "some kind of global government." The *LA Times* grasped the key point, running its story under the headline: "Gorbachev Backs World Government." [20]

• At the opening of the Earth Summit, a *Time* magazine cover story for its June 1, 1992 "Rio: Coming Together to Save the Earth" issue revealed the real purpose for the green hysteria: "Making sacrifices for the good of the planet requires negotiating away some measure of national sovereignty...." The *Time* story even recommended giving "the United Nations broad powers to create an environmental police force for the planet."

1992 Rio Earth Summit

The grand extravaganza known as the Earth Summit, staged in Rio de Janeiro, Brazil, spanned most of two weeks (June 3 to June 14, 1992). Officially titled the United Nations Conference on Environment and Development (UNCED), the Summit drew a crowd variously estimated at between 17,000 to 30,000.

Of course, most of these travelers were not participants in the main conference; instead they came for a side event — the Global Forum — promoted as the "world's fair of environmentalism," but described by one reporter as the Green Woodstock.

Attending the main conference were the delegates from 172 of the world's governments, including the largest gathering of heads of state (108) up to that point in history, and representatives of more than 1,700 accredited NGOs. And, of course, there was the media.

Maurice Strong set the tone for the conference in his opening remarks: "[P]atterns of production and consumption in the industrialized world ... are undermining the Earth's life-support systems.... To continue along this pathway could lead to the end of civilization.... This conference must establish the foundations for effecting the transition to sustainable development." [Translation: We must reduce progress and growth in the industrialized world.]

At Rio, speaker after speaker would insist that industrialization was irreparably damaging nature, without making any effort to substantiate the claim. Speeches both inside and outside were also notable for their virulent anti-Americanism and socialism. (America was cast as the premier polluter of the world and criticized for not doing enough to transfer its wealth to the Third World.)

This radical socialism generally went unreported by the American press, which sought to create a more responsible image for the Summit.

As usual, the compliant media took the proceedings at face value, not inquiring as to hidden agendas, funding, organization, and orchestration. Yet the festivities cried out for such inquiry. Americans were asked to accept, for example, that "representatives" of "indigenous peoples" travelled half way around the world to add their voices to the CFR line that their habitats were suffering from unrestrained industrialization.

Maurice Strong would claim: "[The indigenous peoples] are the guardians of the extensive and fragile ecosystems that are vital to the well-being of the planet." [21] And the Establishment would hold up other foundation-supported NGOs as the legitimate voices of civil society. It was all about creating an illusion of "planetary consensus."

Fallout from Rio

The Rio Conference adopted two formal treaties — the UN Framework Convention on Climate Change (UNFCCC) and the Convention on Biodiversity. The former was signed by President Bush and ratified by the U.S. Senate later that year. Three agreements were also approved at the Summit: The Rio Declaration, Protection of the World's Forests [a set of Forest Principles], and Agenda 21.

The Establishment's *New York Times* wasted no time telling its readers what had been accomplished. On the closing day of the conference, William K. Stevens, reporting from Rio for the *Times*, quoted Richard Benedick of the U.S. State Department and advisor to Maurice Strong: "[The Earth Summit] should not be judged by the immediate results, but by the process it sets in motion." [22]

An example of a process set in motion at Rio was the Agenda 21 non-binding "soft law" agreement.

A Totalitarian Master Plan

The development of Agenda 21 began three years prior to Rio. Advocates would tout Agenda 21 as a comprehensive global action plan for sustainable development, approved at the Earth Summit. The massive document proposes to micro-manage the lives of the entire human population. Even though the delegates voted to adopt Agenda 21, few likely read the final version, which ran to over 700 pages of complex legalese.

An abbreviated version, enthusiastically endorsed by Maurice Strong, was published the following year by Earthpress as: *AGENDA 21: The Earth Summit Strategy to Save Our Planet*. The editor, environmental-activist attorney Daniel Sitarz, wrote approvingly:

AGENDA 21 proposes an array of actions which are intended to be implemented by every person on Earth.... It calls for specific changes in the activities of all people.... Effective execution of AGENDA 21 will require a profound reorientation of all human society, unlike anything the world has ever experienced — a major shift in the priorities of both governments and individuals and an unprecedented redeployment of human and financial resources. This shift will demand that a concern for the environmental consequences of every human action be integrated into individual and collective decision-making at every level.

Among the minority of critics attending the conference who were not caught up in the eco-propaganda was the late former governor of Washington State — Dr. Dixy Lee Ray. A professor of zoology from Stanford, Dr. Ray had been appointed Chairman of the Atomic Energy Commission by President Nixon in 1973.

In her book, *Environmental Overkill*, published in post-Rio 1993, Dr. Ray would assert:

> The objective, clearly enunciated by the leaders of UNCED, is to bring about change in the present system of nations. The future is to be world government, with central planning by the UN.... If force is needed, it will be provided by a UN green-helmeted police force....[23]
>
> First, we must recognize that the environmental movement is not about facts or logic. More and more it is becoming clear that those who support the so-called "New World Order" or World Government under the United Nations have adopted global environmentalism as a basis for the dissolution of independent nations and the international realignment of power.[24]

We certainly do not mean to suggest that rank-and-file environmentalists have no real interest in protecting the environment. But it should be clear from the above that the movement would be a non-starter without Establishment funding and a conspiratorial purpose that has nothing to do with protecting the spotted owl.

Specifically, the alarmists over the post-cold war pretexts always go to the same solutions — more coercive authority in government and more support for international (i.e., UN) institutions.

Terrorism

But it has taken the events in our own wondrous and terrible century to clinch the case for world government.... Each world war inspired the creation of an international organization, the League of Nations in the 1920s and the United Nations in the '40s..... Globalization has also contributed to the spread of *terrorism*, drug trafficking, AIDS and environmental degradation. But because those threats are more than any one nation can cope with on its own, they constitute an incentive for international cooperation. [Emphasis added.] — Strobe Talbott, "America Abroad: The Birth of the Global Nation," *Time*, July 20, 1992

113

In the above essay, soon-to-be Assistant Secretary of State Strobe Talbott (CFR) glibly inverts reality by claiming that the two world wars inspired the creation of international organizations. Instead, designing men seeking to pull America into an international organization looked to war to advance their revolutionary scheme.

The battle against terrorism constitutes another huge deception perpetrated against the American public. For example, the suggestion that either the UN or the former Soviet Union can serve as useful allies in the fight against terrorism is absurd. Indeed, this swindle has required the cover-up of two facts: 1) The Soviet Union launched the international terrorist movement in the 1960s; and 2) the UN welcomes and extols terrorist leaders and groups in its decision-making bodies.

The CFR has aided and encouraged the deception so its team could provide the leadership for "fighting" the new enemy. Let's look at the record.

The Soviet Connection

More than a century and a half ago, Karl Marx wrote: "Only one means exists to shorten the bloody death pangs of the old society and the birth pangs of the new society, to simplify and concentrate them — revolutionary terrorism." [25] Marx's disciples began to apply that principle in the last century by supporting "wars of national liberation," a propaganda substitute for "terrorism."

The actual beginning of the modern-day international terrorist movement can be traced to a 1964 decision of the Soviet Politburo. Following that decision, the Soviet Union began recruiting terrorists from around the world and training them at the Lenin Institute and Lumumba University in Moscow and at various camps in the USSR, Czechoslovakia, East Germany, and Cuba.

In January 1966, Fidel Castro would host the Tricontinental Conference, an international gathering of 513 representatives of 83 terrorist groups. Tricontinental would map out a "a global revolutionary strategy to counter the global strategy of American imperialism." [26]

Before the year was out, terrorist training camps in Cuba, under the direction of a colonel in the Soviet KGB, would be training recruits from throughout Latin America. Among the first graduates were the Sandinista Communists, who would seize power in Nicaragua in 1979.

Claire Sterling, an American foreign correspondent for several major publications, including the *Reader's Digest* and the *Washington Post*, researched these developments. She discovered that "Castro was training the advance guard of the coming European fright decade — Palestinians, Italians, Germans, French, Spanish Basques — and forming guerrilla nuclei in practically every Western Hemisphere state south of the American border." [27]

More training camps would appear in Eastern Europe, the Middle East, and Asia. But the instructors generally came from the Soviet Union, Cuba, and East Germany. And that's where thousands of ruthless terrorists were born.

However, Sterling's exposé was ignored or disputed in government circles. Indeed, Insider plans required that the Soviets not be exposed as the orchestrators of modern terrorism. The world's "superpowers" and the major players among nations had to appear clean for the authority of the "international community" to be respected. Nations who did not fit the required image of responsibility were described as "rogue states" in need of *international* supervision.

So, with the aid of the Establishment media, an effective blackout regarding the Soviet hand in terrorism (likewise for Soviet and Red Chinese orchestration of the international drug menace) has been maintained. Nevertheless, Soviet sponsorship has never been in doubt, nor has it been unknown to American presidents and their advisors.

In her 1981 book, *The Terror Network,* Ms. Sterling quotes Dr. Hans Joseph Horchem of West Germany's antiterrorist Office for the Defense of the Constitution, "considered one of the West's best informed intelligence analysts." Dr. Horchem was particularly blunt regarding Soviet involvement: "The KGB is engineering international terrorism. The facts can be proven, documented, and are well known to the international Western intelligence community." [28]

Ray S. Cline, former deputy CIA director for intelligence (1962–1966) and coauthor of the 1984 book *Terrorism: The Soviet Connection*, also summed up the clear evidence:

It's important to realize that when you say the Soviet Union supports terrorism, you do not mean that they direct and command each terrorist activity. That would be impossible and not very useful. What they do is supply the infrastructure of terror: the money, the guns, the training, the background information, the communications, the propaganda that will inspire individual terrorist groups. [29]

Contrary to the misleading sanitized news regularly offered to the public, there have been no really significant stand-alone terrorist groups. Virtually all the notable groups receive their funding and direction from Russia, China, Cuba, and thinly deniable assets such as Iran, Syria, and formerly Ghaddafi's Libya.

Yet U.S. presidents, influenced by the Insiders, persisted in covering up the Soviet connection. As Sterling noted in 1981: "No Western government has gone so far to indict the Soviet Union. Some have gone pretty far to avoid doing so." [30]

Moreover, since the "collapse" of the Soviet Union, the disingenuousness and willful blindness have reached new heights. Now the former Soviet Union is supposedly our friend and ally in the war *against* terrorism.

In January 1989, a few months before the Berlin Wall came down, Secretary of State George Shultz (CFR) joined representatives of 34 other nations in Vienna to condemn "as criminal all acts, methods, and practices of terrorism, wherever and by whomever committed" and agree that "terrorism cannot be justified under any circumstances." [31]

What a show of contempt for the public! Among the signers of the anti-terrorist agreement were representatives from the Soviet Union, Bulgaria, Czechoslovakia, East Germany, and Hungary — all *supporters* of international terrorism.

The Action Is in the Reaction

As far back as the late 1970s, several notable figures and groups tried valiantly to inform the public of the *real* threat of terrorism and move government to appropriate action. Congressman Lawrence P. McDonald (D-Georgia) offered outstanding leadership in the battle to strengthen America's internal security. His Western Goals

Foundation produced as its first video documentary — *No Place to Hide: The Strategy and Tactics of Terrorism.*

No Place to Hide aired on CNN eight days following the Soviet shootdown of KAL flight 7. Ironically, Congressman McDonald was aboard that flight. He, along with 268 other defenseless passengers, became victims of a Soviet terrorist act — an event hastily swept under the rug by the Establishment.

Congressman McDonald's video documentary explained that terrorism was to be feared not only for its action but also for the expected *reaction.* In fact, it is the reaction of the target government that sponsors of terrorism seek.

Governments normally respond to terrorist acts by cracking down on liberties to try to achieve order. For the Conspiracy, this dramatic pretext for a crackdown provides an ideal opportunity for consolidating power.

CFR Organizes War on Terror

Within hours of the September 11, 2001 terrorist attacks, CFR members began preparing the public for the "revolution in world political arrangements," described by Bloomfield. They insisted that the crisis demanded actions that had long been part of the globalist agenda.

The public was repeatedly told that the U.S. could fight terrorism only through the terrorist-loving United Nations. We were also told that the attacks demonstrated the need for the UN's International Criminal Court. And, perhaps most ominously, that Americans might have to sacrifice some of their liberties to achieve security.

Lawmakers rushed to show bipartisan support for every Insider objective that could be portrayed as fighting terrorism, including the payment of "back dues" to the UN.

The insanity, or rather duplicity, in counting on the UN to fight a war against terrorism was highlighted a few weeks later when the General Assembly voted overwhelmingly to elect Syria to a two-year term on the Security Council! The Bush administration chose not to oppose Syria's election even though our own State Department had included Syria on its list of state sponsors of terrorism.

The CFR response was organized long before the actual attack. On January 31, 2001, a few days after the inauguration of President

George W. Bush, the CFR-dominated Hart-Rudman Commission delivered its proposal for an independent National Homeland Security Agency to the new president and his cabinet. This was several months *before* the nation-shaking attacks of September 11, 2001.

And *just three days* after the attacks, the CFR hosted a meeting in Washington, D.C., which publicized the Commission's recommendation. Six days later, President Bush announced the creation of a new Cabinet-level post, the Office of Homeland Security.

To build and maintain an Orwellian security state, there must be a never-ending stream of enemies. The planned "war on terrorism" fills that role to a tee. Secretary of Defense Donald H. Rumsfeld (CFR 1974-1980), in a *New York Times* op-ed, predicted that the war on terrorism:

> ... will be a war like none other our nation has faced.... [I]t will involve floating coalitions of countries, which may change and evolve.... This is not a war against an individual, a group, a religion or a country. Rather, our opponent is a global network of terrorist organizations and their state sponsors.... Forget about "exit strategies"; we're looking at a sustained engagement that carries no deadlines. [32]

Rumsfeld could just as easily have promised "perpetual war for perpetual peace." It was difficult not to recall Alexander Hamilton's warning in *The Federalist No. 8*:

> Safety from external danger is the most powerful director of national conduct. Even the ardent love of liberty will, after a time, give way to its dictates. The violent destruction of life and property incident to war, the continual effort and alarm attendant on a state of continual danger, will compel nations the most attached to liberty to resort for repose and security to institutions which have a tendency to destroy their civil and political rights. To be more safe, they at length become willing to run the risk of being less free.

Dismantling Our Layers of Internal Security

American Insiders must share a major part of the blame for the terrorist evil that has occurred, because they supported the Bolshevik revolution, caused our government to keep the Soviet Union alive, and even built the Soviet Union into a serious enemy. And American Insiders have actively covered up the Soviet role in creating terrorism.

But there is another part to the indictment — the decades-long campaign to strip America of her multiple layers of internal security so that she would be naked to terrorist attacks and then *using the resulting catastrophes to advance totalitarian measures*.

Until the early 1970s, America could rely on multiple layers of efficient and effective defense against terrorism and subversion. These decentralized protections included state and congressional investigative committees, intelligence departments of major city police, and counter-intelligence departments of the various branches of the armed forces.

This layered protection prevented the oppression that could come from heavily centralized police powers. It also prevented cover-up of real threats and bureaucratic ineptitude.

But America's multi-layered security structure began to unravel in the 1970s. During that decade, radicals in Congress succeeded in abolishing the Subversive Activities Control Board, the Internal Security Division of the Justice Department, the House Internal Security Committee, and the Senate Subcommittee on Internal Security. Congress also killed the counter-intelligence units of the armed forces.

Soon to follow were the investigative committees of state legislatures and the intelligence units of state and local police organizations. In 1981, the Senate briefly reestablished the Subcommittee on Security and Terrorism. However, constantly underfunded, the Subcommittee was scrapped again in 1987.

The FBI's counterintelligence activities and investigations were also crippled in 1976 by the guidelines issued by Attorney General Edward Levi during the Ford administration. Incredibly, Levi had been a member of the National Lawyers Guild, a notorious Communist front that represented Cuba in American courts. [33] Under pressure, subsequent attorneys general would revise the most restrictive of the disastrous Levi guidelines, a small step at restoring some sanity.

In the December 1984 *Reader's Digest*, Eugene Methvin described the pathetic condition of our internal security apparatus:

> While the terrorists were preparing a massive campaign of kidnapping, assassination, and bombing, the United States had virtually disbanded its domestic-intelligence apparatus. Civil-liberty lawsuits had vitiated or destroyed police-intelligence units across the country. In the five years before the Nyack attack, the FBI's informants in political-terrorist groups had been cut from 1,100 to fewer than 50.

Our congressional investigative committees represented a particularly great loss. An important responsibility of Congress is to hold the executive and judicial branches accountable for upholding our laws regarding internal security. However, congressional committees had been so successful in exposing top Soviet agents, such as Alger Hiss, Harry Dexter White, Virginius Frank Coe, and Gregory Silvermaster, that the Communist Party and its allies targeted the committees for destruction.

The committees and their chairmen were accused of "witch hunting," "McCarthyism," and "fascism." Tragically, this propaganda campaign was able to weaken needed support in Congress.

Although the campaign against our internal security apparatus was launched by the Communist Party USA as far back as the 1920s, the Establishment offered no effective resistance and often joined in the attacks, which eventually succeeded in the 1970s.

The campaign was clearly intended to blind law enforcement and intelligence agencies so the terrorists could operate freely. Much of the destruction of our internal security can be traced to organizations, such as the ACLU, supported by Establishment foundations.

Following the September 11, 2001 terrorist attacks, a new, much more intrusive security apparatus was created to fill the vacuum. But it was a sad exchange. The multi-layered system that had been destroyed was *efficient and compatible with liberty*. It provided invaluable redundancy while dispersing power.

Unfortunately, under the post-9/11 system, a broad-based federalization of police powers concentrates the responsibility for America's security in the hands of one department. It will be very difficult to hold this system accountable for failure or abuse.

For more on the war on terror, see Chapter 14 (George W. Bush).

Part III

Harnessing the Executive Branch

Chapter 9

CFR Dominance: Truman, Eisenhower & Kennedy/Johnson Administrations

"[T]he two parties should be almost identical, so that the American people can 'throw the rascals out' at any election without leading to any profound or extensive shifts in policy." [1]
— Establishment Insider Carroll Quigley, 1966

In the aftermath of World War II, the Council on Foreign Relations expanded its domination of the State Department, foreign policy, and related departments of the Executive branch. And through a network of interlocking organizations its influence has extended to domestic affairs as well. As we shall see, members of the CFR have occupied key posts in every administration since FDR — regardless of whether a Republican or Democrat, a liberal or a perceived conservative, has sat in the White House.

With CFR dominance of the media and the leadership of the two major national political parties, the Establishment would gain camouflaged control of both sides of presidential contests and achieve a lockgrip on the Executive branch of government. Since World War II, with perhaps one exception (GOP nominee Barry Goldwater), Professor Quigley's dictum would reflect reality. When the electorate grows weary of one of the Establishment parties, continued Quigley, "it should be able to replace it, every four years if necessary, by the other party, which ... will still pursue, with new vigor, approximately the same basic policies." [2]

And regardless of party affiliation or media created image, every president (and almost all serious contenders) have supported the CFR's creation — the United Nations. To be sure, some presidents have urged reform of the UN, temporarily withdrawn from a UN agency, or even withheld some dues in a show of independence. But none have seriously questioned U.S. participation in this fundamental building block of the Insiders' new world order or any other of the internationalist plans for the world.

Indeed, CFR dominance of the U.S. Executive branch has played a central role in carrying out Insider schemes to transform not only the U.S. but the entire world. It is that dominance that we will examine in this and four of the following chapters.

However, control of the Executive branch is not sufficient by itself to implement revolutionary changes. American public opinion must also be prepared to accept the changes. We have already seen how the CFR and its aligned foundations have sponsored pressure groups and think tanks to help create the right political climate. In Chapters 12 and 13, we will further examine the CFR's influence over education, the media, and other opinion-forming institutions.

Although each administration has worked to advance the CFR agenda, the focus would often change. That focus, and associated deceptions, would depend on several factors, such as the CFR's success in orchestrating perceived crises (e.g., the myth of catastrophic manmade global warming), opportunities created by unforeseen events, and even the need for a president to maintain a particular image with his constituency.

Contrary to the Establishment promoted image, most presidents have become largely figureheads within their own administrations. The real leadership comes from subordinates in whose selection the president may have had little input.

Of course, there are likely exceptions, such as President George H.W. Bush (senior), who had served as a director of the CFR and had been carrying out the CFR agenda during his previous government posts (e.g., as U.S. ambassador to the UN and director of the CIA).

The suggestion that a president may be a mere figurehead is certainly quite different from what the Establishment media and the party organizations would have us believe. However, the notion that the passions and crusades associated with modern presidents (such as NAFTA and the drive for national health care) actually originate within their bosoms strains credibility.

In the sections that follow, we examine the CFR influence in post-war administrations and the steady contribution of those administrations, accompanied by massive deception, toward transforming America into a mere province within a totalitarian world order.

Truman Administrations
(1945 – 1953)

Road to the White House

Harry S. Truman was elected to the U.S. Senate from Missouri in 1934, with the backing of the Democratic political machine of Tom Pendergast. Upon assuming office, Truman was referred to as "the senator from Pendergast." Robert E. Hannegan, who controlled the Democratic Party in St. Louis, helped Truman get reelected in 1940.

As the Democratic National Committee chairman in 1944, Hannegan brokered the deal that put Truman on the FDR ticket. (Shortly after becoming president, Truman returned the favor, appointing Hannegan postmaster general.)

Although there is more to the story of the forces promoting Truman, several Democratic leaders realized that FDR would probably not live out his fourth term, and they didn't want Henry Wallace, Roosevelt's vice president at the time, as president. Indeed, FDR died on April 12, 1945, just four months into his fourth term, and Truman succeeded him as president.

Truman stood for re-election in 1948, but for a number of reasons was not expected to win the contest against Republican nominee Thomas Dewey. Truman, however, confounded the naysayers. The effect of Truman's innovative "Whistle Stop Tour" of rural America on the presidential train escaped the notice of the national press corps. After Election Day, Truman held up the front page of the *Chicago Tribune* that had been typeset with the headline "Dewey Defeats Truman."

CFR Staffing

Upon assuming the presidency in 1945, Truman made no immediate changes in FDR's cabinet. CFR members already in the cabinet included Secretary of State Edward Stettinius, Jr. and Secretary of War Henry L. Stimson. Secretary of the Treasury Henry Morgenthau, Jr. and Secretary of the Navy James V. Forrestal [the last Secretary of the Navy at cabinet level] were former CFR members. Attorney General Francis Biddle would later join the CFR.

During his administrations, Truman filled three significant vacancies from the roster of the CFR: Dean G. Acheson as secretary of state, Robert A. Lovett (formerly CFR) as secretary of defense, and W. Averell Harriman as secretary of commerce.

In 1986, Walter Isaacson and Evan Thomas published *The Wise Men — Six Friends and the World They Made* chronicling the careers of Acheson, Lovett, and Harriman, as well as John J. McCloy, George Kennan, and Charles Bohlen. All six were members of the CFR and the East Coast foreign policy establishment and came together under the Truman administration. Most had known each other at college or on Wall Street. Later, the Establishment would refer to these and other senior "experts" of like mind as "the Wise Men."

• **Dean Acheson** attended Yale with Harriman. But, according to Isaacson and Thomas, "it was not until he studied under Felix Frankfurter at Harvard Law School that his mental agility was honed to the intellectual intensity that was to mark his tenure as Truman's Secretary of State." [3] Quick-witted perhaps, but not in America's interests. Indeed, Acheson would play a prominent role in developing many foreign policy programs advancing internationalist interests, such as the European unification movement, the Marshall Plan, the loss of China to the Communists, and America's no-win war in Korea (see below) and even Vietnam. Acheson first joined the CFR in 1947.

• **W. Averell Harriman** graduated from Yale in 1913, where he had joined the Skull and Bones Society. In 1922, with his inheritance from his father's railroad fortune, Averell established his own banking business, bringing in his brother a few years later. He joined the CFR shortly after its founding in 1923.

Through a merger in 1931, the Harriman firm became the notable international banking firm of Brown Brothers Harriman and Company. George H.W. Bush's father, Prescott Bush, along with Robert Lovett became partners in the firm.

Harriman was one of the early traders with the Bolshevik government. In 1922, he formed a jointly owned shipping firm, the Deutsch-Russische Transport Co., with the Communists and obtained a twenty-year concession to operate the manganese mines in the Caucasus Mountains of Georgia.[4] So Harriman was well known to the Soviet regime when FDR appointed him U.S. ambassador to the Soviet Union in 1943. According to Isaacson and Thomas, Harriman spent more time with Stalin than any other American.[5]

In 1945, Harriman enabled the Communists to come to power in Romania by inducing the anti-Communists to accept a suicidal coalition government with the Reds.[6] In subsequent decades, Harriman would continue to influence U.S. policy adversely, in both official and unofficial roles.

In 1952 and 1956, Harriman contested unsuccessfully for the Democratic presidential nomination. In 1955, he became the 48th governor of New York.

• **Robert A. Lovett** graduated from Yale in 1918 and, like Harriman, was also a member of Skull and Bones. Lovett and Harriman had grown up together. In 1931, Lovett helped with the merger of Brown Brothers (where Lovett was a partner) and Harriman's firm. According to Isaacson and Thomas: "When he came to Washington as Assistant Secretary of War [in December 1940], Lovett operated as he had on Wall Street, discreetly backstage."[7]

Lovett's influence and prestige would grow in subsequent years. In *A Thousand Days* (1965), Special Assistant to the President (JFK) Arthur Schlesinger Jr. candidly referred to McCloy and Lovett as the "present leaders" of "the heart of the American Establishment," "its front organizations, the Rockefeller, Ford and Carnegie foundations and the Council on Foreign Relations...."[8]

Although our primary focus here is on cabinet level appointments, assistant secretaries and undersecretaries often implemented the CFR agenda more aggressively than their more prominent bosses.

Advancing the Insider Agenda

The UN's founding San Francisco Conference would begin within two weeks after Harry Truman was sworn in as President. According to Wikipedia: "As a Wilsonian internationalist, Truman strongly supported creation of the United Nations...." More significantly, the staff Truman inherited and accepted had been, and were, heavily involved in launching the world body.

Other contributions to the Insider agenda included:

• **Betrayal of China**. Following America's launching and entry into the United Nations, the Truman administration's next major gift to the Insiders was the betrayal of China into Communist hands. During World War II, China had been our ally. However, at the end of the war China's leader, Chiang Kai-shek, faced a Communist insurgency led by Mao Tse-tung.

At Yalta, Stalin agreed to enter the Pacific War against Japan if the U.S. would supply the equipment. Ignoring MacArthur's plea to keep the Soviets out of the Pacific war, Roosevelt agreed, and the Soviets entered the war, to no effect, just days before Japan's capitulation. However, as a result of the agreement, Stalin was able to equip Mao's forces with Japanese arms and munitions surrendered in Manchuria as well as with American lend-lease supplies.

Nevertheless, in early 1946 the Nationalist forces had Mao's Reds on the run. However, Truman had sent General George C. Marshall to China to mediate the fighting, and Marshall forced Chiang to accept a cease-fire (one of several). As recorded by Freda Utley:

> In the interval that followed, General Marshall and President Truman took steps to prevent the Nationalist forces from obtaining arms and ammunition. At the end of July 1946 General Marshall clamped an embargo on the sale of arms and ammunition to China. For almost a year thereafter the Chinese Government was prevented from *buying*, and was definitely *not given*, a single round of ammunition. On August 18, 1946, President Truman issued an executive order saying that China was not to be allowed to acquire any "surplus" American weapons "which could be used in fighting a civil war," meaning a war with the Communists. [9]

Marshall would boast: "As Chief of Staff I armed 39 anti-Communist divisions, now with a stroke of the pen I disarm them." [10] Stockpiles of arms on their way to Chiang were actually destroyed in India. The Soviets, meanwhile, equipped Mao with vast stores of U.S. military supplies Truman had provided Stalin for the assault on Japan.

In 1948, when Chiang's situation had become desperate and the American people were more aware of the Communist threat, Congress approved $125 million in military aid for Chiang. But the Truman administration drug its feet for nine months until Chiang's forces had to withdraw to Taiwan, leaving mainland China in Communist hands.

On January 25, 1949, John F. Kennedy, a young second-term congressman from Massachusetts, rose on the floor of the House of Representatives to protest the actions of his party's president:

> Mr. Speaker, over this weekend we have learned the extent of the disaster that has befallen China and the United States. The responsibility for the failure of our foreign policy in the Far East rests squarely with the White House and the Department of State. The continued insistence that aid would not be forthcoming, unless a coalition government with the Communists were formed, was a crippling blow to the National Government.

A few days later, he would summarize his protest in words that could be applied to the future handling of Vietnam: "What our young men had saved, our diplomats and our President have frittered away." [11]

What Representative Kennedy may not have understood at the time was that the betrayal of China was orchestrated by the Establishment he would later serve as president.

An essential element facilitating Washington's betrayal was the deception of the American people by misrepresenting the struggle in China. At the time, Chiang's government was repeatedly portrayed as corrupt, and Mao was described as an agrarian reformer rather than a Communist.

Much of the propaganda originated with the Institute of Pacific Relations (IPR). A Senate Judiciary Committee investigation would determine in 1952 that the IPR "was a vehicle used by the Communists to orient American Far Eastern politics toward Communist objectives." [12] However, Establishment historian Carroll Quigley, who had researched the records of American Insiders, claimed a Wall Street connection:

The influence of the Communists in IPR is well established, but the patronage of Wall Street is less well known....

The headquarters of the IPR and of the American Council of IPR were both in New York and were closely associated on an interlocking basis. Each spent about $2.5 million dollars over the quarter-century from 1925 to 1950, of which about half, in each case, came from the Carnegie Foundation and the Rockefeller Foundation (which were themselves interlocking groups controlled by an alliance of Morgan and Rockefeller interests in Wall Street). Much of the rest, especially of the American Council, came from firms closely allied to these two Wall Street interests, such as Standard Oil, International Telephone and Telegraph, International General Electric, the National City Bank, and the Chase National Bank.[13]

Quigley would also insist: "It must be recognized that the power that these energetic Left-wingers [Communist sympathizers and fellow travelers who had infiltrated an influential network of organizations in the 1930s] exercised was never their own power or Communist power but was ultimately the power of the international financial coterie...."[14]

Also not well known: The IPR could count at least forty members of the CFR among its ranks.

Estimates of the death toll from Communist genocide in China have varied widely. Professor R. J. Rummel of the University of Hawaii estimated the number conservatively at more than 35 million deaths — approximately one of every 20 Chinese.[15]

The undeniable Chinese genocide has not prevented globalist-minded Insiders in this country from supporting their Communist agents in Beijing. Returning from a 1973 trip to China, David Rockefeller had the gall to claim: "Whatever the price of the Chinese Revolution, it has obviously succeeded.... The social experiment in China under Chairman Mao's leadership is one of the most important and successful in human history."[16]

• **The Korean "Police Action."** The Korean War was the first war fought under the newly established UN. The U.S. supplied much of the manpower, but without Congress voting to declare war as required by the U.S. Constitution. The Korean War became the internationalist prototype for future "no-win" wars of limited objectives, including the Viet Nam War. It can be argued that if American forces had been allowed to win the Korean War, there likely would never have been a Viet Nam War.

Although the Truman administration feigned surprise when the North Koreans invaded South Korea on June 25, 1950, there was ample warning. In a 1950 New Year's Day statement, North Korean leader Kim Il Sung announced that this would be Korea's "year of unification," and called for "complete preparedness for war."

In response, on January 12, 1950, Dean Acheson publicly defined the United States "defense perimeter" in the Far East and conspicuously excluded Korea and Taiwan. The U.S. also encouraged the Communist aggression by withdrawing most of its forces from South Korea and not insisting that the Soviets do the same in the North.

Yet our own intelligence units and the South Koreans were well aware of what the North was preparing. According to Robert Welch: "Between June, 1949 and June, 1950 our army general headquarters agency in Korea sent to Washington 1195 consecutive warning reports, an average of three a day, as to what was taking place just above the 38th Parallel." [17]

On June 25, 1950 the UN Security Council condemned the North Korean invasion and two days later approved Resolution 83 recommending that member states provide military assistance to South Korea.

The same day, President Truman directed our forces in the area to go to the aid of the South Koreans.

Chiang Kai-shek, now on Taiwan with his army, volunteered to send 30,000 troops to Korea immediately. But General Marshall refused the offer.

In testifying before the Senate Internal Security Subcommittee on April 9, 1952, former U.S. Ambassador Bullitt was asked by Senator Arthur Watkins if the Free Chinese had a navy. Bullitt replied:

> Oh, yes. As a matter of fact, it has been quite an efficient force, although it is forbidden to act in any way by fiat of our government which has given orders to our fleet to prevent it

from stopping the Communist supply ships going up to Korea. They sail right by Formosa [Taiwan], loaded with Soviet munitions put in the Polish Communist ships in Gdynia. They come all the way around and go right by Formosa and sail past there taking those munitions up, taking those weapons up to be used to kill American soldiers in Korea, and by order of our government the Chinese Navy is flatly forbidden to stop them on their way up there.

The UN Security Council could never have authorized the UN "police action" had the Soviets been present to use their veto. However, for several months the Soviets had been boycotting the Security Council and did not return until after the votes on Korea.

Since the Soviets undoubtedly knew the invasion plans of their North Korean proxy in advance, one must conclude that the Soviets were strategically absent. The Soviets undoubtedly realized that a UN-authorized limited response was no serious threat to Communist control of North Korea.

However, following MacArthur's brilliant Inchon landing, U.S. and South Korean forces held the upper hand. Faced with the threat of massive Red Chinese intervention, MacArthur ordered the destruction of the bridges across the Yalu River. Within hours, General Marshall countermanded MacArthur's order. MacArthur would later state:

> I realized for the first time that I had actually been denied the use of my full military power to safeguard the lives of my soldiers and the safety of my army. To me, it clearly foreshadowed a future tragic situation in Korea, and left me with a sense of inexpressible shock. [18]

Foreshadowing the "rules of engagement" that strangled U.S. forces in the Viet Nam War, MacArthur was forbidden to attack Chinese supplies being amassed across the river or to follow Chinese MIGs retreating across the border into China. Although the reason given for such restrictions was ostensibly to avoid a wider war with China, the effect was just the opposite. General Lin Piao, commander of the Chinese forces, later said:

I never would have made the attack and risked my men and my military reputation if I had not been assured that Washington would restrain General MacArthur from taking adequate retaliatory measures against my lines of supply and communication. [19]

General Mark Clark, who signed the Korean armistice agreement in July 1953, would echo MacArthur's criticism. In his memoirs, Clark declared it was: "beyond my comprehension that we would countenance a situation in which Chinese soldiers killed American youth in organized, formal warfare and yet we would fail to use all the power at our command to protect those Americans." [20]

While men were still dying in the UN "police action," Adlai Stevenson (the soon-to-be Democratic nominee for president and the future U.S. ambassador to the UN under Kennedy) authored an article for the April 1952 *Foreign Affairs*, entitled "Korea in Perspective." In summary, Stevenson stated:

The burden of my argument, then, based on the meaning of our experience in Korea as I see it, is that we have made historic progress toward the establishment of a viable system of collective security. [21]

The cost of that "progress" was enormous in South Korean and American dead.

• **The North Atlantic Treaty Organization (NATO).** At the start of the Cold War, another internationalist creation, NATO, sought to draw the United States into a permanent "collective defense" alliance to oppose the spread of Communism in Europe.

The North Atlantic Treaty, signed in Washington D.C. on April 4, 1949, led to an intergovernmental military alliance headquartered in Brussels, Belgium. However, NATO really got off the ground when the Soviet threat became apparent through the Korean War.

At a NATO Council meeting in New York in September 1950, U.S. Secretary of State Dean Acheson suggested the formation of an international NATO army. On December 9, 1950, the North Atlantic Council announced that it had "completed the arrangements... for the establishment" of such an army.

The Council also announced that it had appointed General Eisenhower Supreme Commander of NATO with the consent of President Truman. Two years later, Eisenhower would ride an anti-Truman, anti-Acheson wave into the White House.

The CFR NATO architects envisioned NATO as having a broader mission than a mere anti-Communist alliance. While Under Secretary of State Robert Lovett was working behind the scenes to establish the NATO alliance, *Foreign Affairs* registered its support: "[A] regional organization of nations, formed to operate within the framework of the United Nations, can only strengthen that organization." [22]

The formation of regional alliances, military or political, operating within the UN framework has been explained many times in *Foreign Affairs* as a steppingstone to world government. [23]

Eisenhower Administrations
(1953 – 1961)

It was almost a forgone conclusion in 1952 that whoever got the Republican nomination would be the next president of the United States. Plagued with scandals, including revelations of Communist infiltration of government, and plummeting popularity due to the stalemated Korean War and his firing of Douglas MacArthur, Truman had decided not to seek re-election to a third term. For the first time since 1932, the Republicans would not face an incumbent president.

However, the Insiders still didn't have a solid grip on the national Republican Party, and one candidate — conservative Senator Robert A. Taft of Ohio ("Mr. Republican") — seriously threatened to derail their agenda. The major Establishment challenge was to stop Taft, and the Insider choice for the GOP nomination was General Dwight David Eisenhower.

Military Road to White House
As the European theater's Supreme Commander Allied Expeditionary Force, Eisenhower was perceived as America's top military leader in our successful victory over the Nazi war machine.

With that background, Eisenhower had enough popularity with the American people in 1952 to become a serious candidate for president.

Indeed, Eisenhower's name had been touted several times as a presidential candidate, but since he had no previous involvement in politics, he was not clearly identified with either party. His credentials as a Republican had to be quickly established.

Robert Welch, a strong supporter of Taft, wrote a blockbuster exposé, *The Politician*, that recounts how the Insiders sidelined Taft and elevated Eisenhower to the presidency (see Recommended Reading). [24] *The Politician* thoroughly documents the real Eisenhower record, but more importantly it highlights the forces that propelled him into the presidency. And it shows how the American people can be hugely deceived by phony media-created images of prominent personalities.

We won't dwell on the tactics that were used to push Eisenhower to the top over Taft (either before or during the convention). But the contest was close. On the first ballot, before shifts, the vote stood at 595 for Eisenhower and 500 for Taft.

California Governor Earl Warren delivered the California vote to Eisenhower and, per apparent agreement, would be appointed to the first vacancy in the Supreme Court, which turned out to be a vacancy for Chief Justice. [25] Many of the Warren Court's decisions favored communist subversion and undermined efforts to bolster our internal security. [26]

Republican Advance

In addition to stopping Taft, a parallel Insider goal was to permanently defang the Republican Party as a challenge to its agenda and, in the process, convert it into an image of the Democratic Party. That effort got off the ground in 1950 with the creation of Republican Advance, bankrolled by Nelson Rockefeller and Sidney Weinberg (of Goldman, Sachs and an earlier organizer of the CFR-aligned Business Advisory Council). [27]

Among the prominent sponsors of Republican Advance were Clifford Case (CFR in 1953), Christian A. Herter (CFR), far-left New York Republican Representative (and soon-to-be Senator) Jacob Javits (CFR in 1960), John Foster Dulles (CFR founder), and

Advance founders Russell Davenport (CFR in 1953) and Richard M. Nixon (CFR in 1961).[28]

Republican Advance drew additional support from the Fabian-Socialist "Americans for Democratic Action" (see Chapter 13), which was also busy infiltrating and influencing the Democratic Party.[29] According to Robert Welch:

Francis Biddle [CFR], one of the most new-dealish of Roosevelt's cabinet members, publicly stated that he would like to see Republican Advance and Americans For Democratic Action become formally affiliated, since "both are working towards the same end."[30]

According to researcher Rose L. Martin: "It was [Republican Advance] which invited General Eisenhower to run for the Presidency in 1952, and which steered him into the White House."[31] Indeed, when "Citizens for Eisenhower" was formed in 1952, the new group gradually absorbed the former.[32]

An Astonishing Ascent
But in 1952, it was certainly not obvious to most Americans that Eisenhower was the Establishment's candidate. However, there had been signs. At the outset of the war (1941), Eisenhower was a lieutenant colonel with no combat experience. Yet by 1943, he become a four-star general and was placed in charge of all the Allied forces in Western Europe. Why the meteoric rise? It can likely be traced to an interview Ike achieved with FDR at the White House in 1940.[33]

During the War, Ike showed that he was willing to play ball with the internationalists. In early 1945, General Patton's forces had reached Pilsen, fifty miles from Prague. Eisenhower ordered Patton to pull back, thus allowing the Soviets to take the capital of Czechoslovakia.[34] Eisenhower also prevented Patton's army from entering Berlin with the same result.[35]

In the aftermath of the war, Eisenhower authorized Operation Keelhaul, which at Stalin's request repatriated 2 million anti-Communist refugees against their will to Soviet control (meaning death and concentration camps), thus eliminating a determined anti-

Communist force in Western Europe. [36]

In November 1945, Eisenhower returned to Washington to become chief of staff of the Army. Eisenhower and his wife Mamie began socializing with the elite. [37] Then in 1948, with no academic background beyond West Point, Eisenhower became president of Columbia University. The following year, Eisenhower would be invited to join the Council on Foreign Relations and serve on the advisory board of *Foreign Affairs* magazine.

In December1950, the North Atlantic Council announced it had "completed the arrangements for ... the establishment" of an international army. With Truman's consent, the Council appointed Dwight Eisenhower as the first Supreme Allied Commander Europe (SACEUR) for the North Atlantic Treaty Organization (NATO).

The 1952 Republican convention nominated Dwight David Eisenhower (CFR) for president, whereas the Democratic convention chose Adlai Stevenson (CFR in 1957) as its nominee. In the October 1952 issue of *Foreign Affairs*, McGeorge Bundy (CFR and future national security advisor to presidents Kennedy and Johnson) praised the outcome:

> Contemplating this remarkable result, many were tempted simply to thank their lucky stars; but it was not all luck. These two nominations were not accidental....
>
> The fundamental meaning of the Eisenhower candidacy can best be understood by considering the nature of the forces he was drafted to stop — for fundamentally he was the stop-Taft candidate....

CFR Staffing

Ike drew his top foreign policy leader from the internationalists at the CFR. His first choice for secretary of state was John J. McCloy, who rejected the offer. McCloy had bigger mountains to conquer. In 1953, McCloy assumed the chairmanship of the CFR on the road to earning the unofficial title of "Chairman of the Establishment."

• **John Foster Dulles.** For secretary of state Eisenhower settled instead on John Foster Dulles, a founding member of the CFR and member of Colonel House's Inquiry, who had accompanied

President Wilson to the Paris Peace Conference. Dulles was a veteran internationalist who had played an important role in the U.S. delegation to the 1945 UN founding conference in San Francisco. In his 1950 book *War or Peace* Dulles wrote:

> The United Nations represents not a *final* stage in the development of world order, but only a primitive stage. Therefore its primary task is to create the conditions which will make possible a more highly developed organization.[38]

Those who pick candidates for high office count on the public having short memories, and they rely on the Establishment media not to bring up embarrassing history.

In 1941, more than a decade prior to his secretary of state post and new reputation as a tough anti-Communist, John Foster Dulles had been active as a leader of the pro-Communist Federal Council of Churches. The Federal Council was the American branch of the Soviet-controlled World Council of Churches. (In 1950, the Federal Council of Churches conveniently changed its name, with minor reorganization, to the National Council of Churches.)

One of the projects of the Federal Council of Churches was to mobilize organized religion on behalf of internationalist goals. The first chairman of the Council's Commission on a Just and Durable Peace was John Foster Dulles. In 1942, a few months after Pearl Harbor, the Federal Council convened a conference of hundreds of delegates from more than 30 denominations. The purpose of the conference, held at Ohio's Wesleyan University, was to mobilize church support for new post-war international institutions.

As reported by *Time* magazine: "The meeting showed its temper early by passing a set of 13 'requisite principles for peace' submitted by Chairman John Foster Dulles and his inter-church Commission...."[39]

Time summarized the conference's conclusions:

> Politically, the conference's most important assertion was that many duties now performed by local and national governments "can now be effectively carried out only by international

authority." Individual nations, it declared, must give up their armed forces "except for preservation of domestic order" and allow the world to be policed by an international army & navy. This League-of-Nations-with-teeth would also have "the power of final judgment in controversies between nations ... the regulation of international trade and population movements among nations."

The ultimate goal: "a duly constituted world government of delegated powers: an international legislative body, an international court with adequate jurisdiction, international-administrative bodies with necessary powers, and adequate international police forces and provisions for enforcing its worldwide economic authority." [40]

With the passing of a decade and the help of a few anti-Communist speeches, the image-builders in the Establishment media were able to transform Dulles into a tough conservative anti-Communist.

• **Christian Herter.** When Dulles died in 1959, near the end of Eisenhower's second term, Eisenhower chose Christian Herter to replace him. Herter, as you will recall, was another member of Colonel House's Inquiry who accompanied President Wilson to the Paris Peace Conference. Herter married into the Standard Oil fortune, joining the CFR in 1929.

In 1961 to 1962, Christian Herter played a major role in the founding of the internationalist Atlantic Union, becoming its first chairman. The following year (1963), he expressed his anti-sovereignty views in *Toward an Atlantic Community*, published for and copyrighted by the Council on Foreign Relations. [41]

Christian Herter represents again the fact that both GOP and Democratic presidents went to the same well for staffing. In November 1962, President Kennedy appointed Herter as his special representative for trade negotiations with nations of the European Common Market.

• **Allen Dulles.** To head up the Central Intelligences Agency, Eisenhower selected John Foster's brother, Allen Dulles, another member of Colonel House's Inquiry who had attended the Paris Peace Conference. Allen Dulles had been president of the CFR from 1946 to 1950.

Other prominent positions filled from the CFR roster included:

- Secretary of the Treasury Robert B. Anderson (1957–1961);
- National Security Adviser Gordon Gray (1958–1961);
- Chairman of the Atomic Energy Commission Lewis L. Strauss;
- Under Secretary of HEW Nelson Rockefeller (1953–1954); and
- U.S. Ambassador to France C. Douglas Dillon (1953–1957).

- **C. Douglas Dillon** was the son of Clarence Dillon of Dillon, Read, and Company (the international banking house) and would later chair the firm. His Establishment connections were obvious. He went to school with the three Rockefeller brothers — Nelson, Laurence, and John D. Rockefeller III — and was a close friend of John, becoming chairman of the Rockefeller Foundation in 1972.

Dillon worked for John Foster Dulles in Thomas E. Dewey's 1948 presidential campaign and provided key support for Eisenhower's 1952 campaign in New Jersey. Eisenhower appointed Dillon U.S. ambassador to France in 1953. In 1958, Eisenhower selected Dillon as under secretary of state for economic affairs and a year later as under secretary of state.

President Kennedy would choose "Republican" Dillon as his secretary of the treasury, and President Johnson retained Dillon in that role. Upon leaving the cabinet shortly after the start of Johnson's second term, Dillon stated: "I am a moderate Republican [Eisenhower's term]. I do not believe there are great differences between that kind of Republicanism and the objectives" of the Kennedy and Johnson administrations. [42]

Dillon would become chairman of the Brookings Institution (1970–1976), the Rockefeller Foundation (1972–1975), and vice chairman of the CFR (1976–1978).

Advancing the Insider Agenda

With President Eisenhower's military background plus "anti-Communist" Nixon as vice president, Americans naturally assumed

142

that the new administration would be tough on Communism. Moreover, John Foster Dulles, with Establishment media cooperation, cultivated the image of an anti-Communist hard-liner willing to engage in "brinksmanship" in negotiating with the Soviets, i.e., take the nation to the brink of nuclear war to force the Soviets to back down.

However, the Ike and Dulles record was quite different from the images crafted for the American people. Ike was an internationalist and, as with the presidents who would follow, did the bidding of the Insiders. And undermining their creation — the worldwide Communist empire — was not in their planning.

• **The Hungarian revolt.** In 1956, the peoples of several of the captive nations of Eastern Europe were restless and demanding independence from Moscow. The Poles revolted in June, but the rebellion was crushed by tanks.

The Hungarians were even more determined to gain their freedom. With the encouragement of U.S. broadcasts behind the Iron Curtain, Hungarian freedom fighters came out in the open and courageously fought Soviet tanks with home-made Molotov cocktails.

Some of the tank commanders, sympathizing with the Hungarian people, even joined the freedom fighters. Incredibly, the Hungarians managed to seize control of their capital city, Budapest. For a brief few days, Hungary stood free and desperately looked to the West for aid.

Soviet reinforcements massed on the border prepared to invade Hungary. But the Soviets, not wanting a confrontation with the West, waited to see whether the U.S. would support the freedom fighters with more than words.

Then came the U.S. betrayal. On November 2, 1956 the U.S. State Department sent an incredible message to Tito, the Communist dictator of Yugoslavia. The message reaffirmed U.S. support for Tito's allegedly moderate regime. But it also signaled our opposition to the creation of anti-Communist governments in Eastern Europe:

> The Government of the United States does not look with favor upon governments unfriendly to the Soviet Union on the borders

143

of the Soviet Union.[43]

With this reassurance, Soviet tanks rolled across the border and crushed the revolt.

Several years later, a *New York Times* editorial would blatantly advocate a reprehensible "moral" standard that supposedly justified such betrayals:

> [W]e must seek to discourage anti-Communist revolts in order to avert bloodshed and war. We must, under our own principles, live with evil even if by doing so we help to stabilize tottering Communist regimes, as in East Germany, and perhaps even expose citadels of freedom, like West Berlin, to slow death by strangulation.[44]

• **Betrayal of Cuba.** In the late 1950s, Herbert L. Mathews (CFR) wrote a series of articles for the *New York Times* painting Fidel Castro as the "George Washington of Cuba" — "a man of ideals" with "strong ideas of liberty, democracy, social justice...."[45] So went much of the American media, which also suddenly depicted Cuban President Fulgencio Batista as a corrupt tyrant.

The U.S. State Department and the Establishment media ignored evidence and warnings (e.g., by U.S. Ambassador to Cuba Earl Smith) that Castro was a Communist. Castro seized control of Cuba in early 1959.

Two decades later, in a letter published in the *New York Times*, Smith once again attempted to correct the history:

> To the contrary, Castro could not have seized power in Cuba without the aid of the United States. American Government agencies and the United States press played a major role in bringing Castro to power.... As the U.S. Ambassador to Cuba during the Castro-Communist revolution of 1957–59, I had first-hand knowledge of the facts which brought about the rise of Fidel Castro.... The State Department consistently intervened — positively, negatively, and by innuendo — to bring about the downfall of President Fulgencio Batista, thereby making it possible for Fidel Castro to take over the

Government of Cuba.[46]

Cuba would become a base for Communist subversion and confrontation (useful to the Insiders) throughout the Southern Hemisphere and give strong support to Communism in Mexico.

Other contributions of the Eisenhower administration to Insider goals included:

• **Department of HEW.** The Eisenhower administration added the giant cabinet level Department of Health, Education, and Welfare to the federal bureaucracy in April of 1953 (a few months into Eisenhower's first term). As noted above, Eisenhower selected Nelson Rockefeller as under secretary of state for the new department.

Following in the footsteps of Presidents Roosevelt and Truman, the Eisenhower administration continued to expand the scope and role of the federal government in domestic affairs, racking up huge peacetime deficits. In June of 1957 (three years into Eisenhower's first term), Norman Thomas, the perennial Socialist Party candidate for president, would contend that "the United States is making greater strides toward socialism under Eisenhower than even under Roosevelt, particularly in the fields of Federal spending and welfare legislation."[47]

• **Federal aid for education.** The Eisenhower administration opened the federal funding spigot for education in 1958. Federal involvement in education had long been advocated by the National Educational Association and the liberal Left. But there was great resistance.

A principal objection was that federal aid would eventually have strings attached, leading to federal control, a fear vehemently denied by proponents. It would take a "crisis" to overcome the resistance.

The "crisis" came with the Soviet launch of Sputnik in October 1957 — the first-ever earth satellite. Americans were quickly told that American technical education needed to catch up with the scientifically superior Soviets. And the Eisenhower administration agreed. Congress responded the following year by passing the "National Defense and Education Act."

One astute congressman, Noah Mason of Illinois, warned of the consequences at the time:

Federal Aid for Education is not a temporary program to meet an immediate emergency. It is an effort to put our whole educational system under Federal control and to keep it there forever. [48]

However, the "crisis" was phony. Whether through interservice politics or subversive intent, the Eisenhower administration had *allowed* the Soviets to be first in space.

During the 1950s, Major General John B. Medaris headed up the Army's missile program. In 1960, Medaris published the significant fact that the United States could have easily launched an artificial satellite a full year (e.g., September 20, 1957) before the Russians: "We didn't do this for the simple reason that we were forbidden to do so." [49]

• **Blocking congressional investigations.** Investigations by both House and Senate subcommittees had rocked the Truman administration by uncovering Communist cells and Soviet agents in high places. But those investigations were beginning to target the Establishment. President Eisenhower played a significant role in thwarting those investigations.

Rene Wormser, counsel to the Reece Committee [the Special Committee to Investigate Tax Exempt Foundations] wrote that "[Democratic Congressman Wayne] Hays told us one day that 'the White House' had been in touch with him and asked him if he would cooperate to kill the Committee." [50]

Biographer Steven Ambrose wrote that Eisenhower "was determined to destroy McCarthy." [51] Working through subordinates, Eisenhower pressured Congress to censure McCarthy. McCarthy was destroyed not because he allegedly ruined the reputation of innocent people but because he was getting too close to the *sponsors* of Communists in government. In his *New York Times Magazine* article on the CFR, Anthony Lukas explained:

Though his nominal targets were Communists in Government,

by the fifties few Communists retained important positions, and as McCarthy bulled ahead it became clear that his real target was the Eastern Establishment, which had run the nation's foreign policy for decades....[52]

When McCarthy sought to question those in the administration who were trying to sabotage his work, President Eisenhower invoked a new claim of "executive privilege," ordering subordinates not to cooperate in sensitive areas with congressional committees.[53]

John F. Kennedy Administration
(1961 – 1963)

Road to the White House

Joseph P. Kennedy, Sr., father of John, Robert, Edward (Ted) et al, was the driving force behind the family financial and political fortunes. Joseph had succeeded in building a large fortune from a variety of investments.

As assistant general manager of Bethlehem Steel during World War I, Joseph Kennedy developed a friendship with Assistant Secretary of the Navy Franklin Roosevelt. A leader, in the Democratic Party, Kennedy received several government appointments while FDR was president.

Although the family fortune was an aid to the political careers of three of his sons, the father was never fully accepted by the New York Establishment, a hurdle JFK had to overcome when he sought the presidency.[54]

John Kennedy studied briefly at the Fabian Socialist London School of Economics, following in his elder brother Joseph's footsteps. He entered Princeton, also briefly. Repeated illnesses interrupted his schooling, however, he eventually graduated from Harvard in 1940.

John was serving as an ensign in the U.S. Navy assigned to the office of the Secretary of the Navy when the Japanese attacked Pearl Harbor. He subsequently served in the Pacific theater as a lieutenant commanding a patrol torpedo boat, receiving several decorations for wartime service.

Following the war, JFK was elected to the U.S. House of Representatives (1946), serving three terms, before successfully challenging for a Senate seat (1952). As a senator, Jack sought and received the opportunity to gain national attention by making the nominating speech for Adlai Stevenson at the 1956 Democratic convention. Then he threw his hat in the ring for the vice presidential spot.

Stevenson won the nomination but decided to let the convention choose the VP nominee. After the first round of balloting, Kennedy was second, behind Estes Kefauver. Then, Lyndon Johnson announced that Texas was switching to Kennedy: "Texas proudly casts its vote for the fighting sailor who wears the scars of battle" giving Kennedy the lead. [55] However, in the end, Kefauver got the convention's nod.

A year later, Kennedy signaled that he deserved Establishment support by writing an internationalist article for the October 1957 *Foreign Affairs*, entitled "A Democrat Looks at Foreign Policy."

In 1960, JFK captured the Democratic Party nomination winning primary contests against Senators Hubert Humphrey of Minnesota and Wayne Morse of Oregon. At the convention in Los Angeles, his main opponent was Lyndon Johnson. Nevertheless, Kennedy chose Johnson as his running mate, largely to obtain Johnson's strength in the South.

A Faustian bargain

Kennedy also sought the support of the party's left wing. His bargain with the Left would advance the socialist drive to control health care and set the stage for Medicare under Johnson. According to Edward Annis, former president of the AMA (1963–64):

> With Kennedy's backing, a founding member and past vice chairman of the ADA [Americans for Democratic Action], Representative Chester Bowles [CFR] of Connecticut, was made chairman of the party's Resolutions and Platform Committee, and he alone appointed the subcommittee to draft the platform. Bowles made himself chairman ... of the subcommittee. He also appointed Joseph Rauh, founding father and national chairman of the ADA, to the subcommittee. The platform was written

behind closed doors long before the convention in Los Angeles, and it contained many planks that had appeared on the ADA's platform for years.[56]

As Mr. Rauh later said, "We got everything we asked for, and it was so easy."[57]

Annis also observed that to secure the ADA support, Kennedy must have provided assurances that he would adhere to the ADA platform, assurances that became apparent after the election:

> The cabinet post most sought after by the left wing, because it provided the greatest opportunity for "socializing" society was head of the Department of Health, Education and Welfare (HEW). That coveted secretaryship went to ADA disciple Abraham Ribicoff, to whom the young president was deeply indebted for serving as his floor manager at the Democratic convention. At the president's right hand as his "special assistant" would be Harvard history professor Arthur Schlesigner, Jr., a founder of the ADA.[58]

Schlesinger had joined the CFR in 1946. Ribicoff would not become a member until 1974.

The Kennedy-Johnson ticket proceeded to defeat the GOP nominee, Richard Nixon, in one of the closest presidential elections of the 20th Century.

CFR Staffing

According to several Establishment sources, President-elect Kennedy offered "wise man" Robert A. Lovett his "choice of three top Cabinet posts — State, Defense, or Treasury" — and Lovett "spurned them all but suggested the three men who ended up in those jobs."

Kennedy also consulted CFR "wise man" Dean Acheson for cabinet recommendations. [59] The three men Lovett recommended were:

• CFR veteran **Dean Rusk**, president of the Rockefeller Foundation, as secretary of state.

- CFR heavyweight **C. Douglas Dillon** (future vice chairman of the CFR) as secretary of the treasury.

- And Ford Motor Company President **Robert Strange McNamara** as secretary of defense. (McNamara would not join the CFR until 1968.)

According to Kennedy Special Counsel and primary speechwriter Ted Sorensen (CFR in 1967), Kennedy regarded McNamara as the "star of his team, calling upon him for advice on a wide range of issues beyond national security, including business and economic matters." [60]

Other significant appointees from the CFR included:

- **McGeorge Bundy** as national security adviser, the powerful super-cabinet position that Henry Kissinger and Zbigniew Brzesinski would hold in later administrations. Gary Allen observed: "Placing McGeorge Bundy in charge of national security was like putting Liz Taylor in charge of marriage counseling.... Under Bundy's influence, many security risks were brought into the Kennedy Administration. When security officers refused to clear them, they were cleared 'on higher authority.'" [61] In 1966, Bundy would serve as president of the Ford Foundation and support numerous leftist causes.

Bundy's older brother, William P. Bundy, also CFR, would serve in the Johnson administration as assistant secretary of state for Far Eastern affairs (1964–1969), playing a major role in "mismanaging" the war in Vietnam. William would later become a director of the CFR and the editor of *Foreign Affairs*. He married Dean Acheson's daughter.

- **Walt Rostow** as deputy national security adviser. In his 1960 book, *The United States in the World Arena*," Rostow argued that it was an "American interest to see an end to nationhood as it has been historically defined." [62]

In June 1961, Rostow informed graduates of the Army's Special Warfare Center that the U.S. should not seek victory over Communism "in the usual sense." He and Rusk would both promote a no-win policy in Vietnam.

• **John McCone** as CIA director.

• **Roswell Gilpatric** as deputy secretary of defense.

• **Paul Nitze** as assistant secretary of defense.

• **Henry Fowler** as under secretary of the treasury.

• **George Ball** as under secretary of state for economic affairs (the number three post). Ball soon advanced to the number two post, under secretary of state, serving as Dean Rusk's "alter ego" and troubleshooter. He would play a lead role in our State Department's betrayal of Katanga. Ball became an established internationalist, serving on the Trilateral Commission, the Atlantic Union, and the Bilderberg Steering Committee.

• CFR "wise man" **Averell Harriman** as assistant secretary of state for Far Eastern affairs.

• **Arthur Schlesinger, Jr.** and **Jerome Wiesner** as special assistants to the president.

• **John J. McCloy** as chief of the U.S. Disarmament Administration (part of the State Department). A former president of the World Bank, McCloy headed up the Ford Foundation in 1953, before turning over the top spot to McGeorge Bundy. He would take the reigns at the Council on Foreign Relations in 1955, handing them over to David Rockefeller in 1970.

Members of the Council on Foreign Relations would dominate the Rusk State Department. Writing for the *New York Times Magazine*, Anthony Lukas noted: "Of the first 82 names on a list prepared to help President Kennedy staff his State Department, 63 were Council members. Kennedy once complained, 'I'd like to have some new faces here, but all I get are the same old names.'" [63]

In describing this elite domination of foreign policy, Pulitzer-prize winning author David Halberstam cited the recollections of John Kenneth Galbraith: "Those of us who had worked for the Kennedy election were tolerated in the government for that reason and had a say, but foreign policy was still with the Council on Foreign Relations people." [64]

Advancing the Insider Agenda

The Insiders dominating the Kennedy administration naturally sought to advance the internationalist agenda abroad and socialism at home:

• **Government-sponsored (controlled) health care.** This agenda of the ADA and socialists would gather steam during the Kennedy administration and see its first major success during the following Johnson administration.

• **American involvement in Vietnam.** Just three weeks prior to his assassination, President Kennedy approved the November 1, 1963 overthrow of South Vietnam's President Diem. "Our complicity in his overthrow heightened our responsibilities and our commitment [in Vietnam]," concluded a secret government study of the war, released maliciously as the *Pentagon Papers*. [65]

• **Securing Communism in Cuba.** While preparing to involve America in a no-win war against Communism in Southeast Asia, the Kennedy CFR team would support socialism and communism in this hemisphere and Africa.

The Kennedy administration managed to ensure that Fidel Castro would have a secure base in Cuba for Communist subversion. The first step was the betrayal of the CIA-organized Bay of Pigs invasion. In the days leading up to the April 1961 invasion by anti-Castro patriots, it was an open secret that the invasion was "in the works." Robert Welch, understanding the Insider support for Castro, predicted the outcome at a public meeting two or three days before the invasion took place. [66] At the last moment, President Kennedy cancelled the promised air support, allowing the invaders to be overwhelmed by Castro's forces.

In the negotiations over the later Cuban Missile Crisis, the U.S. likely provided further assurance that it would not challenge Fidel's reign in Cuba.

In the ensuing decades, Havana became the center for international terrorism in the Western Hemisphere. Cuba would maintain ties with virtually every state sponsor of terrorism: Iran, Syria, North Korea, Libya, Algeria and, of course, with Russia and Red China. And Fidel would support Saddam Hussein. Following the 9-11 attacks, Castro convened a summit in Havana that included representatives from the state sponsors of terrorism and major terrorist groups.[67]

A sad joke would call Cuba the largest country in the world: Its government was in Moscow, its armed forces in Africa, and its population in Miami.

• **The Alliance for Progress.** In March 1961, President Kennedy proposed a ten-year plan for Latin America, which he termed the "Alliance for Progress":

> [W]e propose to complete the revolution of the Americas, to build a hemisphere where all men can hope for a suitable standard of living and all can live out their lives in dignity and in freedom. To achieve this goal political freedom must accompany material progress....

The heroic language announcing the plan provided cover for what amounted to a new Marshall Plan for Latin America. Indeed, some of its CFR architects had helped to put together the original Marshall Plan. And, as with the original, the "aid" would be justified as opposing Communism by assisting "natural" revolution in this hemisphere.

In reality, the massive U.S. aid transfer would support socialist regimes and socialist "land and tax reform" movements at the expense of established allies. It would also entice many Latin American nations into debt to the international bankers and the I.M.F.

Although the Alliance for Progress is commonly thought of as President Kennedy's initiative, it was actually an early step in a long-term agenda for this hemisphere developed by CFR elites. The planning had its roots in the Eisenhower administration and would gain new momentum as the Free Trade Area of the Americas (FTAA) during the George W. Bush administration.

• **Supporting Communism in Africa.** The Kennedy administration would support UN military aggression against the independent province of Katanga. Katanga had seceded from the chaos and reign of terror countenanced by the Moscow-backed Communist central government in Leopoldville. (For more of the Katanga story, see Chapter 16, What Can and *Must* Be Done!)

President Kennedy had been the leading apologist in the Senate for Algeria's National Liberation Front (FLN) and FLN leader Ahmed Ben Bella's war for "independence" from France. The Communist FLN orchestrated a reign of terror primarily against its own Muslim population. The Establishment press would refer to the terrorist FLN as freedom fighters while smearing the French Secret Army Organization (O.A.S.) as terrorists.

Algeria was granted independence on July 1, 1962. Ben Bella quickly consolidated control and in a lopsided election became its premier (later Algeria's first president) on September 20, 1962. Nine days later, the Kennedy State Department extended formal diplomatic recognition to the Communist government. President Kennedy sent Ben Bella his "warmest congratulations" and wishes for "every success."

The following month, Ben Bella visited Washington and received a twenty-one gun salute on the White House lawn. Ben Bella would credit Kennedy with providing invaluable support to the Algerian rebels in 1957 (while senator). The Kennedy administration was embarrassed when the next day Ben Bella flew to Cuba and presented Fidel Castro with Algeria's first "Medal of Honor" and declared: "Algeria is and will be with Cuba."[68]

Algeria would be transformed into an important Soviet base in Africa.

Lyndon Johnson Administrations
(1963 – 1969)

A Crooked Road to the White House

Lyndon Baines Johnson spent most of his adult life working for the government. Nevertheless, he managed to go from modest beginnings to perhaps the wealthiest man to enter the Oval Office at that time. [69] His "family" assets upon assuming the presidency have been estimated at $20 million. [70]

One source of the Johnson family wealth was broadcasting. In 1942, his wife, Lady Bird, used most of her modest ($21,000) inheritance to purchase a small Austin radio station and later a television license. With favorable FEC rulings, the Johnsons parlayed the investment into 7 million by the time Lyndon became president. [71]

Lyndon Johnson was elected to the House of Representatives from Texas in 1937, serving there until 1949. While still in Congress, he became a commissioned officer in the Naval Reserve.

During World War II, President Roosevelt sent him on an inspection mission to the southwest Pacific. On June 9, 1942 Johnson boarded a B-26 as an observer on a bombing mission of Japanese-held New Guinea. The B-26 he almost boarded was shot down with no survivors. There were differing reports of what happened to the plane carrying Johnson. Johnson claimed it came under fire. Other witnesses insisted it returned due to equipment malfunction long before encountering the enemy.

Nevertheless, Johnson was awarded the Silver Star, the nation's third highest military honor. None of the flight crew received a medal. Johnson's biographer Robert Caro, stated:

> The most you can say about Lyndon Johnson and his Silver Star is that it is surely one of the most undeserved Silver Stars in history, because if you accept everything that he said, he was still in action for no more than 13 minutes and only as an observer. Men who flew many missions, brave men, never got a Silver Star. [72]

A Stolen Election

In 1948, Johnson made a second try for a U.S. Senate seat. From that point on, his climb to higher office was marred with charges of corruption. In a three-way Democratic primary, Johnson came in second. But the leader failed to earn a majority, so a run-off was scheduled.

In the subsequent primary run-off, Johnson initially came up the narrow loser, but squeaked out an 84-vote victory on a very questionable recount. The outcome was challenged in court amid allegations of voter fraud on both sides. In one infamous precinct alone [Precinct 13, Jim Wells County], 202 ballots were cast at the close of polling, all in alphabetical order. [73]

The ballot box had obviously been stuffed. The total vote count greatly exceeded the number of ballots officially issued. Among the 202 were several identified as deceased on election day. Others who appeared on the list as having voted denied they had cast ballots.

It was not Johnson's first stolen election. According to Pulitzer Prize winning biographer Robert A. Caro:

> Lyndon Johnson, who was alleged to have won his seat in the United States Senate in a stolen election in 1948, stole his first election in 1930 [to give himself a seat on his college's senior council].... [A] score of political tricks on the same moral level earned him a reputation on campus as a man who was not "straight," not honest; that he was, in fact, so deeply and widely mistrusted at college that his nickname, the nickname by which he was identified in the college yearbook, was "Bull" (for "Bulls**t") Johnson. [74]

Corruption Scandals

Two major corruption scandals would touch Johnson's political career. During most of his time as senator (1949–1961), LBJ would serve in leadership positions, including six years as the Senate majority leader.

Johnson could depend greatly on his friend and aide Bobby Baker for legislative successes. As the Senate's secretary to the majority, Baker was referred to as "Lyndon's boy." Under Lyndon's sponsorship, "Baker's $19,612-a-year salary became a fortune of some two million dollars." [75]

A couple of weeks prior to the JFK assassination, the Senate Rules Committee opened an investigation into Baker for alleged congressional bribery. However, under subsequent pressure from the Johnson White House, the senate voted against a proposal to extend the Baker investigation. The improper activities of a number of senators thus escaped scrutiny.

The other scandal, which gained national attention and threatened to draw in Johnson while vice president, involved his close associate and political supporter, Texas-based financier Billie Sol Estes. In April 1962, Estes was indicted by a federal grand jury for fraud. In 1964, he was sentenced to 15 years in prison (later overturned by the U.S. Supreme Court because of media publicity in the courtroom). [76]

According to biographer Robert Caro:

> For years, men came into Lyndon Johnson's office and handed him envelopes stuffed with cash. They didn't stop coming even when the office in which he sat was the office of the Vice President of the United States. Fifty thousand dollars (in hundred-dollar bills in sealed envelopes) was what one lobbyist — for one oil company — testified that he brought to Johnson's office during his term as Vice President. They placed at his disposal sums of money whose dimensions were revolutionary in politics, and he used it to bend other politicians to his will. [77]

In 1960, Lyndon Johnson tried unsuccessfully to gain the Democratic presidential nomination. However, the nominee, John F. Kennedy, tapped Johnson as his running mate.

CFR Staffing
Upon assuming the presidency following the Kennedy assassination, Johnson made no changes in JFK's Cabinet. However, during his second term Johnson visited the CFR well for the following replacements:

• Henry H. Fowler (CFR) replaced Secretary of the Treasury C. Douglas Dillon (CFR) in 1965.

• Nicholas deB. Katzenbach (CFR) replaced Robert F. Kennedy as attorney general in late 1964 (shortly before the end of Johnson's 1st term). Ramsey Clark succeeded Katzenbach in September of 1966. Clark would show up on the CFR roster in 1971.

After leaving the administration, Clark's left-wing sympathies became public as he repeatedly sided with America's enemies (e.g., supporting North Vietnam on Hanoi radio in 1972).

• John T. Connor (CFR) succeeded Luther Hodges as secretary of commerce.

• John W. Gardner (CFR) was picked as the new secretary of HEW. Gardner was succeeded by Wilbur J. Cohen (not CFR) in 1968. Cohen was a career bureaucrat and a major player in the drive to socialize medicine.

• Arthur J. Goldberg (CFR) to succeed Adlai E. Stevenson (CFR) as the U.S. representative to the United Nations. In 1968, Goldberg was replaced by George W. Ball (CFR).

Dean Rusk (CFR) continued as secretary of state through both Johnson terms. And Robert McNamara (CFR) stayed on as secretary of defense until the last year of the Johnson administration. McNamara would provide disastrous leadership to the Vietnam War (see below).

President Johnson also inherited JFK's team of advisors. Throughout the Vietnam War, Johnson met periodically with an advisory group of 14 he himself called "the Wise Men." Twelve of the fourteen were CFR members. Dean Acheson was perhaps most influential. John J. McCloy, Robert Lovett, and Averell Harriman were also included. [78]

Advancing the Insider Agenda

Lyndon Johnson broke through the political and constitutional barriers that had blocked federal involvement in several areas of American life. With Medicare, for example, the federal government became a third party between a patient and his doctor or hospital, and it would begin to determine everyone's minimum health rights and responsibilities.

President Johnson also created the Cabinet-level Housing and Urban Development Department (HUD), which would provide funds for urban renewal of cities and open the door for federal rent assistance to low-income families. The umbrella for this accelerated power grab was known as:

• **"The Great Society."** Following his decisive win over GOP nominee Barry Goldwater in 1964, President Johnson would start his new term by launching a massive program of federal spending to build what he termed the "Great Society." The Great Society would greatly encourage state and individual dependence on Washington.

In his January 4, 1965 State of the Union address to Congress, President Johnson outlined his proposed national agenda, which included the following:

> I propose that we begin a program of education to ensure every American child the fullest development of his mind and skills.
>
> I propose that we begin a massive attack on crippling and killing diseases.
>
> I propose that we launch a national effort to make the American city a better and more stimulating place to live....
>
> [W]e must open opportunity to all our people.... [T]hrough doubling the war against poverty this year....

The president also promised more help for small farmers, "new programs of help for the basic community facilities and for neighborhood centers of health and recreation," "high speed rail transportation between urban centers," massive efforts to save and beautify the countryside, prevention of "pollution of our air and water," "a National Foundation on the Arts," and more programs to encourage basic science. All while we were still expanding an expensive war half way around the world.

Rather than a war *on* poverty, the president's proposal amounted to a war *of* poverty. At the time of promised "new aid" to the small farmer, for example, almost 100,000 civil servants were already administering the federal government's multi-billion dollar "aid" program for the farms. But that aid, which overthrew natural market forces, came with regulations to fight unwanted surpluses — leading to the prosecution of tens of thousands of farmers for violations each year. Millions of dollars in fines were being collected annually.[79]

The rubber-stamp Democratic Congress gave the President practically everything he asked for, setting new records in deficit spending. And government became the biggest growth area in the nation. By 1966 "one worker in six [was] employed by federal, state, or local government compared to one in seven in 1955, and one in nine back in 1948." [80]

And those figures did not include workers in private industry who owed their jobs to government spending or to those who depended on the government for welfare and benefit income. Of course, huge federal borrowing was required to finance this federal "generosity."

But the Great Society would do even more damage through its assault on the Constitution. When the Department of Housing and Urban Development was created, the *Arizona Republic* protested:

> Nowhere does the U.S. Constitution give the federal government any control over urban affairs....
>
> Scarcely a week passes but some city or county department head goes from Phoenix to Washington to get the answer to a problem which, a few years ago, would have been solved in city hall or the court house. [81]

Norman Thomas, the Socialist Party leader, declared that he did not need to run for president in 1964, because Lyndon Johnson was carrying out his program. Regarding the Johnson "War on Poverty" program, Thomas declared: "I ought to rejoice and I do. I rub my eyes in amazement and surprise. His war on poverty is a Socialistic approach and may be the major issue of the 1964 campaign." [82]

• **No-Win War.** The War in Vietnam was not a project of anti-Communist "hawks," but of CFR "wise men," who had helped and would continue to help Communism. While Americans fought a frustrating war halfway around the globe, Communism was allowed to flourish 90 miles away in Cuba, from where Fidel Castro exported his revolution to Latin America and even Africa.

In Vietnam, McNamara and company hobbled our Armed Forces with a defensive strategy that could not win, while preventing a strategy that could. Americans have been repeatedly told that winning was not feasible. Yet few are aware of counterclaims by America's top military leaders. In December 1965, General John P. McConnell, the Chief of Staff for the Air Force, publicly claimed that victory was possible, "but was muzzled by McNamara before he could reveal the details of his proposed win-fast strategy." [83]

In late 1966, former Air Force Chief of Staff, General Curtis

LeMay, fed up with the Administration's "nibbling around the edges" strategy, which was unnecessarily sacrificing thousands of lives and scores of billions of dollars, published an outspoken article in *U.S. News & World Report*, offering a blueprint of the Air Force-sea power strategy for victory. [84]

According to Admiral Chester Ward: "The thrust of the plan is simple: Destroy by conventional bombing the entire capability of the North Vietnamese Communist Government to make or support a war, and even its ability to supply the population with food; blockade the entire coast, especially Haiphong Harbor. Substantially all professional military opinion, retired and active, supports this strategy or something very similar to it." [85]

But such an objective was contrary to the firm intentions of the Insiders running the war. Even worse, the McNamara team invoked an insidious micromanagement of the war from Washington and imposed Rules of Engagement that ensured our forces could not have victory. They would win every major battle, but were not allowed to win the war.

Not until 1985, thanks to the initiative of Senator Barry Goldwater, was the text of the Rules of Engagement declassified. [86] In a speech to a symposium in Washington D.C. on April 30, 1985, J. Terry Emerson, legal counsel to Barry Goldwater, described "How Rules of Engagement Lost the Vietnam War":

> One rule told American pilots that they were not permitted to attack a North Vietnam MiG sitting on a runway. The only time it could be attacked was after it was in flight, was clearly identified, and showed "hostile intentions.".... Another rule ordered that SAM missile sites could not be struck while they were under construction but only after they became operational and dangerous! [87]

During the War, the administration also made sure that the Soviets would be able to provide their peasant national ally with the means to continue the war. As an example of news that should have set off alarm bells, during the build-up of the Vietnam War the *Chicago Tribune* reprinted the dispatch of a West German newspaper:

Weapons of the Polish armed forces are being shipped from Stettin harbor in Poland in ever increasing quantities to ... North Vietnamese harbors.... While on one side of the Stettin harbor American wheat is being unloaded from freighters, on the other side of the same harbor weapons are loaded which are being used against American soldiers.... The Poles receive the wheat [from the U.S.] on credit and they in turn ship their weapons to North Viet Nam on credit.[88]

Defense Secretary Robert McNamara defined such policies as good strategy: "The trade that we have had with members of the Communist bloc in Europe has, in my opinion, loosened the ties of those countries to the Soviet Union. I strongly support the President's proposal to expand trade with the Communist bloc in Europe."[89]

Not everyone agreed. Senator Karl E. Mundt (R-South Dakota) told the Senate on March 14, 1967:

If increasing the armament of those fighting against us is the shortcut to peace, every American President in history except Lyndon B. Johnson has been totally and completely in error; because he is the first to propose it.

Chapter 10

CFR Dominance: Nixon, Ford, and Carter Administrations

Richard Nixon Administrations
(1969 – 1973) (1973 – 1974)

A "Rocky" Road to the White House

Scandal and defeat afflicted the political career of Richard Milhous Nixon, yet he repeatedly managed to rebound.

A practicing attorney, Nixon joined the U.S. Navy after Pearl Harbor, serving in the Pacific theater. Following the war, he entered politics, defeating five-term congressman Jerry Voorhis in a 1946 election to represent Southern California's 12th congressional district.

Nixon rose to national prominence in 1948 when, as a member of the House Committee on Un-American Activities, he seized the opportunity to push the investigation of Alger Hiss to conclusion. The Left would never forgive him for his role in exposing one of their own.

In the 1950 elections, aided by his new national prominence, Nixon decided to contest for a vacant U.S. Senate seat from California. His successful campaign against Democratic representative and former actress Helen Gahagan Douglas was notably contentious. Nixon called his opponent a left-wing sympathizer and "pink right down to her underwear."

The Nixon campaign employed questionable and misleading tactics, earning Nixon the nickname "Tricky Dick," a derisive label he could never shake. While building his credentials as an anti-Communist, Nixon also took pains to establish himself as an internationalist. In 1947, he travelled to Europe as part of the [Christian] Herter Committee that helped prepare Congress and public opinion for the Marshall Plan.

Two years later, his reputation as a tough anti-Communist would earn him the VP spot on the Eisenhower for President ticket.

However, shortly thereafter accusations of improprieties relating to a fund established by Nixon's financial backers threatened to eliminate him from the ticket.

Nixon took the offensive by going on national television to deliver his famous "Checkers speech." Addressing the charges, Nixon attacked his opponents and urged his audience to contact the Republican National Committee and tell it whether he should remain on the ticket. The speech, heard by an estimated 60 million Americans, resulted in an outpouring of public support, securing his position.

In 1960, following Eisenhower's second term, Nixon won the Republican nomination for president, but lost a very close race to Senator John F. Kennedy. At a critical point in the campaign, Nixon flew to New York to meet with Nelson Rockefeller, during which meeting Nixon sold out the Republican platform.

Senator Barry Goldwater termed the meeting the "Munich of the Republican Party." Nationally syndicated columnist Edith Kermit Roosevelt would write: "It was not as a Standard Oil heir, but as an Establishment heir ... that Nelson Rockefeller forced the Republicans to rewrite their platform. Thus the Republican platform was in effect a carbon copy of the Democratic platform drawn up by Chester Bowles, CFR member and former trustee of the Rockefeller Foundation." [1]

Two years later, Nixon sought to preserve his national stature by relocating back to California and campaigning for governor. Nixon easily won the Republican nomination only to suffer an embarrassing defeat in the general election at the hands of a man of little political stature — incumbent Democratic Governor Edmund G. "Pat" Brown (senior).

Following this defeat, a bitter Nixon told reporters that he was quitting politics and that they wouldn't have Nixon to kick around anymore. He then returned to New York and went to work in the law firm of John Mitchell, Nelson Rockefeller's attorney (and later Nixon's attorney general). He also moved into Nelson Rockefeller's apartment building. During this time his personal wealth grew considerably.

As a presidential candidate again in 1967, Nixon won Establishment favor with a *Foreign Affairs* article that advocated opening diplomatic relations with China. In 1968, Nixon won most of the state primaries and reached the Republican convention with enough delegate strength to gain the nomination on the first ballot.

President Johnson had decided not to seek another term, so Nixon would face Vice President Hubert Humphrey in the general election. With Americans concerned about revolutionary violence in the cities, Nixon campaigned as the "law and order" candidate. Throughout the campaign Nixon cultivated the image of the experienced senior statesman, refusing to engage in televised debates. Regarding Vietnam, he merely said he had a "secret plan" to end the war. The tactic worked.

Nixon's Second Term
During Nixon's reelection campaign, burglars at the Democratic offices in the Watergate hotel were arrested (June 17, 1972). The emerging story didn't seriously touch the president that year, and he was overwhelmingly re-elected in November.

However, the ensuing investigations, trials, and near constant coverage in the daily press fueled a growing scandal. Adding to the president's woes, the past caught up with Nixon's vice president, Spiro Agnew.

During his fifth year as vice president (1973), Agnew was charged with accepting bribes before, during, and after his time as governor of Maryland. As part of a plea bargain, Agnew resigned his vice presidential post. To fill the Agnew vacancy, President Nixon chose veteran House Minority Leader Gerald Ford.

When Nixon was forced to release White House tapes of his conversations regarding the Watergate break-in, the end was near. Nixon lost top GOP congressional support and moves began for his impeachment. At that point Nixon decided to resign, handing the presidency over to Vice President Ford on August 8, 1974, more than two years after the attempted burglary and wiretapping.

Several years after Watergate, Nixon's image was rehabilitated to some extent in the Establishment media.

CFR Staffing
The two appointments that most reflected Nixon's subservience to the Establishment were CFR members Peter G. Peterson as secretary

of commerce (1972) and Henry Kissinger as national security advisor (and later secretary of state).

• **Peter G. Peterson.** Following a one-year stint as secretary of commerce, Peterson was selected as chairman and CEO of Lehman Brothers (from 1973 to 1984). The following year (1985), Peterson would replace an aging David Rockefeller as chairman of the Council on Foreign Relations.

• **Henry Kissinger.** President Nixon's most controversial appointment with the greatest long-term ramifications undoubtedly was Henry Kissinger.

When Nixon tapped Kissinger as his national security advisor, Kissinger already had a long relationship with the Rockefellers. Indeed, Kissinger had been serving as Nelson Rockefeller's chief foreign policy advisor in support of Rockefeller's presidential aspirations. Kissinger would dedicate his memoir, *White House Years*, to Nelson, describing him as "the single most influential person in my life."

Kissinger graduated from Harvard in 1950 with help from the Rockefeller Foundation Fellowship for Political Theory. In 1956, he was invited into the CFR. In 1987, J. Robert Moskin, author of the *U.S. Marine Corps Story*, examined the Council's influence for *Town & Country* magazine:

> It was principally because of his long association with the Rockefellers that Henry Kissinger became a force in the Council. The *New York Times* called him "the Council's most influential member," and a Council insider says that "his influence is indirect and enormous— much of it through his Rockefeller connection." [2]

• **Other Nixon appointments** drawn from the ranks of the CFR included cabinet-level officers Elliot Richardson (secretary of HEW); James Thomas Lynn (secretary of Housing and Urban Development in Nixon's 2nd term); Dr. Paul McCracken (chairman of the Council of Economic Advisors); and Charles Yost (U.S. ambassador to the United Nations).

Also, on the foreign policy side, President Nixon selected Jacob Beam (CFR) as U.S. ambassador to the Soviet Union, Gerard Smith (CFR) to head up the Arms Control and Disarmament Agency (McCloy's old stomping grounds) and security-risk (and friend of Alger Hiss) Harlan Cleveland (CFR) as U.S. ambassador to NATO. Nixon even retained George Ball (CFR), who had served in the Kennedy and Johnson administrations, as a consultant on foreign policy. So much for any real separation between Republican and Democratic presidents.

And last we mention Nixon's selection of Arthur Burns (CFR) to chair the Federal Reserve Board.

Advancing the Insider Agenda
Richard Nixon exemplified the old saying that once you get a reputation as an early riser, you can get up as late as you want. As president, Nixon could rely on his conservative, anti-communist image to neutralize conservative opposition, while he implemented the internationalist-socialist agenda.

While most conservative opinion leaders were reluctant to criticize Nixon, a few Establishment-aligned spokesmen let the cat out of the bag. Within the first month of the Nixon presidency, Roscoe Drummond (CFR) wrote in his nationally syndicated column:

> The most significant political fact of the hour is now so evident it can't be seriously disputed: President Richard M. Nixon is a "secret liberal"....
>
> Lyndon Johnson initiated and Congress approved the largest volume of social legislation of any president in history. And Nixon prepares to carry forward every major Johnson measure.[3]

Not quite two years later, Keynesian socialist and Harvard economics professor John Kenneth Galbraith (CFR) wrote approvingly:

> Certainly the least predicted development under the Nixon administration was this great new thrust to socialism. One encounters people who still aren't aware of it. Others must be rubbing their eyes, for certainly the portents seemed all to the

contrary. As an opponent of socialism, Mr. Nixon seemed steadfast....[4]

New York Times columnist James Reston (CFR) echoed Galbraith's astonishment:

> The Nixon budget is more planned, has more welfare in it, and has a bigger predicted deficit than any other budget in this century.[5]

Nixon's Senate floor leader, liberal GOP Senator Hugh Scott (Penn.), once summed up the "new" Nixon nicely: "We [Liberals] get the action and the Conservatives get the rhetoric."[6]

On the domestic scene, President Nixon advanced a number of Insider/Left goals for a more expansive and intrusive federal government. He created the anti-industry Environmental Protection Agency by executive order, imposed wage and price controls on the American people, and signed into law the bill establishing the Occupational Safety and Health Administration (OSHA).

• **Federal control of health care.** The Nixon administration also supported the socialist agenda of expanding federal control of health care. Indeed a *White House Report On Health Care Needs* released July 10, 1969 sounded as if it had been drafted forty years later by the Obama administration:

> This nation is faced with a breakdown in the delivery of health care unless immediate concerned action is taken by Government....
>
> Our task now as a nation is to acknowledge the extreme urgency of the situation, to take certain steps....

• **Removing the gold restraint.** In August 1971, President Nixon issued an executive order closing the gold window to foreign central banks. Henceforth, the value of the dollar would float in international markets. This action removed a critical restraint on Federal Reserve inflation of the money supply.

Domestically, the value of the dollar has declined significantly since its tie to gold was broken, and internationally its value as a reserve currency is seriously threatened. The U.S. also shifted from a creditor nation in 1971 to a debtor nation today.

One of the key figures at the meeting where the plans were worked out for the suspension of gold convertibility was Paul Volcker, at the time Treasury Undersecretary for International Monetary Affairs. [7] The following year, Volcker would be invited to join the CFR. In addition to his CFR membership, Volcker would become a founding member of David Rockefeller's Trilateral Commission (see Jimmy Carter, below). President Carter appointed him chairman of the Federal Reserve in 1979.

• **Viet Nam.** Nixon was elected in 1968 on a promise to achieve "peace with honor" in Viet Nam. When he took over as commander and chief of U.S. Armed Forces, Nixon used American military force more aggressively than the McNamara-Johnson team, raising initial hopes among the troops that perhaps they would be allowed to win.

As an example, in mid-1970, Nixon authorized a surprise military campaign against Communist sanctuaries in Cambodia. The anti-war Left reacted with massive anti-Nixon hysteria, boosting Nixon's image in conservative circles.

Although the Cambodia campaign hurt the Communist North Vietnamese plans temporarily, Nixon refused to expose the revolutionary organization behind the domestic propaganda undermining public support for the War. Ultimately, the Left, their allies in Congress, and the Establishment media provided Nixon with enough covering pressure to sell out Southeast Asia to the Communists.

Immediately before assuming the post of national security advisor in the Nixon administration, Henry Kissinger wrote "The Viet Nam Negotiations" for the January 1969 issue of *Foreign Affairs*. Not surprisingly, Kissinger was allowed to negotiate an end to American military involvement in Viet Nam. But it was not peace with honor.

The Paris Peace Accords resulted in the abandonment of South Vietnam, and ultimately Laos and Cambodia as well, to Communist forces. Moreover, the Communists were allowed to get away without accounting for all of our POW's, many of whom were known to have been captured alive. Although the North Vietnamese returned

591 POWs, not one returned from Laos.

During the war, the Pathet Lao had acknowledged holding American POWs, and the American government knew the prison locations in Laos of at least 68. [8] But our government never even opened negotiations for their return. They were simply forgotten. The lesson: A government that will betray its men in uniform will betray the nation. For his role in the Southeast Asia perfidy, Kissinger would receive the Nobel Peace Prize.

• **Opening doors to Red China.** While Nixon failed to keep his promise of "peace with honor" in Viet Nam, he did deliver on his "promise" to the Insiders to open relations with Communist China. In July 1971, Henry Kissinger secretly visited Beijing and prepared the groundwork for Nixon's visit the following February.

During his one week visit to China, Nixon met many times with Zhou Enlai, but only once with a weakened Mao Tse Tung. Secretary of State William P. Rogers was excluded from the meeting with Mao, but one other American accompanied Nixon — Winston Lord, a member of the National Security Council's planning staff.

Lord had accompanied Kissinger on his secret trip to Beijing in 1971. Lord would join the CFR in 1973 and serve as its president between 1977 and 1985.

Nixon thus began a U.S. policy spanning several administrations of building Red China into a modern world power. Favored U.S. firms were encouraged to invest in China, even relocating operations to China where they could operate more profitably, with their investments protected by the U.S. government.

The Insider-created policy toward China contributed to the de-industrialization of this country, while also providing a "carrot" (reinforced by U.S. regulatory "sticks") to encourage *manufacturing* flight. The result has been a significant erosion of the American middle class. Cheaper goods in the stores, hasn't offset declining opportunities for quality jobs.

• **Building an enemy.** The month following Nixon's return from China, the Republican National Convention in Miami Beach handed him, as expected, its nomination for a second term. However, the Convention still had its drama.

In developing a "consensus" platform, various subcommittees commonly hold hearings and gather testimonies from experts, often with media coverage. One testimony at the 1972 Convention turned out to be a blockbuster.

The expert was Antony C. Sutton, Ph.D., a little known research fellow at Stanford University's Hoover Institute. However, before Sutton could address the Party's National Security Subcommittee, the television cameras were removed from the hearing room, the press was excluded, and the press conference, which the Subcommittee had scheduled for Dr. Sutton afterwards, was canceled.[9]

What Dr. Sutton had to say was political dynamite, because he had impeccable credentials to back up his statements. For more than a decade, Sutton had researched the connection between Western technology and Soviet economic development. By 1972, Dr. Sutton had written three dry, very scholarly and technical volumes on the subject, each covering a different span of years.[10] Sutton would later update his findings in books more accessible to the public. The title of one summarizes its message: *The Best Enemy Money Can Buy*.

Here is a portion of the professor's politically embarrassing testimony:

> In a few words: there is no such thing as Soviet Technology. Almost all — perhaps 90–95 percent — came directly or indirectly from the United States and its allies. In effect the United States and the NATO countries have built the Soviet Union. Its industrial *and* its military capabilities. This massive construction job has taken 50 years.... It has been carried out through trade and the sale of plants, equipment and technical assistance....
>
> The United States is spending $80 billion a year on defense against an enemy built by the United States and West Europe.[11]

Dr. Sutton went on to present specific examples and to show how we had continued to build up that enemy during the Vietnam War and how substantial aid was continuing right along under the Nixon administration. He pointed in particular to U.S. aid that was then helping the Soviets build the massive Kama River truck factory —

the largest such plant (36 square miles) in the world, capable of turning out 100,000 ten-ton trucks per year. Trucks from this factory would support the 1979 Soviet invasion of Afghanistan.[12]

What the professor did not identify at the time was the Insider axis, including the Council on Foreign Relations and international banking firms, that had promoted the transfer.

A decade later Republican Senator William Armstrong (R-Colo.) revisited the topic from the Senate floor:

> The great irony for Americans who will be asked to tighten their belts in order to pay for our defense needs is that much of the additional money that must be spent on defense is required to offset Soviet weapons that probably could not have been built without our assistance.[13]

The GOP senator cited the following example:

> In 1972, President Nixon authorized the sale to the Soviet Union of 164 precision ball bearing grinders manufactured by the Bryant Chucking Grinder Corp. of Vermont. These grinders can manufacture tiny ball bearings to remarkably precise specifications — a 25-millionth of an inch — the precision necessary to build the inertial navigation systems for multiple warheads on intercontinental ballistic missiles (ICBM's)....
>
> Shortly after the sale of the Bryant grinders, the Soviets began deploying a new generation of ICBM's which were 10 times more accurate than their predecessors, and which, for the first time, were capable of carrying multiple warheads.[14]

Gerald Ford Administration
(1974 – 1977)

A Backdoor to the White House

On October 10, 1973, Spiro Agnew resigned as vice president according to his plea bargain agreement with the U.S. attorney's office in Baltimore. When a vice president resigns, Section 2 of the 25th Amendment to the Constitution stipulates that "the president shall nominate a Vice President who shall take office upon confirmation by a majority vote of both Houses of Congress."

President Nixon nominated Gerald Ford, who was subsequently confirmed — the first time the procedure had been used. So when President Nixon resigned less than a year later, Vice President Gerald Ford became president (per Section 1 of the 25th Amendment).

Although the Establishment media often referred to House Minority Leader Gerald Ford as a conservative, such a label was unwarranted. Ford offered no threat to the international-socialist agenda. Indeed, Nixon would never have selected Ford for VP, if the Insiders had felt their control of the presidency might be in jeopardy. Even without Watergate, Ford would have had a leg up as VP on securing the Republican presidential nomination in 1976.

Moreover, Ford could never have maintained his position as House minority leader for eight years (1965–1973) if the Insiders couldn't count on his support for their agenda. In fact, as president, Nixon had always relied on Ford to promote his agenda in the House.

As still another indication that Ford was solidly in the internationalist corner, Ford was known to have attended at least three of the invitation-only Bilderberger conferences (1962, 1964, 1970) prior to his selection as VP.

CFR Staffing

When Gerald Ford began his abbreviated term as president, he, of course, inherited Nixon's Cabinet. However, by the end of his term, only Henry Kissinger (CFR) and Secretary of the Treasury William E. Simon (CFR) remained.

So Ford put his own stamp on his administration, but it was a CFR stamp. Perhaps most reflective of Ford's true allegiances was his appointment of Nelson Rockefeller (CFR and brother of future CFR Chairman David Rockefeller) as *his* vice president. Having campaigned for the presidency three times (1960, 1964, and 1968), Nelson's strong liberal political colors were well known nationally.

When Ford took over as president, Henry Kissinger had been filling two roles: secretary of state and national security advisor. Ford would continue to rely on Kissinger's "internationalist" leadership in foreign policy. In his address to the nation immediately following President Nixon's televised resignation speech, Ford praised Kissinger extensively, noting: "I've known Henry Kissinger for a great many years. I knew him before he came with the Nixon Administration." [15]

President Ford regularly visited the CFR well for prominent positions within his administration (or selected individuals suitable for future CFR membership) including:

- Donald Rumsfeld as secretary of defense to follow James Schlesinger from the Nixon administration;
- Donald Rumsfeld and Richard B. "Dick" Cheney (CFR in 1982) as successive chiefs of staff, replacing Nixon holdover Alexander Haig (CFR);
- Elliot Richardson as secretary of commerce. (Richardson had resigned as attorney general during the Nixon administration after serving as Nixon's secretary of HEW, then his secretary of defense);
- Brent Scowcroft, replacing Kissinger as national security advisor in 1975;
- George H.W. Bush as director of the CIA, replacing Nixon holdover William Colby in 1976. (Colby would join the CFR in 1975);
- Carla A. Hills as secretary of Housing and Urban Development, replacing Nixon holdover James Thomas Lynn (CFR). (Hills would join the CFR in 1993 and become its co-chair in 2007);
- William T. Coleman Jr. as secretary of transportation;
- Daniel Patrick Moynihan and William W. Scranton (CFR in 1977) as successive ambassadors to the United Nations, replacing Nixon administration holdover John A. Scali (CFR).

Another significant CFR Ford holdover from the Nixon administration was Russell E. Train, the second administrator of the EPA. Train was the founder chairman emeritus of the World Wildlife Fund (WWF), a major player in the foundation-financed eco-lobby.

William K. Reilly (CFR in 2010), EPA administrator under President George H. W. Bush, would also come from the WWF (its president). (In 2010, President Obama selected Reilly to co-chair the commission charged with investigating the BP Deepwater Horizon oil spill in the Gulf of Mexico.)

Advancing the Insider Agenda
The Ford administration continued the Nixon/Kissinger foreign policies of detente with the Soviet Union and engagement with Red China.

• **The Captive Nations.** In mid-1975, President Ford and Secretary of State Kissinger attended an international summit conference in Helsinki, Finland. Thirty-five states, including the USA, Canada, and all European states except Albania and Andorra signed an agreement known as the "Final Act."

In essence, the Helsinki Agreement provided formal acceptance of Soviet conquests in Europe, something the Soviet Union had sought for years. The Brazilian newspaper *La Opinion* saw the reality of the agreement. Its coverage of the conference carried the headline: "Brezhnev Has Won What The Soviet Union Could Not Gain On The Battlefield In 1945." Refugees from the captive nations protested the event with candlelight vigils in the U.S. and Western Europe.

• **Domestic agenda.** President Ford also continued President Nixon's domestic agenda. He signed a $25 billion reauthorization of the Elementary and Secondary Education Act of 1965, originally launched as part of President Johnson's "Great Society." And he supported the socialist piecemeal approach to nationalizing health care by advocating a national health insurance program.

The economy became a major concern during the Ford administration. In response, the president called inflation "domestic public enemy number one" while launching a Whip Inflation Now (WIN) campaign calling on the public to restrain consumer spending.

Of course, the real cause of "rising prices" was monetary inflation by the Federal Reserve in financing government deficits. Nevertheless, the Ford administration proposed ever-larger budgets with ever-larger deficits.

President Ford gave his full support to state ratification of the dangerous federal power grab cleverly titled the Equal Rights Amendment.

• **Undermining internal security.** One of the most outrageous of President Ford's appointments was his selection of Edward Levi as attorney general. As noted in Chapter 8, Levi was a former member of the National Lawyers Guild, cited by the House Committee on Un-American Activities as "the foremost legal bulwark of the Communist Party, its front organizations, and controlled unions." [16]

As attorney general, Levi embarked on a war against the counter-intelligence division of the FBI, and his infamous Levi guidelines did great damage to our internal security. Levi would eventually indict acting FBI Director L. Patrick Gray, former Chief of Counterintelligence Edward Miller, and former acting Associate Director W. Mark Felt on charges of "conspiring to injure and oppress citizens of the United States." The FBI investigations originated with the 1972 bombing of the Pentagon and targeted members of the terrorist Weather Underground.

President Ford's decision to pardon Richard Nixon, the man who had appointed him vice president, did not sit well with many voters, helping to set the stage for a Democrat to be elected in 1976.

Jimmy Carter Administration
(1977 – 1981)

An Insider Track to the White House
In 1976, with the Republican Party still feeling the sting of the Watergate scandal and voters unhappy over the economy and President Ford's pardon of Nixon, the prospects for a Democrat to regain the presidency were especially good. With no clear front-runner, a record number of Democrats competed for their party's presidential nomination.

According to the Gallup organization: "Prior to the Jan. 26, 1976 Iowa caucuses, just 4% of national Democrats said they were likely to support Carter for the nomination, well behind [former Vice President] Hubert Humphrey (27%) and George Wallace (22%)." In less than seven months, the Georgia governor rose from relative obscurity to having more than enough delegate strength to claim the nomination on the first ballot.

Although Carter would campaign as the consummate outsider — a humble peanut farmer from Georgia with no ties to the Establishment — the truth was quite different. Indeed, Jimmy Carter owed his spectacular rise to the presidency precisely to Insider ties.

In 1973, David Rockefeller, then Chairman of the CFR, and Zbigniew Brzezinski (CFR) were looking over prospects for membership in a new organization they were creating — the Trilateral Commission, an offshoot of the CFR.[17] Carter passed the screening and was accepted as a founding member.

In his 1979 personal and political memoirs, Barry Goldwater, the 1964 GOP presidential nominee, wrote:

> David Rockefeller and Zbigniew Brzezinski found Jimmy Carter to be their ideal candidate. They helped him win the nomination and the presidency. To accomplish this purpose, they mobilized the money power of the Wall Street bankers, the intellectual influence of the academic community — which is subservient to the wealth of the great tax-free foundations — and the media controllers represented in the membership of the CFR and the Trilateral.[18]

Brzezinski took up the task of grooming Carter to be president. Brzezinksi was aided by Trilateralist and CFR-member Richard N. Gardner, who served as a campaign advisor to Carter and tutored him in foreign policy. During the campaign, Jimmy Carter would be featured on the cover of the Establishment's *Time* magazine three times and the Washington Post Company's *Newsweek* twice.

The Trilateral Commission
Since the Trilateral Commission would figure so prominently in the Carter administration, a little background is appropriate. Brzezinski floated the idea in the October 1970 issue of *Foreign Affairs*:

> A new and broader approach is needed — creation of a community of the developed nations which can effectively address itself to the larger concerns confronting mankind.... A

council representing the United States, Western Europe and Japan, with regular meetings of the heads of governments as well as some small standing machinery, would be a good start. [19]

That same year, Brzezinksi elaborated his arguments in *Between Two Ages: America's Role in the Technotronic Era*: "To sum up: Though the objective of shaping a community of developed nations is less ambitious than the goal of world government, it is more attainable." [20]

The Rockefeller-Brzezinski steppingstones rest on a foundation of indifference to tragedy and the lessons of freedom. Along with his globalist advocacy, Brzezinski also states:

Marxism represents a further vital and creative stage in the maturing of man's universal vision. Marxism is simultaneously a victory of the external, active man over the inner, passive man and a victory of reason over belief.... [21]

In 1973, Rockefeller and Brzezinski launched their Trilateral Commission, recruiting as members a select group of leaders in business, banking, government, and the media from North America, Western Europe, and Japan. Barry Goldwater summarized what several other critics had recognized:

In my view the Trilateral Commission represents a skillful, coordinated effort to seize control and consolidate the four centers of power — political, monetary, intellectual, and ecclesiastical....

What the Trilaterals truly intend is the creation of a worldwide economic power superior to the political governments of the nation-states involved.... As managers and creators of the system they will rule the future. [22]

During his campaign for the presidency, Jimmy Carter delivered his first major foreign policy speech to the Foreign Policy Association in New York City. It began: "The time has come for us to seek a partnership between North America, Western Europe, and Japan." The *Los Angeles Times* identified a dozen members of a task force that had helped Carter prepare the speech. All 12 were members of the Council on Foreign Relations. [23]

CFR & Trilateral Staffing

Following his election, President Carter drew so heavily on the Trilateral Commission to staff his administration that even Gore Vidal (a prominent liberal political activist, author, and playwright with Washington connections) was prompted to protest the betrayal:

Not long after the Trilateral Commission came into being, I started to chat about it on television. Although I never saw anything particularly sinister in the commission itself (has any commission ever *done* anything?), I did think it a perfect symbol of the way the United States is ruled. When Trilateral Commission member Carter was elected president after having pretended to be An Outsider, he chose his vice-president and his secretaries of state, defense, and treasury, as well as the national security adviser, from Chase Manhattan's commission. I thought this pretty bold — even bald. [24]

At a Carter-for-President Rally in Boston early in the campaign, Carter had the audacity to declare:

The people of this country know from bitter experience that we are not going to get ... changes merely by shifting around the same group of insiders.... The insiders have had their chance and they have not delivered. [25]

And top Carter advisor Hamilton Jordan commented following Carter's election victory:

If, after the inauguration, you find a Cy Vance as Secretary of State and Zbigniew Brzezinski as head of National Security, then I would say we failed. And I'd quit. But that's not going to happen. [26]

But that is just what did happen, and Jordan, rather than resigning, continued to advise Carter during his administration, eventually becoming Carter's chief of staff in 1979.

In his White House memoirs, Zbigniew Brzezinski candidly acknowledges: "Moreover, all the key foreign policy decision makers of the Carter Administration had previously served in the Trilateral Commission...."[27]

Specifically, Jimmy Carter chose the following Council on Foreign Relations members for key posts, with many holding dual membership in the Trilateral Commission (TC):

- National Security Advisor: Zbigniew Brzezinski (TC)
- Secretary of State: Cyrus Vance (TC) (In 1985, Vance would become vice president of the CFR.)
- Vice President: Walter Mondale (TC)
- Secretary of Defense: Harold Brown (TC)
- Secretary of the Treasury: W. Michael Blumenthal (TC)
- Federal Reserve Chairman: Paul Volcker (TC)
- Deputy Secretary of State: Warren Christopher (TC)
- Under Secretary of State: Richard Cooper (TC)
- Assistant Secretary of State: Richard Holbrooke (TC)
- Under Secretary of the Treasury: Anthony M. Solomon (TC)
- Ambassador to the UN: Andrew Young (TC)
- Deputy Secretary of Energy: John Sawhill
- Special Assistant to the President: Hedley Donovan (TC)
- Ambassador to Italy: Richard N. Gardner (TC)
- Ambassador at Large: Henry Owen (TC)
- Ambassador at Large: Elliot Richardson (TC)
- Ambassador at Large: Gerard Smith (TC)
- Director of Arms Control and Disarmament Agency & SALT negotiator: Paul Warnke (TC)
- Director of the Central Intelligence Agency: Stansfield Turner
- Secretary of HEW: Joseph Califano
- Panama Treaty negotiator: Sol Linowitz.

In total, Carter appointees included more than 70 members from the CFR and over 20 from the more exclusive Trilateral Commission.[28] The CFR's 1980 *Annual Report* would count 340 of its members as U.S. government officials, up from 284 in 1978.

Advancing the Insider Agenda

Right out of the starting box, the Carter administration undertook an aggressive campaign to make the world less safe for America. In just four short years, the Carter administration managed to undercut an incredible number of friends and allies, while providing strategic support to America's enemies.

The Carter "foreign policy" toppled the anti-Communist regime of Anastasio Somoza in Nicaragua, helping the Communist Sandinistas come to power.

It pushed the pro-Western Shah out in Iran, allowing a virulent anti-American religious fanatic, the Ayatolla Khomeni, to seize control (and Khomeni militants to storm our embassy and take our embassy staff hostage).

The Carter administration also took the ongoing betrayal of Nationalist China another big step further, helped Soviet-sponsored forces transform pro-Western Rhodesia into Marxist Zimbabwe ruled by the terrorist Robert Mugabe, and surrendered the Panama Canal to the Marxist regime of Omar Torrijos.

The Carter administration also joined in the international campaign to remove President Ferdinand Marcos of the Philippines. [29] His overthrow eventually cost us the strategic U.S. Naval Base in Subic Bay and Clark Air Base.

Since David Rockefeller had propelled Carter to the White House and since Carter had selected Trilateralists and CFR members to run his foreign policy, it must be assumed that the Carter foreign policy had Rockefeller support.

• **Betrayal of Allies.** To topple friendly regimes in favor of a radical or Communist insurgency, it was first necessary to deceive the American people. Typically a heavily orchestrated international propaganda campaign would vilify the head of state, alleging corruption or rights abuses.

When president-elect Carter announced his selection of Trilateralist Cyrus Vance as his secretary of state, Vance promised that U.S. foreign policy would be guided by "a deep concern for human rights" — one of Carter's campaign pledges. [30]

The Carter "human rights" concern was completely hypocritical, as the administration would embrace the worst violators among the totalitarian regimes, such as Red China, while supporting the trumped-up charges of communist insurgents against the pro-Western regime they were seeking to provoke.

• **Betrayal of Nicaragua.** Nicaraguan President Anastasio Somoza was one of our most friendly allies in Latin America, having been educated in the U.S. since early childhood and having graduated from West Point. Moreover, Nicaragua was a constitutional republic patterned after the U.S.

However, during the late 1970s, the Cuban- and Soviet-backed guerilla forces of the Sandinista National Liberation Front targeted the Somoza government. Concurrently, media reports began depicting Somoza as a corrupt dictator and gross violator of human rights.

In response to the anti-Somoza propaganda, the Carter administration instituted an international arms embargo against Somoza's army. The Carter administration even forced Israel to recall an arms shipment. It also pressured the IMF and World Bank to withhold credit from Nicaragua and embargoed Nicaraguan exports of beef and coffee.

Aided by the Carter embargoes, the well supplied Sandinistas were able to defeat the Nicaraguan National Guard in a "civil war" lasting only seven weeks. According to Somoza, President Jimmy Carter gave the orders that forced him out of Nicaragua and put the Sandinista Communists in power. [31]

Following his resignation in July of 1979, President Somoza fled to Miami, where Deputy Secretary of State Warren Christopher (CFR) denied him the sanctuary that had been promised him. [32] Somoza then fled to Paraguay, where he was killed by a Communist assassination team the following year.

The overthrow of Somoza brought to power the brutal regime of Daniel Ortega, which immediately received substantial U.S. aid. The Ortega regime declared itself "a revolution without borders," and began to support guerrilla forces in neighboring El Salvador.

The overthrow of Somoza set the stage for another battle, this time between the Sandinistas and the Contras. Subsequent chapters in the story would be played out in the U.S. Congress during the Reagan administrations.

• **Ousting the Shah of Iran.** By pursuing a similar strategy, the Carter administration succeeded in ousting Shah Muhammad Reza Pahlavi, one of our strongest allies in the Middle East. An Iranian diplomat in Washington summarized the betrayal: "President Carter betrayed the Shah and helped create a vacuum that will soon be filled by Soviet-trained agents and religious fanatics who hate America." [33]

The Soviets had lusted over Iranian oil and Iran's warm-water ports for years. In the seventies, Soviet-backed guerrilla forces supplied one part of the pressure to topple the Shah. The Soviet campaign was joined by the United Nations, the Western media, and the phony worldwide "human rights" lobby.

In late 1978, riots and street demonstrations ensued. As the Iranian military was preparing to stabilize the situation, President Carter sent Air Force General Robert Huyser and George Ball (CFR) to Tehran to convince the Iranian generals not to intervene and the Shah to resign. The Shah fled his country in January of 1979.

When Khomeni took power, Iran's top generals who did not escape were brutally executed. In addition to holding America hostage, the Khomeni regime would employ torture and execution in a crackdown on human rights previously enjoyed under the Shah. And it would sponsor worldwide terrorism.

Nevertheless, Jimmy Carter, the great advocate of human rights, would not protest the execution of former Iranian officials (and America's loyalist friends) following "trials" in Khomeni's kangaroo courts.

• **Betrayal of Taiwan.** The Republic of China (ROC), whose government fled to Taiwan, was our ally against Japan in World War II and a founding member of the United Nations. For decades, the U.S. government under a watchful American public had refused Communist demands to recognize Red China as the legitimate government of all China, including Taiwan.

However, the handwriting was on the wall. The ascendancy of Communist power in China had been supported from the beginning by CFR elites. In 1971, the ROC was forced out of the UN, and its seat as a permanent member of the Security Council was given to Communist China.

In December of 1978, President Carter announced on national television that the U.S. would be extending diplomatic recognition to the Communist Peking regime and withdrawing formal diplomatic recognition from our ally on Taiwan. President Carter proceeded unilaterally to cancel our treaties with Taiwan, including the Sino-American Mutual Defense Treaty.

Earlier that year, the Senate had voted 94 to 0 that it must be consulted before any such action were taken to change our agreements with Free China. So the president waited until the Senate was recessed. When it reconvened in early 1979, the U.S. Congress reacted by passing the Taiwan Relations Act, giving Taiwan a measure of continued support.

• **Panama Canal giveaway.** Another immense perfidy of the Carter administration was its gift of the strategic U.S.-owned "Panama" Canal and Canal Zone to Panama, then ruled by "Marxist" dictator Omar Torrijos. In fact, the "Communist" tilt of Torrijos was well established. [34]

The Panama Canal had long been a monument to U.S. engineering ingenuity, built following the failed French effort, which lasted from 1883 until 1899. For successful construction the U.S. had to conquer mosquito-borne disease in the region. The resulting waterway became a service to the world.

By virtue of the 1903 Hay-Bunau-Varilla Treaty with Panama, the U.S. had acquired sovereign rights "in perpetuity" over the Canal and Zone. In return, the Republic of Panama, recently separated from Columbia, received a U.S. guarantee of independence as a sovereign nation. Panama also received an initial sum of money plus annual payments. The U.S. investment, development, and operation of the Canal enabled Panama to achieve the highest standard of living in Latin America.

Although control of the world's strategic waterways had long been a goal of the Communists, the surrender of the Canal to Panama was actually engineered by the U.S. Establishment.

President Carter deserves credit for the culmination of the betrayal, but he could not have succeeded were it not for the groundwork laid in administrations going back to Truman — both Republican and Democratic.

In 1971, with the GOP ensconced in the White House, Henry Kissinger proposed that a "termination formula" be developed for ceding control of the Canal to Panama. Nixon then signed National Security Memorandum 131, calling for a new treaty with Panama, and assigned Kissinger the project. [35]

In 1974, Kissinger met with Torrijos and signed a "Principles of Agreement" with Panama's foreign minister, recognizing the Canal as rightfully Panamanian territory, a contention totally unsupported by history.

Following Carter's successful election two years later, David Rockefeller and Sol Linowitz, chairman of the Rockefeller Foundation's private Commission on U.S.-Latin American Relations, also met with Torrijos. Subsequently, they urged President-elect Carter to adopt the Commission's report as the basis for U.S. policy. The Linowitz report recommended that the U.S. give up the Canal.

On his first day in office, President Carter signed an order to begin negotiations for the surrender of the Canal. He appointed Sol Linowitz (CFR) and Ellsworth Bunker (CFR) to negotiate the treaties.

The new treaties were swiftly "negotiated." Before the end of Carter's first year, the president and Omar Torrijos met in Washington D.C. (September 7, 1977) to sign the two Panama Canal treaties. However, President Carter would have a tough time gaining Senate approval in the face of strong public opposition.

In his memoirs, Carter wrote: "I thanked God when we got the 67th vote [needed for ratification]. It will always be one of my proudest moments, and one of the greatest achievements of the United States." [36]

Incredibly, after the final Senate vote of approval, Omar Torrijos announced that he had ordered the National Guard to "attack and blow up the Canal if the Senate had rejected our agreement." [37]

There was a great voter backlash to Senate ratification of the Panama Canal treaties, reminiscent of the backlash at the polls over ObamaCare. Of the sixty-eight senators who voted for the treaties, twenty-nine no longer held office following the 1978 and 1980 staggered elections!! And the Panama Canal giveaway played a big part in holding President Carter to one term.

During a campaign debate with President Ford, Carter had declared: "I would never give up complete control or practical control of the Panama Canal Zone." [38] Then again, he had promised: "I would never lie to you."

• **Carter's war on energy.** The Carter energy policy can be summarized as a campaign to deny America use of its own energy resources, create dependence on foreign suppliers, and create shortages leading to government rationing. However, just as the effort to give away our Panama Canal didn't begin with President Carter, so the federal government's war on energy also started much earlier.

Indeed, actions of the Nixon administration precipitated the 1973 "energy crisis," with its attendant long lines at gasoline stations. [39] Already in 1973 there was talk of rationing energy, as part of a plan to establish a federal Department of Energy headed by an "energy czar," who would have the power to decide the fate of every manufacturing and industrial enterprise in America.

Jimmy Carter merely took the anti-energy campaign one step further. Shortly after President Carter moved into the White House, the *New York Times* reported: "The Federal Energy Administrator, John F. O'Leary, told the American people today that the Carter Administration's energy policy would call for higher prices, less comfort at home, and some way to take some of the fat out of the driving habits in this country." [40]

In August of 1977, Carter signed legislation establishing the Cabinet-level Department of Energy (DOE), and the following year he signed into law his National Energy Act. James Schlesinger (secretary of defense under Nixon and Ford and CFR in 1986) became the nation's first secretary of energy.

That same year (1977), a delegation of General Electric executives visited the new secretary in Washington. Edward Hood, G.E. vice president for power generation, reportedly told Schlesinger that, "without nuclear energy, we will have blackouts and brownouts. And according to a G.E. executive, Schlesinger replied: 'That's what we want. It's the only way to teach the people a lesson.'" [41]

The new department would not produce any energy and instead would create a myriad of obstacles to domestic energy production.

The Chicago Tribune reported in March of 1979:

> For more than a century, the U.S. was the world's leading oil producer. In fact, before the 1973 Arab embargo the U.S. had oil to export, and maintained quotas to restrict imports of cheap foreign oil. While the U.S. continues to be the world's biggest consumer, it has slipped to the position of No. 3 behind the Soviet Union and Saudi Arabia. [42]

In addition to creating policies that would lead to energy shortages, the new bureaucracy would come at a terrible cost to taxpayers. As the *Wall Street Journal* reported:

> [T]he $10.6 billion budget of the proposed new Department of Energy ... is about double the value of all the oil the U.S. imported from Saudi Arabia last year.... It is equivalent to about $3 a barrel of domestic crude oil production, which means ... that you could decontrol all domestic crude oil prices and still end up paying less for oil than for the federal energy bureaucracy.... [43]

• **New Cabinet-level Education Department.** President Carter also took the federal government's intrusion into education, launched under the Eisenhower administration, a big step further. On December 17, 1979, he signed into law the Department of Education Organization Act. This Act split the Department of Health, Education, and Welfare into the two Cabinet-level departments — the Department of Education and the Department of Health and Human Services (HHS), which we have today.

The National Education Association (N.E.A.) (together with the A.F.L.-C.I.O) provided much of the pressure from below for the creation of the new $14 billion department.

The Department of Education would initially employ twenty-four thousand federal bureaucrats without any reduction in personnel for the parent HHS. It would be expanded greatly during the George W. Bush administration with passage of the "No Child Left Behind Act of 2001." (See Chapters 13 and 14.)

Centralization of government control of education in Washington had long been a CFR/Insider goal (see Chapter 13). It has also been a

187

Communist goal. In 1932, U.S. Communist Party leader William Z. Foster wrote:

> The schools, colleges, and universities will be coordinated and grouped under the National Department of Education and its State and local branches. The schools will be revolutionized, being cleansed of religious, patriotic and other features of the bourgeois ideology. [44]

A radical federal agenda would draw support from UN-conferences and UNESCO, which set policies in education for nations to follow.

Chapter 11

CFR Dominance: Reagan, Bush, & Clinton Administrations

We don't claim to know the hearts of men. In fact, men may not even know their own hearts, and they often behave differently in one setting than in another. But we can look clearly at their track records, taking pains not to be swayed by hype and stirring speeches. Experience shows that past behavior is generally the best predictor of future behavior.

Ronald Reagan Administrations
(1981 – 1989)

Road to the White House

Going into the 1980 GOP convention in Detroit, former California Governor Ronald Reagan had accumulated enough votes in the primaries that his presidential nomination was a forgone conclusion. The big question was whom would Reagan choose as his vice presidential running mate. Conservatives were naturally expecting that Reagan would live up to his public promises and choose someone who shared his conservative philosophy.

So many Reagan supporters felt betrayed when early Thursday morning on the last day of the convention Reagan presented his choice: Rockefeller Republican George H.W. Bush, Reagan's rival in the primary contests. Top Reagan supporters Senator Paul Laxalt and Joseph Coors felt even more betrayed, because just two weeks prior to the convention, Reagan had assured them personally that under no circumstances would he choose George Bush.[1]

Indeed, by choosing the Establishment's man, Reagan set the stage for Bush, who had failed twice to win a U.S. Senate seat, to become president in 1988. Reagan (who would turn 70 shortly after his inauguration) had made it very difficult for a conservative to succeed him as president.

But the handwriting was on the wall, and Reagan supporters shouldn't have been surprised at this latest sellout to the internationalists. Four years earlier, Reagan had also stunned his campaign supporters.

In 1976, Reagan was running a strong challenge to steal the nomination away from incumbent president Gerald R. Ford. What surprised Reagan supporters was Reagan's announcement, issued just before the opening of the convention in Kansas City, that if he received the nomination he would choose Pennsylvania Senator Richard Schweiker as his running mate to create a more balanced ticket. Idaho's conservative congressman Steve Symms responded: "I'm sick." [2]

New York Times columnist Tom Wicker explained why conservatives were shocked: "Some of Reagan's more devoutly conservative supporters will find Schweiker, with his ninety-nine out of one hundred score in the Americans for Democratic Action ratings, too liberal by half." [3] Senator George McGovern, then president of the Americans for Democratic Action reacted by suggesting that if Reagan didn't get the nomination, he wanted Schweiker as *his* vice presidential candidate.

Although Senator Schweiker was claiming to have shifted his views, he had a long way to go to earn the confidence of conservatives. In 1975 he was the only Senator to receive a 100 percent rating from Big Labor's Committee on Political Education (COPE). [4] He thus earned a more liberal rating than Senators McGovern and Kennedy.

Reagan's CFR Appointments

The Reagan sellout to the internationalists was also apparent in the choices Reagan made to staff his administration. "His" choices should not have been surprising, since the post-election Reagan transition team included twenty-eight CFR men, among them the "Chairman of the Establishment," John J. McCloy. [5]

Reagan's campaign manager, Bill Casey (CFR) would head up the CIA. During the Nixon administration, Casey had run the Export-Import Bank, which provided the Soviets with $153 million to build their Kama River truck factory. Earlier Casey had been an associate of Armand Hammer, the Soviet's favorite capitalist. [6]

When Casey resigned in 1987, following surgery for a cancerous brain tumor, Reagan chose Casey's deputy, Robert M. Gates (CFR), to succeed him. (Gates had good Establishment credentials. He would go on to serve as secretary of defense, succeeding Donald Rumsfeld in the George W. Bush administration. And President Obama would choose Gates to continue as his first secretary of defense.)

President Reagan selected his 1976 would-be running mate, Senator Richard Schweiker (not CFR), for the post most prized by the Fabian Socialist Americans for Democratic Action (see Chapter 13) — secretary of Health, Education, and Welfare.

As his chief of staff, Reagan selected James A. Baker III, the campaign manager for George W. Bush. President Bush would later pick Baker as his secretary of state, a pretty good indication of Baker's acceptance by the Establishment. However, Baker would not formally join the CFR until 1998.

For Treasury secretary, Reagan went to the CFR well, choosing Donald T. Regan (CFR).

Several conservatives tried to block the nomination when it was learned that Regan had recently made campaign contributions to liberal Democrats including $1,000 to the 1980 re-election campaign of Jimmy Carter *against* Ronald Reagan. [7] (Later Regan and Baker would switch jobs.)

The key post of secretary of state initially went to Alexander Haig (CFR). But Reagan replaced Haig in 1982 with a director of the CFR — George P. Shultz. (The "P." stands for Pratt from the Pratt family. Mrs. Harold Pratt donated the Pratt House to the CFR for its headquarters.)

For secretary of defense, Reagan chose fellow California Republican Caspar Weinberger, a member of David Rockefeller's Trilateral Commission. During the presidential campaign, Ronald Reagan had made an issue of Jimmy Carter staffing his administration with Trilateralists. Weinberger would join the CFR the following year. In 1987, Reagan replaced Weinberger with Frank Carlucci, also CFR.

Other Reagan appointees from the CFR well included Malcolm Baldridge as Commerce secretary, William Brock as Labor secretary, and Alan Greenspan as Federal Reserve Board chairman

(Greenspan was also a Trilateralist).

During his second term, Reagan would select Winston Lord, president of the CFR, as the U.S. ambassador to China. Lord, a former Kissinger aide, had accompanied Kissinger on his historic secret trip to China in July 1971. Mr. Lord's nomination was confirmed in the Senate by a vote of 87 to 7.

The Reagan Performance

The difficulty most conservatives had in evaluating Ronald Reagan was that they listened to his speeches. And certainly, no one can deny that Ronald Reagan articulated some of the most stirring defenses of limited government and conservative principle. And conservatives also listened to the Establishment media chorus and the politicians who repeatedly characterized Ronald Reagan as a great conservative leader.

However, actions *should* speak louder than words. Unfortunately, most busy Americans receiving their news from Establishment sources were unfamiliar with the actions.

Reagan's performance as governor of California was anything but conservative. In fact, the strongly conservative United Republicans of California refused to support Reagan's candidacy for president. Even some of Reagan's political opponents in California acknowledged the disparity between Reagan's words and actions. Democrat Bob Moretti, speaker of the California Assembly when Reagan was governor, conceded: "The way he acted as Governor didn't resemble his rhetoric." [8]

Certainly, one of the great Reagan myths, perpetrated on the American people by the Establishment, is that President Reagan almost single handedly won the Cold War. In reality, Reagan's greatest blow to Soviet plans for world domination seems to be that he had once referred to the Soviets as the Evil Empire.

Conservatives also make a mistake, if they imagine that Ronald Reagan was actively in charge of and on top of his administration. A political career (let alone an acting career) rarely equips politicians with executive skills.

However, as with Nixon, Reagan's conservative, anti-Communist image allowed him, or rather his administration, to deliver for the Establishment:

• **Strategic aid to Red China.** Ever since Nixon opened trade relations with China, the CFR has promoted massive transfers of capital and technology to the Red regime, helping it to become a new "superpower," while decimating America's industrial and manufacturing capacity.

On August 30, 1982, President Reagan signed a determination that "it is in the national interest for the Export-Import Bank of the United States to extend a credit and guarantee in the aggregate amount of $68,425,000 to the People's Republic of China in connection with its purchase of steel making equipment and related services." [9]

• **Deficit spending.** During the 1980 presidential campaign, Ronald Reagan vowed to balance the federal budget by the end of his first term. The peak deficit under Jimmy Carter was $78.9 billion (FY 1981). Under President Reagan the red ink hit a record of $127.9 billion in 1982, before heading into the stratosphere. The deficits in 1985 and 1986 each totaled more than $200 billion.

In fact, during Reagan's eight years in the White House, not once did he even *propose* a balanced budget. Here are Reagan's own *proposed* deficits: fiscal 1982 budget, $59 billion; 1983 budget, $107 billion; 1984 budget, $203 billion; 1985 budget, $195 billion; 1986 budget, $180 billion; 1987 budget, $144 billion; 1988 budget, $108 billion; 1989 budget, $129 billion.

By 1984, economist Lester Thurow was able to write in *Newsweek* that "President Reagan has become the ultimate Keynesian." Thurow continued:

> Not only is the Reagan Administration rehabilitating exactly the economic policies it pledged to bury when entering office, it is applying them more vigorously than any Keynesian would have dared. Imagine what conservatives would be saying if a liberal Keynesian Democratic president had dared to run a $200 billion deficit. [10]

• **Taiwan.** When President Jimmy Carter severed all diplomatic ties with the Republic of China on Taiwan, Ronald Reagan correctly termed the action an "outright betrayal of a close friend and ally." [11]

However, as president, Reagan made no effort to reverse the Carter betrayal, and U.S. trade with the Red regime continued to increase.

Moreover, in August 1982, Reagan issued a joint communiqué with Peking stating that the U.S. "does not seek to carry out a long-term policy of arms sales to Taiwan." Adding insult to injury, in 1986, the Reagan administration got Congress to approve the sale of $560 million in advanced electronics to Red China, giving its fighters an all-weather capability superior to Taiwan's.

Of course, in a couple of areas Reagan appeared to show some conservative, anti-Communist promise: the invasion of Grenada, for example, and some of his appointments to the federal court. But the overwhelming direction favored the Establishment.

Several theories have circulated to explain the Reagan disappointment. The theories are interesting but do not change the bottom line. The Reagan administration continued the same CFR-sought policies that have been leading this nation to disaster ever since FDR. And moreover, Reagan did it while putting most conservatives to sleep.

George H.W. Bush (Sr.) Administration (1989 – 1993)

"George Bush, in fact, has been a dues-paying member of the Establishment, if it is succinctly defined as the Council on Foreign Relations and the Trilateral Commission."
— Sidney Blumenthal, *Washington Post*, February 10, 1988

The "Establishment's Man"
Born in Milton, Massachusetts, George Herbert Walker Bush was one of five children of Prescott Sheldon Bush and Dorothy Walker Bush.

Bush's father, Prescott, became a partner of the international banking firm of Brown Brothers Harriman & Co. Prescott was also active in politics and from 1952 to January of 1963 served as a liberal GOP senator from Connecticut. Prescott graduated from Yale, as did his son George H.W. Bush and his grandson George W. Bush. All three were members of Yale's Skull and Bones Society, perhaps the most exclusive of the nation's secret fraternities.

George H.W. Bush served with distinction as a Navy pilot in World War II, the youngest Naval aviator at the time. After graduating from Yale, he moved his family to West Texas and became wealthy in the oil business. He entered politics and was elected twice to the U.S. House of Representatives. As a representative from Texas, Bush would take many conservative positions, quite at odds with his later stance as president.

Following a second unsuccessful effort to gain a U.S. Senate seat, Bush was appointed by President Nixon as ambassador to the United Nations, embarking on a path to national political prominence outside of elective office. That same year (1971), Bush would join the Council on Foreign Relations.

After two years as chairman of the Republican National Committee, Bush would be appointed by President Ford as envoy to Communist China and then director of the Central Intelligence Agency. Following his stint at the CIA, Bush would be selected as a director of the CFR (1977).

In 1979, while preparing for a run at the presidency, George Bush relinquished his membership in the Council on Foreign Relations and the Trilateral Commission, in an obvious effort to deflect a potentially negative campaign issue. Asked about his memberships during the campaign, he replied: "Clearly I would never have belonged to any organization that had devious designs or favored one-world government." [12]

However, Bush had also served as a director of the Atlantic Council of the United States — founded in 1961 by Christian Herter (CFR), Will Clayton (CFR), and others — another organization whose mission has been to submerge the U.S. in a world government.

After serving as President Reagan's vice president for eight years, George H.W. Bush would campaign successfully for the presidency in 1988, defeating his Democratic opponent, Massachusetts Governor Michael Dukakis (CFR in 1989).

The Atlantic Council
The Atlantic Council is the successor to the Federal Union movement, which changed its name to the Atlantic Union

Committee and then to the Atlantic Council of the United States. It thus inherits the movement motivated by Clarence Streit's Establishment-promoted books, *Union Now* (1939) and *Union Now with Britain* (1941). Streit was a Rhodes Scholar and *New York Times* correspondent.

As Table 11.1 illustrates, the Atlantic Council is heavily interlocked with the CFR. All of the directors and honorary directors listed are, or in Kissinger's case have been, also members of the CFR. Moreover, the current (January 1, 2012) president and CEO of the Atlantic Council is Frederick Kempe (CFR).

Looking at the Atlantic Council International Advisory Board, the current chairman is Brent Scowcroft (a former director of the CFR and Bush's choice for national security advisor, see below). The current Advisory Board also includes CFR members Zbigniew Brzezinski, Jimmy Carter's former national security advisor and Rupert Murdoch, chairman and CEO of News Corp.

CFR/Trilateralist Staffing
Identifying George Bush atop an administration should be sufficient by itself to demonstrate Establishment domination. However, as one would expect, Bush appointed numerous CFR members and several Trilateralists to key posts. Some of the more noteworthy CFR members included:

- William H. Webster as director of the CIA (Bush's old stomping grounds);
- Brent Scowcroft as national security advisor (also a Trilateralist);
- Robert M. Gates as deputy national security advisor;
- Nicholas Brady as secretary of the Treasury;
- Richard G. Darman as director of the Office of Management and Budget;
- Dick Thornburgh as attorney general;
- General Colin L. Powell as chairman of the Joint Chiefs of Staff;
- Thomas J. Pickering as U.S. ambassador to the United Nations; and
- Lawrence S. Eagleburger as deputy secretary of state (a Trilateralist).

Unlike President Reagan, Bush was not trying to distance himself

Atlantic Council*
(Overlap with CFR)

Board of Directors	Notable U.S. Position
Wesley K. Clark	Supreme Allied Commander Europe of NATO (Clinton)
Chuck Hagel: Chairman	Chair of Obama's Intelligence Advisory Board
Robert L. Hutchings	Chair of the National Intelligence Council (Bush Jr.)
Henry Kissinger	Secretary of State (Nixon & Ford)
Barry R. McCaffrey	"Drug Czar" (Clinton)
Thomas R. Pickering	U.S. Ambassador to the UN (Bush Sr.)
Anne-Marie Slaughter	Dir. of Policy Planning — State Department (Obama)
John C. Whitehead	Deputy Secretary of State (Reagan)
R. James Woolsey	Director of the Central Intelligence Agency (Clinton)
Anthony C. Zinni	Commander in Chief/U.S. Central Command (Clinton)
Honorary Directors	**Notable U.S. Position**
Madeleine K. Albright	Secretary of State (Clinton)
James A. Baker	Secretary of State (Bush Sr.)
Frank C. Carlucci, III	Secretary of Defense (Reagan)
Colin L. Powell	Secretary of State (Bush Jr.)
Condoleezza Rice	Secretary of State (Bush Jr.)
James R. Schlesinger	Secretary of Defense (Nixon & Ford)
George P. Shultz	Secretary of State (Reagan)
William H. Webster	Director of FBI, then CIA (Carter & Reagan)

*As of July 18, 2011

Table 11.1

publicly from Henry Kissinger's influence. Eagleburger (above) was wooed away from his job as president of Kissinger Associates, while Scowcroft (also above) had been vice-chairman.

Two other important Bush appointments would later be accepted into the CFR: Secretary of State James A. Baker III (midterm in 1991) and Counselor at State Robert B. Zoellick (also in 1991).

President Bush initially picked Senator John Tower to be his secretary of defense, but Tower was shot down by the Senate. Then Scowcroft recommended Cheney, who had been serving with Scowcroft as a director of the CFR. Cheney would rise to national prominence during the Gulf War.

Richard Cheney

During the Nixon administration Cheney served in the Office of Economic Opportunity (the federal poverty agency) under Donald Rumsfeld (CFR). He hitched his wagon to Rumsfeld (and later Scowcroft). Rumsfeld brought Cheney with him into the Ford White House and when Ford picked Rumsfeld for secretary of defense, Cheney became Ford's chief of staff.

With the election of Jimmy Carter in 1976, Cheney returned to Wyoming and two years later ran successfully for Wyoming's sole seat in the U.S. House of Representatives. Cheney would be elected to five terms, compiling an outstanding conservative voting record. However, Cheney had already made his Establishment connections and was invited into the CFR in 1982. In December 1988, he was elected House minority whip, serving only two-and-a-half months before Bush chose him for secretary of defense.

Advancing Insider Objectives

President Bush took office at the beginning of 1989, while Gorbachev and company were implementing major changes in the Soviet Union. By the end of the year, the Berlin Wall would come down. As president, Bush was in prime position to help the Insiders implement their strategic change in pretexts for a UN-dominated world government, euphemistically referred to as the "new world order."

• **Empowering the UN.** Indeed, on September 11, 1990, George Bush would proclaim:

The crisis in the Persian Gulf, as grave as it is, also offers a rare opportunity to move toward an historic period of cooperation. Out of these troubled times, our fifth objective — a new world order — can emerge.... We are now in sight of a United Nations that performs as envisioned by its founders. [Of course, the UN founders envisioned a world government dominated by the UN.]

In fact, strong evidence suggests that empowering the UN and gaining a U.S. foothold in the Middle East were the real reasons behind Mr. Bush's decision to use military force in the Persian Gulf.

On January 31, 1992 the UN Security Council convened for the first time ever at the level of heads of state. At the meeting, which was designed to build support for increased UN-peacekeeping capability, President Bush stated:

For most of its history the United Nations was caught in a cold-war crossfire.... Today all that has changed. The collapse of imperial communism and the end of the cold war breathe new life into the United Nations.... It was just one year ago that the world saw this new invigorated United Nations in action as the Council stood fast against aggression, and stood for the sacred principles enshrined in the United Nations Charter. [13]

The Establishment's man was actively advancing Insider strategies on other fronts as well:

• **Negotiating NAFTA.** Although President Clinton would push Congress to approve the NAFTA treaty, the signed agreement had been handed to him by President Bush. The Bush administration negotiated the misnamed "free trade" agreement, which would destroy many American jobs.

Most significantly, NAFTA would finally give the Insiders' regionalism strategy a foot in the door in this hemisphere. Chapter 20 of the agreement between the U.S., Mexico, and Canada called for a North American "Free Trade Commission" and a vast bureaucracy under this commission — the "Secretariat."

The NAFTA treaty plus its annexes and footnotes consisted of more than 1700 pages of bureaucratic intervention designed to regulate, control, and decide policy on virtually every industrial, agricultural, environmental, and labor matter affecting trade. Rather than freeing up trade, NAFTA is designed to enforce uniform socialism.

However, to forestall conservative opposition, the agreement was cast as a conservative proposal. And to help in that task the Establishment called upon its anointed voice of the conservatives, William F. Buckley, Jr. (CFR).

In his September 4, 1992 syndicated column, Buckley wrote that NAFTA "gives us an important leverage in the looming trade wars in Eastern Europe. It will prove less tempting to discriminate against American goods when to do so would be to provoke at least the northern half of the western hemisphere."

• **"Voluntarism."** On November 16, 1990, President Bush quietly signed the National and Community Service Act. Although promoted mostly by liberal Democrats, the final version (S. 1430) sponsored by Senator Ted Kennedy was actually a response to President Bush's campaign call for "1000 points of light." After becoming President, George Bush championed a new government responsibility — to call Americans into community service:

> Today I announce a new initiative calling on all levels of government — both sectors, public and private — to enlist in a new crusade to bring national service into every corner of America. This crusade begins with a simple truth: From now on, any definition of a successful life must include serving others. [14]

The Kennedy measure passed the House by a vote of 235 to 186 on October 24. Representative Steve Gunderson (R-Wis.) saw correctly what was involved and addressed his fellow representatives: "We are authorizing a program of ... new money to set up grants and bureaucracy for voluntarism. My colleagues, have we lost our minds?"

In view of its collectivist origins, some analysts fear that government-sponsored volunteerism will lead to mandatory social regimentation. Already we hear of "volunteer" problems for "government" to solve, such as high volunteer drop-out rates and the need to prioritize volunteer activity. [15] Other critics point out that most of the problems government claims to want to solve were actually created or exacerbated by government (e.g., a minimum wage that creates unemployment).

Not surprisingly, every successor president, Establishment-approved of course, has sought to expand President Bush's trailblazing program, starting with President Clinton and his AmeriCorps. In October of 2009, President Obama met with former President Bush at Texas A & M University to celebrate the 20th anniversary of Bush's "thousand points of light" initiative. Reporting on the event, the *Christian Science Monitor* stated: "Under the bipartisan Edward M. Kennedy Serve America Act of 2009, Obama seeks to triple the size of AmeriCorps...." [16]

• **National industrial policy.** President Bush implemented another assault on limited government — a "national industrial policy" — which has since become a staple under the Obama administration. On April 25, 1991, the White House quietly announced a major shift in government's relationship to the free market, authorizing federal funds to advance commercial technology. As the foot in the door, a list of 22 technologies was cited as "critical to economic prosperity and national security."

Mr. Bush hired Allan Bromley (CFR) as his science advisor to help break through the historic barrier against this government intrusion in our market-based economy. To get by the "ideological" objections to this step toward a bureaucratically controlled economy, Bromley advocated investing only in technologies that are "pre-competitive" or "generic." And grant seekers quickly caught on to the pretense — their proposals carefully avoided the term "industrial policy" in favor of the Bromley verbiage. According to the *Wall Street Journal*:

> While stoutly denying that it is in the business of picking technological winners and losers, the Bush administration is doing just that by pushing technology programs in Congress that would subsidize makers of supercomputers, software and electric cars....

The line between what's acceptable ideologically and what isn't is faint, if not invisible. That vagueness allows the administration to stick to its free market rhetoric while starting to endorse some of the industrial policy programs of its opponents. [17]

• **"Read my lips."** Two years into the Bush administration, even government economists would agree that American business was in a recession. But, of course, the culprit was disputed. Nevertheless, strong contributors were a major tax increase approved in late 1990, increased regulation supported by the Bush administration, and a huge increase in federal spending.

In his acceptance speech at the 1988 GOP convention, Mr. Bush would utter his memorable "read my lips, no new taxes" pledge:

I'm the one who will not raise taxes .... And my opponent won't rule out raising taxes. But I will and the Congress will push me to raise taxes, and I'll say no, and they'll push, and I'll say no, and they'll push again. And I'll say to them: Read my lips, no new taxes.

Nevertheless, on June 26, 1990 the President agreed to a "deficit reduction" increase, one of the largest tax increases in our nation's history. On September 30, President Bush announced a budget agreement with Democratic leaders and explained his reversal:

Sometimes you don't get it the way you want.... But it's time we put the interests of the United States of America here and get this deficit under control.... If we fail to enact this agreement, our economy will falter, markets may tumble and recession will follow.... [18]

• **Record federal spending.** On February 4th of the following year (1991), the president submitted his Fiscal Year 1992 budget to Congress. His record-shattering proposal called for $1.446 trillion in federal spending. The proposed budget brought *domestic* spending to $970 billion, a whopping increase of $300 billion over the final year ($670 billion) of the Reagan administration. Among the areas receiving large increases were liberal favorites —

education and housing.

Two days later (February 6, 1991), Mr. Bush sought to reassure the nation: "True, the deficit is high — unacceptably high .... But thanks to the budget reforms that began last fall, the deficit will be virtually eliminated by 1995." Which confirms the old adage that the more things change, the more they stay the same. Politicians count on the public having a short memory.

Nevertheless, it is vital to understand the real agenda behind the perpetual betrayal. While campaigning for the presidency in 1932, FDR stated:

> I accuse the present Administration [Hoover's] of being the greatest spending Administration in peace time in all American history.... We are spending altogether too much money for government services which are neither practical nor necessary.... I regard reduction in federal spending as one of the most important issues of this campaign. [19]

As would Bush, almost six decades later, President Roosevelt immediately changed his tune after gaining office, repudiating our constitutional system and initiating a wholesale flight into socialism. Two years later (January 4, 1935), President Roosevelt summarized his New Deal in his annual message to Congress:

> We have undertaken a new order of things.... We have proceeded ... a measureable distance on the road toward this new order.... The outlines of the new economic order, rising from the disintegration of the old, are apparent.

Similarly, while campaigning for the presidency in 1988, Mr. Bush would wear the clothes of a fiscal conservative while characterizing his Democratic opponent, Michael Dukakis, as a profligate big-spender. However, the ensuing parallel to FDR should have set off alarm bells.

In the introduction to the Fiscal 1992 Budget, Richard Darman (CFR), director of the Office of Management and Budget, observed: "Though less grand than a New World Order, steps toward a new domestic order can continue to be advanced — at least at the margins of practicable change."

Under the heading "Reformist Steps — Toward a New Domestic Order," Darman enthusiastically endorsed Bush's proposed expanded federal role, while affirming America's "historic mission" (anticipating the rhetoric of today's GOP "young guns") of "protecting freedom, accelerating innovation, assuring fairness, increasing growth and opportunity, while limiting the expansion of intrusive and inefficient government...."

Foretelling the collectivist arguments of a President Obama, a Harry Reid, or a Nancy Pelosi, Bush and Darman justified their explosion in domestic spending as "investments in human capital" that "will help members of the next generation maximize their human potential." Indeed, the more things change, the more the Insiders' web tightens.

Bill Clinton Administrations
(1993 – 2001)

Scandal Dogs Road to White House

Had Bill Clinton faced an unfriendly press during his campaign for the presidency, he would never have gained even his party's nomination. In sharp contrast to its normal behavior, the Establishment media either ignored the personal scandals that surfaced or gave them short play, writing them off as unimportant. The media seemed to adopt the attitude that a little thing like character flaws should not deprive the nation of Clinton's impressive talents.

The scandals, ranging from draft dodging to anti-war protesting, philandering, and marijuana use, as well as dishonesty regarding all of the above, are too numerous to describe here. A couple of examples (omitting much indicting detail) should suffice to illustrate candidate Clinton's vulnerability.

• **Draft-dodging.** In the summer of 1968, with the Vietnam War in full swing, Bill Clinton had just graduated from Georgetown University, thus losing his deferment. As a student, Clinton had been working on the staff of U.S. Senator and Rhodes Scholar J. William Fulbright (D-Ark.). Fulbright fixed Bill up with a Rhodes scholarship and arranged a deferment of nearly a year from the local draft board. So Bill was off to England to study at Oxford.

Upon his return, following his first year at Oxford, Bill's efforts to get another deferment failed, so he applied for admission into the ROTC program at the University of Arkansas Law School. [20] The interviewing commander of the ROTC unit, Colonel Eugene Holmes, a survivor of the Bataan Death March and more than three years as a POW of the Japanese, accepted Clinton for the fall term and Clinton obtained a deferment to attend ROTC.

However, instead of following through on his ROTC commitment, Clinton left the country and returned to England. He didn't bother to enroll again at Oxford, but travelled all over Europe and participated in/organized anti-war demonstrations. (The extent of Clinton's involvement became the source of other controversy.)

Two days after Clinton was awarded a safe lottery number for the draft, he wrote a long overdue letter to Colonel Holmes, apologizing for the lack of contact and admitting he had never been interested in the ROTC program, but had applied only to avoid the draft. When Clinton's letter surfaced in February 1992, Ted Koppel read it in its entirely on Nightline but accepted the excuse from his guest, Governor Clinton, that Bill was only 23 years old at the time. The rest of the media generally ignored the letter, which is available in the *Congressional Record*. [21]

In an affidavit, released on September 16, 1992, Colonel Holmes says he had not spoken up earlier because of poor health, however "present polls show that there is imminent danger to our country of a draft dodger becoming the Commander-in-Chief of the Armed Forces of the United States. While it is true, as Mr. Clinton has stated, that there were many others who avoided serving their country in the Vietnam War, they are not aspiring to be president of the United States." [22] The affidavit was generally ignored by the major news organizations.

• **Anti-war protesting.** Candidate Clinton tried repeatedly to downplay his participation in anti-war demonstrations. In October of 1992 on the Phil Donahue show he stated: "I have said repeatedly that I was in two or three marches during the course of my life as an opponent of the Vietnam War.... I did go to a couple of rallies.... I was not a big organizer of anti-war activities."

However, other evidence suggests much greater involvement. For example, Father Richard McSorley, a professor from Georgetown University and one of Bill Clinton's anti-war comrades, writes of meeting Clinton the day following a demonstration in front of the U.S. Embassy in London. According to Father McSorley, Bill Clinton, while studying at Oxford, was one of the organizers.[23]

One of the groups supporting the demonstration was the British Peace Council, a Soviet-front directed by the KGB. Although anti-war, the demonstrations were also anti-American, pro-Vietcong, and pro-Hanoi. During the winter of 1969–70, Bill Clinton would visit Moscow, ostensibly for sightseeing (a strange destination for winter tourism).

• **Other radical sympathies.** Questions regarding Clinton's true sympathies persisted right up to his campaign for president. Italian journalist Antonio Socci claims to have interviewed Governor Clinton at the 1992 Democratic convention. Socci's interview was published in the Italian newsweekly *Il Sabato* under the title "Comrade Bill." According to the article, Governor Bill Clinton had visited Italy in 1987 to study the communist co-op at Legga, Italy, then returned to put together about 70 youth cooperatives in Arkansas.[24]

An isolated account? Perhaps. But look at Derek Shearer, a longtime friend of Bill Clinton and an economic adviser for Clinton's campaign. Shearer is an associate fellow at the "Marxist" Institute for Policy Studies in Washington, D.C. and an admirer of Italian communist theorist Antonio Gramsci. In 1980, Shearer co-authored *Economic Democracy* with fellow IPS associate Martin Carnoy. *Economic Democracy* champions the same Italian cooperatives that Clinton was alleged to have visited and used as a model in Arkansas.[25]

In his detailed 1987 exposé *Covert Cadre: Inside the Institute for Policy Studies*, Dr. S. Steven Powell discusses Shearer:

> Shearer has also served on the board of Jane Fonda/Tom Hayden's Campaign for Economic Democracy.... Shearer frankly says, "Socialism has a bad name in America, and no amount of wishful thinking on the part of the left is going to

change that in our lifetimes." Thus he pleads, "the words economic democracy are an adequate and effective replacement." [26]

At Oxford, Bill Clinton didn't earn a degree, but he did make connections that would prove important to his political ambitions. (Bill would meet Hillary at Yale where both would earn law degrees.) While governor of Arkansas, Clinton was invited to join the CFR (1989) and by 1991 was accepted into the even more exclusive Trilateral Commission.

The connections Clinton had accumulated paid off during his campaign for president. After Clinton received the Democratic nomination, retired Admiral William J. Crowe Jr., a director of the CFR, would endorse Clinton for president. Crowe had served as the chairman of the Joint Chiefs of Staff in the Reagan and Bush administrations. President Clinton appointed Crowe as U.S. ambassador to England.

Chinagate

Although Clinton would withstand evidence of character flaws in his 1992 campaign, shortly into his second term serious new revelations threatened to remove him from office. Extensive evidence of illegal contributions to both the 1992 and 1996 Clinton-Gore campaigns, in return for selling out America's national security to the Red Chinese, became known as Chinagate. (The Chinagate umbrella also included charges of obstruction of justice in response to the ensuing investigation.)

Congressional researchers Edward Timperlake and William Triplett documented much of the developing evidence in their blockbuster 1998 exposé *Year of the Rat: How Bill Clinton Compromised U.S. Security for Chinese Cash.* [27] Setting the stage, the authors note:

> Before Bill Clinton took office the United States was the prime obstacle to the CCP's [Chinese Communist Party's] ambitions to dominate East Asia. After he was elected, the CCP expressed two major needs — political and economic intelligence on the United States, and assistance with its military modernization

program. The Clinton administration has met both Chinese Communist goals.[28]

Incredibly, John Huang, who had raised much of the illegal campaign cash from Red Chinese sources, was given a top-secret security clearance in the Clinton Commerce Department. House Rules Committee Chairman Gerald Solomon charged on June 11, 1997 that "John Huang committed economic espionage and breached our national security by passing classified information to his former employer, the Lippo Group."[29]

The scope and credibility of the evidence against President Clinton never reached most of the American public, thanks to Clinton's media allies, who sought desperately to contain a scandal that resisted containment. Political cowards (or those subject to blackmail, etc.) within the Republican Party also aided the cover-up.

The media finally succeeded in deflecting national attention from the criminal charges in Chinagate to other scandals such as Whitewater and Clinton's affair with an intern (Monica Lewinski). With the latter, the media generally ignored the more serious issue of perjury and framed the whole matter as just "lying about sex."

While the momentum of the revelations was still rocking the Clinton administration, House Republicans forced the Judiciary Committee to initiate an impeachment inquiry. Once the impeachment process began, however, pressures were applied from Establishment circles to subvert the process and focus attention on the less serious charges.

Following its investigation, the Committee recommended four articles of impeachment to be voted on by the full House, completely ignoring Chinagate, which the media had disparaged as a campaign financing issue. The House passed two of the four articles (President Clinton was thus impeached) and a trial was scheduled in the Senate.

However, with the media successfully framing the action as motivated by cheap GOP partisanship, even many of the representatives who voted for impeachment soon lost their appetite for the battle and wanted it to end as soon as possible.

In that atmosphere, the Senate steamrolled the public trial, with Senate leaders ridiculing the lower chamber for forcing the action, and on February 12, 1999 voted to acquit the president on both charges. (A two-thirds vote (67) was needed to convict. The votes were 45 to 55 and 50 to 50 to convict.)

CFR Staffing

President-elect Clinton chose Vernon Jordan (CFR) and Warren Christopher (former vice chairman of the board of the CFR) to head up his 48-member transition team to develop recommendations for administration posts.

Although such radicals as Derek Shearer and Johnnetta Cole were also on the team (Cole was a member of the KGB-directed World Peace Council), Clinton largely went to the Establishment for the major posts.

Clinton brought more than 20 **Rhodes Scholars** into his administration, many with CFR credentials. The Rhodes Scholars included: Strobe Talbott (CFR), see below; Robert Reich as secretary of labor; R. James Woolsey (CFR) as CIA director; Ira Magaziner as senior policy advisor for policy development (and chief health care adviser); George Stephanopoulos (CFR) as White House communications director; and the ubiquitous Richard N. Gardner (CFR) as U.S. ambassador to Spain.

• **Economic team.** To head up his economic team, President Clinton chose Senate Finance Committee Chairman Lloyd Bentsen (former CFR) as his Treasury secretary and Roger C. Altman (CFR) as Bentsen's deputy. Altman was vice chairman of the Blackstone Group (a New York investment firm co-founded by Peter G. Peterson, former secretary of commerce under Nixon and chairman of the CFR in 1985).

Robert E. Rubin (co-chairman of Goldman, Sachs) would serve as Clinton's senior economic adviser. Two years later, Rubin succeeded Bentsen as secretary of the Treasury. And in 2007, Rubin would succeed Peter G. Peterson as co-chairman (alongside Carla A. Hills) of the Council on Foreign Relations. Clinton clearly knew he had to enlist up-and-comers in the Establishment.

Laura D'Andrea Tyson (CFR), a professor at the University of California at Berkeley, would serve as chair of the Council of Economic Advisors.

President Clinton tapped Representative Leon Panetta, chairman of the House Budget Committee, for director of the Office of Management and Budget. Although not CFR himself, Panetta would be assisted by Alice Rivlin (CFR director 1989–1992), an economist at the Brookings Institution and former director of the Congressional Budget Office.

The incoming president would also reappoint Alan Greenspan (a CFR director 1982–1988) as chairman of the Federal Reserve. President Reagan had first appointed Greenspan to head up the Fed in 1987.

• **Foreign policy.** For his secretary of state, President Clinton chose his transition team leader — Warren M. Christopher (CFR director 1982–91 and former vice chairman of the board).

As deputy secretary of state under Carter, Christopher had worked with Cyrus Vance to topple pro-Western governments in Nicaragua and Iran (see Chapter 10). In 1991, following the Rodney King affair, Christopher had headed up a commission to "investigate" the LAPD, as a steppingstone to federal control.

President Clinton would also bring his former roommate at Oxford, Strobe Talbott, into his administration. Talbott, a CFR director since 1988 and a member of the Trilateral Commission, would serve in a new post — Ambassador-at-Large to the states of the former Soviet Union (as aid coordinator) and special adviser to the secretary of state. As 1993 came to a close, Christopher would select the relatively inexperienced Talbott as his deputy secretary of state (the number two post), replacing Clifton R. Wharton (CFR), a former trustee and chairman of the Rockefeller Foundation.

In announcing the Talbott nomination, Christopher would comment: "Strobe and I have been friends for 15 years.... We served together on the board of the Council on Foreign Relations, and now, of course, we have worked closely together over the course of the last year." [30]

Winston Lord, former president of the CFR, joined the Clinton administration as assistant secretary for East Asian and Pacific Affairs. The post of under secretary for political affairs went to Peter Tarnoff, president of the CFR since 1986 and member of the Trilateral Commission.

And Madeleine K. Albright (CFR) would be tapped for U.S.

ambassador to the United Nations. Albright succeeded Christopher as secretary of state for Clinton's second term.

Defense/National Security Staffing
A similar pattern of CFR/Trilateral domination could be found in the military/national security and intelligence branches. Clinton selected R. James Woolsey (CFR) as CIA director. Woolsey was a longtime ally of the new secretary of defense — Les Aspin. Representative Les Aspin, chairman of the House Armed Services Committee, had run as a peace candidate in 1970, opposed to the Vietnam War.

President Clinton chose General John M. Shalikashvili (CFR) as the new chairman of the Joint Chiefs of Staff. Blatant security risk W. Anthony Lake (CFR) filled the post of assistant for national security affairs. President Clinton later tried to elevate Lake to head up the CIA, but Lake finally withdrew his nomination rather than face more tough questioning in the Senate. Samuel R. Berger (CFR) was selected as deputy assistant for national security affairs.

Other important cabinet selections drawn from the CFR rolodex included:

- Donna Shalala (also TC) as secretary of Health and Human Services;
- Henry Cisneros for secretary of Housing and Urban Development (former TC); and
- Bruce Babbitt as secretary of the interior (former TC).

The CFR annual report just prior to the end of Clinton's 2nd term (2000) would claim 548 of its members as U.S. government officials. Hundreds were in important positions.

Vice President Al Gore
We can't leave the topic of the Establishment influence in the Clinton team without taking a look at the vice president. Although Al Gore has no direct ties to the Establishment's Council on Foreign Relations or Trilateral Commission, he has clearly been promoting the Establishment's domestic and internationalist agenda.

Of course, Al Gore's big issue has been the threat of environmental apocalypse. Early in 1992, Al Gore published *Earth in the Balance: Ecology and the Human Spirit*, which called for a "Global Marshall Plan" that would "require the wealthy nations to allocate money for transferring environmentally helpful technologies to the Third World and to help impoverished nations achieve a stable population and a new pattern of sustainable economic progress." [31]

Advancing Insider Objectives

President Clinton's support for **NAFTA** provided early evidence that he was carrying the Establishment's ball. Clinton would gain congressional approval before his first year was up. In the process, he enlisted the support of all five living former presidents (Nixon, Ford, Carter, Reagan, and Bush) to help him promote the pact. [32]

Here are several among many Clinton priorities and attacks on our constitutional system:

• **The WTO.** Following up on his NAFTA victory, President Clinton would convince Congress (1994) to commit America to the World Trade Organization — "a United Nations of world trade" — a serious attack on America's right to develop an independent trade policy and a further step toward "global governance."

• **HillaryCare.** During his campaign, Bill Clinton embraced the socialist challenge of further nationalizing health care. Once in office he set up the National Task Force on Health Care Reform, headed by Hillary Clinton and supported by chief health care policy adviser Ira Magaziner.

On November 20, 1993, Representative Richard Gephardt introduced the "Health Security Act" (H.R. 3600), Clinton's plan for government mandated health insurance. The act ran to more than 1,000 pages.

Even before the detailed proposal was unveiled, attention focused on rationing guidelines. The *New York Times* reported:

> Hillary Rodham Clinton said [before the Senate Finance Committee on September 30th] that she hoped the nation would engage in a serious discussion about what is appropriate medical care in cases where very expensive treatments do nothing for the patient's quality of life.... If the plan creates "the

kind of health security we are talking about," she said, "then people will know they are not being denied treatment for any reason other than it is not appropriate — will not enhance or save the quality of life." [33]

Great opposition to the Clinton plan ensued and congressmen introduced several alternative plans. In August 1994, Senate Majority Leader George Mitchell declared his compromise plan dead for that session. With the Republicans taking control of both houses of Congress in the 1994 elections, Clinton's health care "reform" would go nowhere during his terms of office.

Nevertheless, the plan was not really dead. The administration would implement portions of its plan in other legislation and by administrative decision.

• **UN treaties.** With heavy CFR/Trilateral staffing in the foreign policy arena, one would expect to see the administration pushing the Establishment's internationalist agenda on multiple fronts.

And indeed, the Clinton foreign policy team would strive to entangle America in a host of new UN treaties dealing with human rights, the environment, economic development, drugs, terrorism, and disarmament.

One of the potentially most damaging is the treaty that would bind the U.S. to the International Criminal Court. During the last few days of the Clinton presidency, David Scheffer (CFR), Clinton's ambassador for the International Criminal Court signed the extremely subversive treaty for the United States. Of course, the U.S. Senate still must ratify it, and that won't happen until the Insiders have preset the dials of public opinion.

• **NATO expansion.** The administration's "Partnership for Peace" plan, engineered by Strobe Talbott, was designed to bring the former members of the Warsaw Pact, including Russia, into "partnership" status in an expanding NATO. The plan was presented as a "go slow approach" toward formal membership and "the security guarantees that come with it." [34]

• **Environmental activism.** On the campaign trail Bill Clinton had declared that his environmental opinions coincided with those of his running mate. Early evidence of a shared vision was President Clinton's appointment of Carol Browner to head the EPA.

An environmental activist-lawyer Browner had served as the legislative director for Senator Gore until 1991 when Florida Governor Lawton Chiles appointed her to head up the Florida Department of Environmental regulation. Browner led the EPA throughout both of President Clinton's terms. In 2009, President Obama would appoint Browner to the new post of "energy czar" in his administration.

• **Deepening NAFTA.** A series of NAFTA side agreements was negotiated on August 13, 1993. Mickey Cantor, the chief U.S. negotiator for the accords proudly proclaimed: "No nation can lower labor or environmental standards, only raise them...." Two months later, Carol Browner testified before the Senate: "The NAFTA package will dramatically increase enforcement. The environmental agreement obligates countries, for the first time, to enforce environmental laws, and backs these obligations up with sanctions."

• **Executive Orders.** Much of the Clinton administration's domestic assault was conducted through a campaign of Executive Orders. Expanding presidential authority through Executive Orders was an old practice, but President Clinton brought it to a new level as he neared the end of his second term. The White House called the strategy "Project Podesta" (named after chief of staff John Podesta). The *Christian Science Monitor* observed:

> It's been a mark of the Clinton administration to rule by executive fiat, circumventing a hostile Congress by signing presidential orders that affect everything from patients' rights to conservation to a war against Yugoslavia.

Incredibly, the *Monitor* would assert: "The Constitution speaks only vaguely about the president's powers, designating Congress as the body that makes the laws and the executive branch as the one that carries them out. Nowhere does it define or limit the president's power to rule by executive order." [35]

Part IV

Controlling the People

Chapter 12

Organized Subversion at Home

Although the CFR was formed to control the "foreign" relationships of the United States, domestic subversion was essential to its program. Indeed, the goal of entangling the U.S. in international institutions required molding public opinion while undermining expected resistance.

Just as J.P. Morgan sought to keep a foot in all camps, so the architects of a new world order have used every revolutionary principle to advance their cause. Pursuing one of those principles, the Insiders sought to control the opinion forming institutions of society — education, book publishing, the media of communications.

One objective of controlling the news media was to create the illusion of consensus and allow revolutionary cadres to represent public opinion or even expert opinion. This pressure from below would enable cooperative politicians to promote revolutionary measures while posturing as responsibly reacting to public opinion. And the pressure would tend to stifle resistance.

Another objective of media domination was to keep dissent within acceptable bounds. Often the Insiders would create or control their own opposition. Domination of the media would allow them to channel expected resistance into following "respectable," non-threatening "leadership."

But to create rock-solid insurance against potentially catastrophic opposition, the Insiders would need to rewrite the Constitution, eliminating its checks on unrestrained power, and destroy America's independent middle class. Several proven revolutionary strategies, in addition to economic strangulation, have targeted the middle class:

• Undermining the supporting culture of religion, morality, and independence;

• Dumbing down the electorate through control of education; and

- Changing the role of government from servant to a gatekeeper to basic necessities, such as health care and energy.

In pursing these objectives, the Establishment has sponsored a multi-pronged attack from a myriad of interlocked organizations, as well as from revolutionary, particularly socialist, organizations. At first glance, these latter organizations appear to represent the "little people" or anti-Establishment interests, which aids the deception and confuses resistance.

Let's take a look at how this multi-pronged attack has been organized.

Control of Education

Among the minutes of the Carnegie Endowment, Reece Committee investigator Kathryn Casey discovered a plan to control education in the United States. According to Norman Dodd, director of research for the Committee:

> The war was over. Then the concern became, as expressed by the trustees, seeing to it that there was no reversion to life in this country as it existed prior to 1914. And they came to the conclusion that, to prevent a reversion, they must control education. And then they approached the Rockefeller Foundation and they said, "Will you take on the acquisition of control of education as it involves subjects that are domestic in their significance? We'll take it on the basis of subjects that have an international significance." And it was agreed.
>
> Then, together, they decided that the key to it is the teaching of American history and they must change that. So, they then approached the most prominent of what we might call American historians at that time with the idea of getting them to alter the manner in which they presented the subject.[1]

Author William McIlhany, who had interviewed Dodd, writes that after encountering initial opposition, "the Carnegie trustees resolved to build their own stable of kept historians, and they even got a working agreement with the Guggenheim Foundation to grant scholarships to their selected candidates who were seeking degrees."[2] McIlhany continued:

> Carnegie Trustee James T. Shotwell organized the National Board for Historical Service, which was designed to line up all the historians in the Allied cause and in support of Wilson's interventionist policies. Though encountering resistance at first, this group succeeded gradually in capturing more influence in the American Historical Association and affiliated circles.[3]

Shotwell, you may recall, was a member of Colonel House's Inquiry. He joined the CFR in 1923, was a member of the U.S. delegation to the founding of the UN, and became president of the Carnegie Endowment in 1949.

Hidden Censorship in America
Following World War II, the internationalists again sought to publish their history of the war and provide a spirited defense of Roosevelt policies. On a grant by the Rockefeller Foundation, the CFR hired Harvard professor William Langer to develop a chronicle of the war.

In the wake of the First World War, several historians did bring out books challenging the Carnegie line. However, this time the internationalists were better organized and took pains to ensure that alternate viewpoints would either not reach the American people or would be denigrated. In a 1947 *Saturday Evening Post* article, one of America's most famous historians, Charles A. Beard, blasted this conspiracy:

> The Rockefeller Foundation and Council on Foreign Relations ... intend to prevent, if they can, a repetition of what they call in the vernacular "the debunking journalistic campaign following World War I." Translated into precise English, this means that the Foundation and the Council do not want journalists or any other persons to examine too closely and criticize too freely the official propaganda and official statements relative to "our basic aims and activities" during World War II.[4]

A former president of the American Historical Association with socialist credentials, Beard was for a while a darling of the

Establishment. However, he opposed the dishonesty of the Roosevelt administration in dragging America into war. The Establishment reacted with venom to ensure Beard's fall from grace.

Harry Elmer Barnes, another historian who refused to go along with the Establishment, ran into the censorship. In a 1953 book, published by a non-Establishment firm in Idaho, he described how the process worked:

> The methods followed by the various groups interested in blacking out the truth about world affairs since 1932 ... fall mainly into the following patterns or categories: (1) excluding scholars suspected of revisionist views from access to public documents which are freely opened to "court historians" and other apologists for the foreign policy of President Roosevelt; (2) intimidating publishers of books and periodicals, so that even those who might wish to publish books and articles setting forth the revisionist point of view do not dare to do so; (3) ignoring or obscuring published material which embodies revisionist facts and arguments; and (4) smearing revisionist authors and their books....
>
> The book clubs and the main sales outlets for books are controlled by powerful pressure groups.... These outlets not only refuse to market critical books in this field [American foreign policy since 1933] but also threaten to boycott other books by those publishers who defy their blackout ultimatum. [5]

The Ivy League Colleges

At the opening of the Twentieth Century, the Establishment was already able to dictate the direction of higher education in America. In *Tragedy and Hope*, Professor Carroll Quigley explains how the international bankers led by the J.P. Morgan firm came to have enormous influence in the big name universities during the period from the 1880s to 1930s [after which the Rockefeller interests assumed the leadership role]:

> Their connection with the Ivy League colleges rested on the fact that the large endowments of these institutions required constant consultation with the financiers of Wall Street (or its

lesser branches on State Street, Boston, and elsewhere).... As a consequence of these influences, as late as the 1930's, J.P. Morgan and his associates were the most significant figures in policy making at Harvard, Columbia, and to a lesser extent Yale, while the Whitneys were significant at Yale, and the Prudential Insurance Company (through Edward D. Duffield) dominated Princeton....

The chief officials of these universities were beholden to these financial powers and usually owed their jobs to them. Morgan himself helped make Nicholas Murray Butler president of Columbia; his chief Boston agent, Thomas Nelson Perkins of the First National Bank of that city, gave Conant his boost from the chemical laboratory to University Hall at Harvard; Duffield of Prudential, caught unprepared when the incumbent president of Princeton was killed in an automobile in 1932, made himself president for a year before he chose Harold Dodds for the post in 1933. At Yale, Thomas Lamont, managing partner of the Morgan firm, was able to swing Charles Seymour [a member of Col. House's Inquiry] into the presidency of that university in 1937.[6]

Control of the Media

At the beginning of the last century, media meant newspapers, books, and magazines. Owners of print publishing naturally invested in radio and later television when these technologies were getting off the ground. So it still pays to look at the Establishment's domination of the print media to understand total media control.

One of the Establishment's early moves to control print publishing appears to have been driven by the desire to entangle the U.S. in World War I. However, as suggested by three-term Congressman Oscar Callaway (D-Tex.), the objectives of the control did not end there. In 1917, Callaway inserted the following statement in the *Congressional Record*:

In March, 1915, the J. P. Morgan interests, the steel, shipbuilding, and powder interests, and their subsidiary organizations, got together 12 men high up in the newspaper world and employed them to select the most influential newspapers in the United States and sufficient number of them to control generally the policy of the daily press of the United States.

These 12 men worked the problem out by selecting 179 newspapers, and then began, by an elimination process, to retain only those necessary for the purpose of controlling the general policy of the daily press throughout the country. They found it was only necessary to purchase the control of 25 of the greatest papers. The 25 papers were agreed upon; emissaries were sent to purchase the policy, national and international, of these papers; an agreement was reached; the policy of the papers was bought, to be paid for by the month; an editor was furnished for each paper to properly supervise and edit information regarding the questions of preparedness, militarism, financial policies, and other things of national and international nature considered vital to the interests of the purchasers....

This policy also included the suppression of everything in opposition to the wishes of the interests served. [7]

The Establishment's *New York Times*

For more than a century, the *New York Times* has topped the list of the nation's most influential newspapers. Its influence extends far beyond New York readers. Indeed, the *Times* has long been regarded as "The Important Paper For Important People Everywhere."

Moreover, what appeared in the *Times* would later appear in many other places. During the middle of the last century, Alice Widener, a columnist for *Barron's*, explained:

It is a fact that most editors and newsmen on the staffs of *Life*, *Look*, *Time*, *Newsweek*, etc., and most editors, reporters, and commentators at NBC, CBS, and ABC take their news and editorial cues from the *New York Times*. Technically, it is a great newspaper; but it reports much of the news in conformity with its editorial policies. [8]

And what are those editorial policies? The late Hermann Dinsmore could answer that with authority. Dinsmore worked at *The New York Times* for 34 years, serving nine years (1951–1960) as editor of its

International Edition. Dinsmore became angry at what he saw at the *Times* — a deliberate, systematic distortion of the news as a matter of official *Times* policy. He was particularly outraged over the *Times* coverage of the Vietnam War. And so in 1969 Dinsmore wrote a critical analysis of the *Times*, titled appropriately *All the News That Fits*.[9]

While at the *Times*, Dinsmore had every reason to consider himself well informed. As editor of the International Edition, it was his duty to be aware of every story reported in the paper. However, his further investigation after leaving the *Times* led him to an awareness of important events that had not been reported. With new insight, Dinsmore would acknowledge the existence of a Conspiracy and write a much more enlightened exposé entitled *The Bleeding of America*.[10]

The ownership of the *Times* is unassailably Establishment. With financial backing from international bankers J.P. Morgan, August Belmont, and Kuhn, Loeb's Jacob Schiff, Adolph Ochs was able to take control of the *Times* in 1896, and the modern history of the *Times* began.

In his published recollection of the Kennedy years while special assistant to the president, Arthur Schlesinger Jr. (CFR) also acknowledged the Establishment's domination of the *New York Times*:

> [T]he New York financial and legal community ... was the heart of the American Establishment.... [I]ts front organizations [were] the Rockefeller, Ford and Carnegie foundations and the Council on Foreign Relations; its organs, the *New York Times* and *Foreign Affairs*.[11]

T*imes* membership in the CFR was not limited to the top echelon. The *Times* could count among its editors and prominent journalists numerous CFR members. Indeed, Leslie H. Gelb (CFR 1973+), who was assistant secretary of state during the Carter administration, returned to the *Times* in 1981, first as a national security correspondent, then a deputy editorial page editor, an op-ed page editor, and finally a columnist. Gelb would later serve as president of the CFR for a decade (1993-2003) and is currently its president emeritus.

Among the journalists at the *Times* have been several whose apologies for Communist dictators have seriously misled Americans: Walter Duranty covering up the Soviet-orchestrated Ukrainian famine; Herbert L. Matthews championing Fidel Castro; and Harrison Salisbury (CFR) (regarding Moscow and Hanoi), to name three of the most blatant.

A horrific example of misleading reporting was the media coverage of the unfolding Khmer Rouge regime in Cambodia, which ultimately murdered a third of its population in the "killing fields." The American press aided that Communist revolution by insisting that America withdraw its support from the embattled Cambodia government.

In 1975, four days before the Communists seized control of the Cambodian capital of Phnom Penh, the *New York Times* echoed the Khmer Rouge propaganda line in a story carrying the headline: "Communist Rule Is at Least Uncertain; Napalm is Not; Indochina Without Americans: For Most, a Better Life." [12] As the genocide unfolded in 1976, the nightly television news, on which so many Americans rely to be informed, barely mentioned the atrocity (NBC never, ABC once, and CBS twice).

An honest study of the *Times* illustrates the fact that Establishment-owned institutions have often supported Communist causes. The natural first reaction might be that Communists had infiltrated the institutions, duped the owners, and co-opted the operations for their own purposes. The much better answer, however, is that they were working toward the same goals.

The development of the wire services and later the Internet has not diminished the prominence of the *Times*. Its website is one of America's most popular online newspaper websites.

The Wall Street Journal

The late Robert L. Bartley provides an excellent example of the controlled opposition. Bartley served as the editorial page editor of the *Wall Street Journal* for 30 years (from 1972 to 2002). Adopting the image of a conservative free-market Republican, Bartley would use the *Journal* to promote internationalism (NAFTA, WTO, the IMF and World Bank) to its mostly conservative readership.

Bartley was invited to join the CFR in 1979. He also showed up on the membership roles of the even more selective Trilateral Commission and attended the internationalist Bilderberg meetings.

Bartley would cleverly argue the wisdom of sacrificing national sovereignty to the *Journal's* readers. "I think the nation-state is finished," Bartley once told Peter Brimelow, senior editor for *Forbes* magazine and Bartley's former colleague at the *Journal*. "I think [Kenichi] Ohmae is right," Bartley continued.

In "The Rise of the Region State," an essay for the Spring 1993 issue of *Foreign Affairs*, Ohmae had written: "The nation state has become an unnatural, even dysfunctional, unit for organizing human activity and managing economic endeavor in a borderless world." Apparently Brimelow had not recognized Bartley's agenda:

> I was thunderstruck. I knew the fans of the *Journal's* editorial page, overwhelmingly conservative patriots, had no inkling of this. It would make a great *Wall Street Journal* front-page story: *Wall Street Journal* Editor Revealed As Secret One-Worlder — Consternation Among Faithful — Is Pope Catholic? [13]

In later years, Bartley would become even more open in his advocacy of internationalist goals: In an editorial for July 2, 2001, entitled "Open NAFTA Borders? Why Not?" Bartley wrote:

> Reformist Mexican President Vicente Fox raises eyebrows with his suggestion that over a decade or two NAFTA should evolve into something like the European Union, with open borders for not only goods and investment but also people. He can rest assured that there is one voice north of the Rio Grande that supports his vision. To wit, this newspaper....
>
> Indeed, during the immigration debate of 1984 we suggested an ultimate goal to guide passing policies — a constitutional amendment: "There shall be open borders." [14]

Astute readers of the *Journal* could have noticed another betrayal of conservative principles by Robert L. Bartley — his promotion of the neo-con revolution.

The neo-cons were a group of ex-Trotskyite socialists who sought to assume the leadership for conservatives. They gained power in the Republican Party and were influential in many so-called conservative organizations, audaciously taking over the conservative label. The acknowledged "godfather of neoconservatives" Irving Kristol defined what it meant to be a "neoconservative" in his 1995 book, *Neoconservatism: The Autobiography of an Idea*:

> [We] are conservative, but different in certain respects from the conservatism of the Republican Party. We accepted the New Deal in principle, and had little affection for the kind of isolationism that then permeated American conservatism.

When Bartley became editorial page editor in 1972, he opened up the pages of the *Journal* to Kristol, who would write a regular column promoting internationalism.

In December 2003, a week before Bartley succumbed to cancer, President George W. Bush awarded Bartley the Presidential Medal of Freedom, America's highest civilian honor. Although the Establishment media eulogized Bartley as a leading voice of conservatism and one who had shaped modern economic thought, Bartley was in reality just an agent of the Insiders, effectively retailing their internationalist propaganda.

Current CFR members on the *Journal's* editorial staff include: Daniel P. Henninger, deputy editor of the *Journal's* editorial page, succeeding George R. Melloan (CFR), who held the position for 33 years, Assistant Managing Editor Gerald F. Seib, and Washington Bureau Chief John Bussey. Karen Elliot House, publisher of the *Journal* from 1991 to 2006, was a member of the CFR. In 2007, Rupert Murdoch's (CFR) News Corporation purchased the Dow Jones & Company, parent company for the *Wall Street Journal*.

CFR Members in the Media

We could look at many more publications and outlets and show their Insider connections, but let's allow the CFR to suggest the totality of its media influence. In its published *Annual Reports*, the CFR breaks down its membership into several categories (which have changed over the years). Its 1994 *Report* claimed a total of 3,126 members. The largest group consisted of business executives (760) with "academic scholars and administrators" close behind at 693. Another 463 were U.S. government officials and 575 administered nonprofit institutions. But a total of 330 (a little over 10 percent) were members of the media.

Another important way the Establishment influences the media is through its support for Left-wing schools of journalism. The Ford Foundation has, for example, supported journalism schools at Harvard and Columbia with multi-million dollar grants. In 1970, among just the graduates of the Columbia School of Journalism could be found 45 newspaper publishers, 152 newspaper editors, and 71 magazine editors.[15]

The rise of television did not seriously threaten Establishment control of the media. Although the three major TV networks would compete for viewers, they would all retail the Establishment line. Under the guidance of founder William S. Paley, CBS became one of the largest radio networks in the country and then the largest of the big three television networks. Paley joined the CFR in 1935.

In 1946, Paley promoted Frank Stanton (38) to president of CBS, a position Stanton held for 25 years, as CBS expanded into television. Stanton would join the CFR in 1965.

Fox News

Just as the *Wall Street Journal* plays to conservative readers, so Fox News has become the TV network of choice for conservatives. With the proliferation of television channels due to technological advances, many conservative viewers, tired of the liberal diets fed them by the news anchors at NBC, CBS, and ABC, were eager for an alternative.

Then in 1996, media mogul Rupert Murdoch created the Fox News Channel. It provided a platform for several conservative pundits. Fox would also cover many stories that never saw the light of day on the other Establishment networks. In 2008, Fox News enhanced its conservative viewership when it lured Glenn Beck away from CNN.

Unfortunately, busy, frustrated conservatives often want to rely on these articulate heroes, who take on the liberals before huge audiences, to carry the freedom fight. Yet even with no other reason to be suspicious, those who are aware of the Establishment's deceptions and its historical domination of the media should be wary of the perspectives and "leadership" they get from Fox.

However, there is one other good reason to be wary — Fox News Network owner Rupert Murdoch.

Rupert Murdoch

In 1985, the Australian born media mogul switched his citizenship to American. According to *New York Times* columnist William Safire: "To meet the legal requirements for [television] station ownership — and apparently for no other reason — [Murdoch] intends to become an American." [16] Less than a decade later (1994), Murdoch was inducted into the Establishment's Council on Foreign Relations.

The following year, at the height of the anti-Clinton conservative reaction that brought Republican control of the Congress, Murdoch would launch a new ostensibly "conservative" magazine, *The Weekly Standard*. *The Weekly Standard* would be edited by neo-con William Kristol, son of Irving Kristol, the "godfather of neoconservatives," and Fred Barnes, former senior editor and White House correspondent for the "liberal" *New Republic*.

Also in 1995, Murdoch's News Corporation set up a joint venture with the *People's Daily* — the official organ of the Chinese Communist Party.

By 2000, Fox News had developed a reputation for hard-hitting reporting critical of the Clinton-Gore Administration. The Establishment, which loves to create leaders for its opposition, seized the opportunity to cast Murdoch as an "über-Republican" and "legendarily conservative." Yet that year, Murdoch's personal money went to support the presidential campaign of Al Gore. He even served as "Vice Chair" of a Gore fundraiser at Radio City Music Hall in New York.

Also in 2000, Murdoch's News Corporation sponsored a New York City conference entitled "Global Forum: America's Role in the World." The event attracted dozens of Establishment heavyweights from the CFR and Trilateral Commission. Panelists included Henry Kissinger, World Bank President James Wolfensohn, and Mikhail Gorbachev. *The New Republic* described the conference as Murdoch's "own personal Council on Foreign Relations." [17]

In 1984, more than a decade before Fox, *Newsweek* criticized Murdoch's hands-on chairmanship of his media empire: "Murdoch runs his operation like a one man band.... There are tales of his dictating editorials, demanding that people be fired, but such direct control is hardly necessary." [18]

Conservatives shouldn't imagine for a minute that Murdoch doesn't insist that Fox programming conform to his guidelines.

Impact of Media Control

The proliferation in news and entertainment options over the last two decades appears to offer a diversity of choice. But numbers of outlets alone do not guarantee diversity if through corporate mergers and buyouts the dominant views expressed stem from the same cartel.

The Insiders know that to control the world they must first conquer public opinion. Media promotion of Insider objectives is not limited to foreign policy. It extends, for example, to supporting an attack on "the right of the people to keep and bear arms." One way it does so is by focusing on *crimes committed* with guns, while ignoring *crimes prevented* by armed citizens or the deterrent value of an armed citizenry.

If there is one theme that dominates the Establishment media, it is the collectivist vision of the glory of the state. Gone is the emphasis of our Founding Fathers on the danger of unlimited government. One writer described the message as "The saga of Government as Savior. On nearly every conceivable issue, domestic or foreign, news stories are designed to encourage readers and viewers to look to government intervention as a solution." [19]

Chapter 13

Mobilizing the Attack Forces

Following the demise of the Reece Committee investigations, the Establishment's tax-exempt foundations continued to support revolution and subversion. Sometimes, the foundations would sponsor programs directly, as when the Rockefeller Brothers Fund underwrote the task force responsible for the *Unfinished Agenda* (see Chapter 8). But often the support would be indirect.

For example, the foundations regularly fund think tanks, such as the Aspen Institute and Brookings, that provide intellectual support and manpower for radical programs. They even provide financial support for the CFR itself.

In addition, the foundations support frontline revolutionary organizations, particularly when an organization is just getting off the ground, until the organization can develop its own funding or obtain federal funding.

Ford-Funded Revolution
Among the major recipients of Establishment "generosity" have been revolutionary groups seeking to undermine immigration enforcement and radicalize the immigrant Hispanic population.

By examining the flow of funds, one sees that the Ford Foundation virtually created the radical Chicano movement, which advocates open borders, uncontrolled immigration from Mexico, and the de facto reconquest by Mexico of the Southwest portion of the United States, termed Atzlan by the radicals.

Ford has funded the radical Mexican-American Legal Defense and Education Fund (MALDEF) and the Southwest Council of La Raza Unida. In fact, La Raza Unida was founded with a $630,000 Ford Foundation grant. A California Senate Subcommittee identified the Council's one-time head, Maclovio Barraza, as a member of the Communist Party.[1]

The militant and subversive Southwest Council has since evolved into the National Council of La Raza, with continued Ford Foundation funding. On July 25, 2011 President Barak Obama addressed the annual conference of the National Council of La Raza, seeking its support.

While President Obama's appeal to a radical constituency may create little surprise, what about the "conservative" GOP side? On March 8 of 2005, Alberto R. Gonzales, President George W. Bush's selection for U.S. attorney general to replace John Ashcroft, also addressed the National Council of La Raza, which had supported him for the position. Gonzales had been affiliated with the National Council for many years.

Fabian Socialism

A major workhorse within the revolutionary network is the little known Fabian Society. The Fabian Society has supplied many of the cadres and much of the strategy and supporting ideology for the network in the United States.

While the Fabians seek the same goals as other members of the network — central control of virtually every human activity (socialism) and world government — they prefer to keep their organization in the background.

The Fabian Society was founded in 1884 in London by a group of radical intellectuals eager to impose socialism on the British people and then the world. Since its formation, the Fabian Society has advocated and pursued a strategy for achieving socialism through deception and patient gradualism.

Through this strategy, the Fabians hope to prevent their victims from recognizing the destination until it is too late. Appropriately, the Fabian Society adopted the wolf in sheep's clothing and the tortoise as its symbols.

Immediately after its founding, the Fabian Society drew significant leadership talent to its socialist cause. Author and playwright George Bernard Shaw came on board, as did author H.G. Wells, Theosophist Annie Besant, and social-psychologist Graham Wallas. At the core was the team of Sidney and Beatrice Webb.

The Fabians would develop their own brand of Marxism. Nevertheless, when the Communist revolution was successful in Russia, the Webbs often looked to the emerging Soviet Union as a model socialist society. Indeed, in their final work, *Soviet Communism: A New Civilization*, published in 1935, the Webbs would extol the virtues of the Soviet experiment.

Beginning in 1911, the British Fabians called for the creation of a universal health care system. By the middle of the last century, Fabian socialist "successes" would affect daily life in England.

A favored component of Fabian strategy involves "penetration" and "permeation" of political parties, academe, the press, government, and social institutions (including the churches). At one time, with a Labour government in power, the Fabian Society could count among its membership "10 Cabinet Ministers, including the Prime Minister, 35 Under Secretaries and other officers of State, and 229 of 394 Labour Party Members of Parliament." [2]

The Labour Party Platform of 1964, written by Fabians, brazenly announced: "For us World Government is the final objective...." [3]

While keeping a low profile, the Fabian Society has exported its revolution throughout the free world. To attract mainstream support, Fabian-controlled parties often avoid the explicit socialist tag, instead calling themselves Labour or Social Democrats.

Today, through its domination of the (fifth) Socialist International (re-established in 1951 and headquartered in London), the Fabian Society provides leadership to "162 political [social democratic, socialist and labour] parties and organizations from all continents." [4] In 1962, the Congress of the Socialist International stated: "The ultimate objective of the parties of the Socialist International is nothing less than world government." [5]

U.S. Roots

In the United States, Fabian-inspired organizations have operated under different names. The first *organizational* roots were planted in 1905 with the founding of the Intercollegiate Socialist Society (ISS). In 1921, a growing public wariness of radical activity caused the ISS to change its name to the League for Industrial Democracy.

In 1947, leaders from the American Fabian Socialist movement helped found a political action arm known as the Americans for Democratic Action (ADA). Although the ADA has "usually chosen to deny its lineage and to disclaim its Socialist purpose," the connections have been obvious. [6] ADA members generally preferred to call themselves liberals rather than socialists.

By September 1961, at least 36 high officials of the Kennedy administration were past or present members of the Americans for Democratic Action. According to author/researcher Rose Martin:

> The tally included two Cabinet members, three White House aides, Under Secretaries and Assistant Secretaries to various departments of government, and holders of other policy-making posts ranging from ambassadors to the director of the Export-Import Bank.[7]

Establishment Ties

The Fabian Society is not an independent force whose objectives just happen to coincide with those of top Insiders. Indeed, from the earliest beginnings of the Fabian movement, the American Establishment has provided close cooperation and support.

In 1895, Fabian Society leaders Sidney and Beatrice Webb and George Bernard Shaw founded the London School of Economics (and Political Science) (LSE). LSE acts as a transmission belt for Fabian theories of state economic dictatorship and plays a central role in the Fabian strategy to socialize and control the world.

Within a few decades of its founding, LSE was drawing substantial support from the international banking families in New York. For many years, the heaviest contributor to LSE was the Rockefeller Foundation. Indeed, the London School of Economics became one of the world's most influential centers of Socialist indoctrination thanks in large part to Rockefeller money.

The London School of Economics (LSE) serves an exclusive international clientele. After graduating from Harvard, David Rockefeller would study economics at LSE. John F. Kennedy studied there, as did his assistant secretary of labor, Patrick Moynihan (as a Fulbright Fellow). (Moynihan would also serve on President Nixon's White House staff and on the national board of directors of the Americans for Democratic Action.)

One of the most popular and prominent lecturers at the London School during the period 1920 to 1950 was British Marxist Harold Laski. Laski was highly regarded in socialist circles, even serving as an executive member of the Fabian Society. In January 1945, prior to leaving for Yalta, Franklin Roosevelt wrote Laski: "Our goal is, as you say, identical for the long range objectives...."[8]

A common reaction of readers who first become aware of wealthy support provided to socialist, even Communist, movements is that the radicals must be *using* the capitalists. Carroll Quigley insists that the use is consensual:

> More than fifty years ago the Morgan firm decided to infiltrate the Left-wing political movements in the United States. This was relatively easy to do, since these groups were starved for funds and eager for a voice to reach the people. Wall Street supplied both. The purpose was not to destroy, dominate or take over but was really threefold: (1) to keep informed about the thinking of Left-wing or liberal groups; (2) to provide them with a mouthpiece so that they could "blow off steam," and (3) to have a final veto on their publicity, and possibly on their actions, if they ever went "radical." [9]

However, as revealing as Quigley's history is, he cannot be trusted to tell the whole story straight up. For example, his extensive history of the first half of the last century fails entirely to mention the Fabian Society.

The New Republic

Quigley even ignores Fabian influence in his account of "the best example of this alliance of Wall Street and Left-wing publication" — *The New Republic*. [10]

The New Republic was founded in 1914 by Morgan agent Willard Straight using money from his wife Dorothy [Payne Whitney] Straight's Standard Oil fortune. According to Quigley:

> The original purpose for establishing the paper was to provide an outlet for the progressive Left and to guide it quietly in the Anglophile direction. This latter task was entrusted to a young man, only four years out of Harvard, but already a member of the mysterious Round Table group.... This new recruit, Walter Lippmann, has been, from 1914 to the present [1966], *the authentic spokesman in American journalism for the Establishments on both sides of the Atlantic in international affairs....* [11] [Emphasis added.]

But Quigley neglects to mention that Walter Lippmann was also a clearly identifiable Fabian Socialist (see next).

The Straights pursued other designs for the international bankers. In 1919, Dorothy Straight helped found the (radical Marxist) New School for Social Research in New York City. The Rockefeller Foundation also supplied major funding. Emphasizing the strangeness of the alliance, the interior walls of the institution were decorated with portraits of Lenin, Stalin, and marching Soviet soldiers. [12]

The Lippmann Link

The career of Walter Lippmann provides compelling evidence of the link between Fabian Socialism and the American Establishment.

An especially bright young man, Walter Lippmann entered Harvard College in 1906 at age 17. As an undergraduate he was greatly influenced by the teachings of several radical professors, including especially Graham Wallas. Wallas, one of the founders of the Fabian Society in Britain, came to Harvard as a visiting professor during Lippmann's senior year.

As a result of the Wallas influence, Lippmann quickly became known on campus as the most brilliant and articulate socialist intellectual. When Lippmann returned to Harvard for post-graduate work, American Fabian Socialist Lincoln Stephens asked him to organize a chapter of the Fabian Intercollegiate Socialist Society, which Lippmann did with great success, while serving as the chapter's president.

Lippmann put together his own ideas on socialism in his first book, *A Preface to Politics*, published in 1913. *A Preface* provided the philosophical and practical guidelines for a serious plan to transform the United States into a socialist state through the "creative statesmanship" of a strong national executive. [13]

Lippmann's book brought him together with Herbert Croly, who was preparing to launch *The New Republic* in 1914. That same year, Lippmann's Fabian professor at Harvard, Graham Wallas, published *The Great Society*, which included a preface in the form of a dedicatory letter to Walter Lippmann. [14]

Decades later President Johnson would adopt the title of the Wallas book as the name for his domestic agenda. Interestingly, on his return from the Kennedy funeral, the newly sworn-in president would make an unscheduled 40-minute stop at the Georgetown home of Walter Lippmann. [15]

In *Philip Dru* (published in 1912), Colonel House had also advocated a transformation of America into a socialist state. We do not know when House and Lippmann first met, but by 1916, Lippmann, as an associate editor for *The New Republic*, was in regular contact with House.

The next year (1917), America entered World War I, and Colonel House decided to organize a secret Study Committee — later called The Inquiry — to draw up proposals for the post-war settlement. House chose his brother-in-law, Sidney Mezes, to head up the Committee and Walter Lippmann as the Committee's secretary to act as a liaison between himself and the Committee.

Mezes and Lippmann then staffed the Committee, drawing heavily on socialist academics. Among their selections were: James T. Shotwell of Columbia, Charles H. Haskins of Harvard, Charles Seymour of Yale, Stanley K. Hornbeck of the University of Wisconsin, Archibald Coolidge of Harvard, Isaiah Bowman of Johns Hopkins, and Norman Thomas (later head of the American Socialist Party). [16]

Part of the Committee's work, specifically Lippmann's, included drafting Wilson's famous Fourteen Points. But Wilson's proposal was actually taken point by point from a Fabian publication, *Labour's War Aims*, written by Fabian Sidney Webb. [17] Similarly, when Colonel House drafted the American version of a "convention" for the League of Nations, he drew heavily on another Fabian document, *International Government*, written by Leonard Woolf. [18]

In 1919, Lippmann remained with House in Paris for the meetings with fellow British internationalists that led to the creation of the Council on Foreign Relations. Lippmann would be welcome as an official member of the CFR, from its founding until three years before his death in 1971.

However, Quigley tells us (see above) that by the time of the CFR's founding, Lippmann was already a member of the elite American Round Table group, one notch up in the Insider hierarchy.

When the Intercollegiate Socialist Society (I.S.S.) became the League for Industrial Democracy (L.I.D.) to escape the "socialist" label, it drew its new name from the title of Fabian leader Sidney Webb's socialist treatise, *Industrial Democracy*." [19] Among the founders of the renamed I.S.S. was Walter Lippmann.

The Fabians have made strong inroads into several areas of American life. We will focus on two — health care and education.

Americans for Democratic Action

In 1941, eight months before the Japanese attack on Pearl Harbor, American socialists decided to form a political action arm. According to Edward R. Annis, past president of the AMA who fought Fabian efforts to control health care during the Kennedy administration:

> The Union for Democratic Action (UDA), named after a similar Fabian "permeation" group in London, was formed in 1941 by members of the Socialist party, including prominent party leader Alfred B. Lewis, and members of the [League for Industrial Democracy].... The primary focus of the organization was to pressure Congress and the administration to assure the security of the Soviet Union. [20]

However, the Union attracted a strong core of Communists and soon became identified as a Communist front. So in 1947, the Union decided to change *its* name. (Note: there were *two* founding PR meetings — one on January 3 and the other on March 30.) According to Dr. Annis:

> [T]he Union for Democratic Action underwent an incredible metamorphosis. Not only would the group be anticommunist, it would no longer be recognizable as socialist. This sudden feat was not accomplished through any mind alterations on the part of the membership, but through a name change, or more descriptively, through a rebirth. The old organization would be dissolved overnight and a new organization formed, retaining the same membership, but called Americans for Democratic Action.
>
> A special meeting was called to reorganize the Union for Democratic Action on January 3, 1947, and the following day labor leader Walter Reuther of the United Auto Workers met

with a small group to prepare a policy statement for the reborn organization. [21]

Readers may well recall Walter Reuther as the tyrannical labor boss, but Reuther's lengthy background in the socialist movement is likely less familiar. Along with Walter Lippmann, Reuther was an early chapter leader for the I.S.S. — Lippmann at Harvard, Walter Reuther at Wayne University.

Also among the ADA's founding members was Harvard history professor Arthur Schlesinger Jr. (no Ph.D.), who had been invited into the Council on Foreign Relations the year before. Schlesinger would serve as the ADA's national chairman from 1953 to 1954. (Illustrating, the phony nature of the conflict between Wall Street and organized labor, Reuther would be accepted into the CFR in 1966.)

Joining Reuther and Schlesinger in "founding" the ADA were Eleanor Roosevelt, Chester Bowles (future CFR), Schlesinger's longtime friend and Keynesian economist John Kenneth Galbraith (CFR), and Minneapolis Mayor (and future senator and vice president) Hubert Humphrey (future CFR). Also notable among the ADA founders were several prominent journalists, such as Stewart and Joseph Alsop (Joseph: future CFR) and Marquis Childs (CFR).

In 1949, Humphrey was elected national chairman of the ADA (1949–1950), in which role he toured the country speaking on the ADA's behalf and raising money. For two decades, Humphrey was one of the ADA's most active members.

In the words of Chester Bowles, the ADA set out "to establish liberal control of the Democratic party." [22] The Establishment was quite supportive of the ADA and its socialist agenda. Among the ADA founders was Herbert H. Lehman (CFR 1922–1963), a son of one of the three founders of the Lehman Brothers international banking firm (a satellite of the European Rothschilds) and a close associate of Colonel House.

Nationalization of Health Care
In the presidential election of 1948, most experts had written off Harry Truman. But the Americans for Democratic Action coordinated the efforts of local AFL and CIO unions on Truman's behalf, organized college campuses through Students for Democratic

Action, and ADA volunteers worked the precincts.

Not only was Truman victorious, but that same year 79 representatives endorsed by the ADA were elected to the U.S. Congress "and nine new House members were actually ADA members.... The big prize for the ADA was the election of Hubert Humphrey to the U.S. Senate." [23]

President Truman was beholden to the ADA. According to Annis:

> Surely it was no coincidence that Truman would address Congress with an eleven-item wish list, and that eight of those items would appear on the platform adopted at the ADA annual convention. And surely it was no coincidence that the most sweeping proposal on that wish list and on the ADA platform was a renewed call for socialized medicine through national health insurance, and that the same proposal had first appeared two decades before on the platform of the Socialist party of America. [24]

Although the American people were not yet ready to accept such unconstitutional federal usurpation of power, the Fabian turtle kept marching on.

The next major effort toward socialized medicine came with the election of President Kennedy in 1960. The ADA members of the Kennedy administration could count on a substantial number of allies in Congress and the organizing efforts of Walter Reuther. In his painstakingly compiled *Biographical Dictionary of the Left*, Francis X. Gannon, Ph.D. profiled Reuther as follows:

> [Reuther] is today the virtual boss of the Democratic Party on federal and state levels. He has spent millions of dollars of union funds either to elect or defeat candidates for governorships, mayoralties, state legislatures, the Congress of the United States, and the Presidency. In blunt terms, Walter Reuther has the Democrats in his back pocket along with the leftwing of the Republican party. [25]

In 1962, Reuther applied his tremendous influence and organizational talent on behalf of socialized medicine. Union organizers planned five thousand speeches nationwide to create an atmosphere of crisis, leading up to a nationally televised speech by President John F. Kennedy on May 20 from Madison Square Garden. [26]

A turning point in the socialist drive, came when Dr. Annis delivered the physician's rebuttal in a televised talk, also from Madison Square Garden, to an audience estimated at 30 million Americans. The public responded with some 42,000 letters to Congress and King-Anderson (Medicare) was dead — for the moment. [27]

However, in the wake of the Kennedy assassination, the bill's socialist proponents and President Johnson seized upon the natural sympathy for the slain president to identify Medicare as Kennedy's wish and push it into law. Dr. Annis, later concluded:

> The Socialist party of America, where the plan for national health insurance was hatched, never garnered more than 6 percent of the popular vote for its specious programs. But through the cunning of the Americans for Democratic Action, aided by an assassin's bullet, King-Anderson became the law of the land known as Medicare. [28]

But Medicare was only the foot in the door for the socialists. President Clinton *attempted* to enlarge the program (see HillaryCare in Chapter 11), while Clinton's successor, "conservative" George W. Bush, was able to sneak through a significant expansion. Of course, the next *major political battle* in the socialist drive to control health care was launched by President Obama (see Chapter 15).

However, these political highlights ignore the essential day-to-day groundwork of Left-wing organizations, with Establishment media support, to propagandize the public regarding our health care "crisis." Indeed, almost a century ago, Walter Lippmann argued that a successful "socialist" plan of action must seek to indoctrinate the masses.

"Permeation" of Education
In her classic 1966 study of Fabian influence in America, Rose Martin emphasizes that Fabian strategists seek to reach every segment of

modern society, from pre-school children to senior citizens.

Martin further explains that the Fabian strategy for doing so "calls for permeation of the colleges, universities, and religious seminaries by Fabian Socialist-oriented educators and administrators, as well as the introduction of uniform 'standards' and 'guidelines' into federally financed educational systems. For total effect, it requires total control of communications and entertainment media...." [29]

British Fabian Socialist John Atkinson Hobson extolled the value of the university professor as a strategic weapon in socialist revolution. Mrs. Martin records the strategy's impact in this country:

> All across the continent at the turn of the century, little clusters of college professors had begun studying socialism in secret, because an open avowal of such interest might have led to their dismissal. Recalling his youth as an instructor at the University of California, Dr. Harry [Allen] Overstreet — long a professor of Philosophy at City College of New York and sponsor of many Socialist causes — said: "We were studying Socialism and didn't want anyone to know we were doing it." [30]

Martin examined the impact of several prominent professors and concluded: "The professor is still the main channel through which the Fabian Socialist outlook percolates to society at large." [31]

European socialists and utopians had long viewed government education as the means to transform society. Intellectual agitation for "socializing" education in America actually began in the early part of the 19th Century, predating the Fabian Society by several decades. In the early 20th Century, the Fabians and the Establishment would co-opt, finance, and offer organizational direction to the movements these intellectuals had spawned.

Dewey and Progressive Education

At the opening of the Twentieth Century, the most prominent of the new educational philosophers was John Dewey (1859–1952), who earned the title "father of progressive education." Dewey would also embrace the Fabians, becoming vice president of the Fabian's League for Industrial Democracy in the Thirties and its president in 1941.

Dewey played a major role in shaping progressive education in the

United States and building an education establishment. "Progressive education" may sound benign, but its basic tenets included: a faith in the Darwinian concept of man; "a belief that children could be taught very much like animals in accordance with the new behavioral psychology; [and] a conviction that there was no place for religion in education and that traditional values were an obstacle to social programs which had to be removed." [32]

In 1919, Dewey helped launch the Fabian Socialist New School for Social Research (see above), whose first president was Alvin Johnson, an early editor of *The New Republic*. The New School would offer Dewey a venue for testing out his theories. Other Fabian Socialist intellectuals who taught future professors there included Graham Wallas and Harold Laski. Professor Harry Overstreet of City College, mentioned earlier, taught in the continuing education program of the New School.

In 1928, Dewey made a trip to Soviet Union (he was vice president of the American Society for Cultural Relations with Russia). [33] In a survey of the Soviet educational system for *The New Republic* that year, Dewey applauded the Soviet design because it served "to create habits so that persons will act cooperatively and collectively as readily as now in capitalistic countries they act 'individualistically.'"

In 1904, Dewey acquired a professorship at the University of Columbia. Its affiliated Teachers College became his primary professional identification until his death in 1952. His influence there would be immense. In his 1954 *A History of Teachers College*, Establishment historian Lawrence A. Cremin wrote:

> With one hundred thousand alumni, Teachers College has managed to seat about one-third of the presidents and deans now in office at accredited U.S. teacher training schools. Its graduates make up about twenty percent of all our public school teachers. Over a fourth of the superintendents of schools in the one hundred and sixty-eight U.S. cities with at least fifty thousand population are Teachers College-trained.

During the 1920s and 30s, the progressives were working to transform the public school curriculum. At a meeting of the American Political Science Association in 1931, University of

Chicago's Charles Judd announced that the organized educational profession was promoting "a movement to bring to full realization the project of socializing the whole body of instructional material in schools and colleges."

The following year, John Dewey, Charles Judd, and other progressives gathered at a National Education Association (NEA) meeting in Washington, D.C. A reporter covering the meeting wrote: "Here, in the very citadel of capitalism ... this group of outstanding spokesmen of American education talked a remarkably strong brand of socialism." [34]

In 1929, the American Historical Association sponsored a five-year investigation into how social studies should be taught, aided by a $340,000 grant from the Carnegie Foundation. In its 1934 report, the Commission on the Social Studies in the Schools stated:

[T]wo social philosophies are now struggling for supremacy: individualism, with its attending capitalism and classism, and collectivism, with planned economy and mass rights. Believing that present trends indicate the victory of the latter the Commission on the Social Studies offers a comprehensive blueprint by which education may prepare to meet the demands of a collectivist social order without submerging the individual as a helpless victim of bureaucratic control. [35]

Fabian Socialist Harold Laski candidly assessed the AHA/Carnegie effort: "At bottom, and stripped of its carefully neutral phrases," this project was "an educational program for a socialist America." [36]

Indeed, Establishment foundations were working hand in glove with the Fabians and progressives to turn education to their purposes. René Wormser, who acted as general counsel to the Reese Committee investigating the Foundations, observed:

Research and experimental stations were established at selected universities, notably Columbia, Stanford, and Chicago. Here some of the worst mischief in recent education was born. In these Rockefeller-and-Carnegie-established vineyards worked many of the principal characters in the story of the suborning of

American education. Here foundations nurtured some of the most ardent academic advocates of upsetting the American system and supplanting it with a Socialist state. [37]

Nationalizing Education

The socialists and Insiders have followed the Fabian strategy of patient gradualism to achieve federal control over teachers and the curriculum. A major steppingstone along that path has been to establish federal standards for teachers and teaching that would bind the states.

In 1986, the Carnegie Corporation released its report, "A Nation Prepared: Teachers in the 21st Century." One of the proposals in the plan was to create a *private* "National Board for Professional Teaching Standards," which would work with the NEA and AFT (American Federation of Teachers) to certify elementary and secondary school teachers.

When President Bush (Sr.) promoted his "Equity and Excellence in Education Act of 1990," the bill included federal funding for the Carnegie-created Board. The measure (S. 695) passed the Senate by a vote of 92 to 8, but was never reconciled with the House-passed version.

In 2001, a top item on the domestic agenda of newly elected Republican President George W. Bush's was expansion of federal aid to education. His proposal, the "No Child Left Behind Act" enjoyed huge bipartisan support in the House and Senate (see next chapter). Republican John Boehner was chairman of the critical House Education and Workforce Committee working with leftist Democrat George Miller to pass the bill.

It is well to realize that both neocons and Fabian Socialists support federal control of education. And so does Newt Gingrich, John Boehner's mentor, and Arne Duncan, President Obama's secretary of education.

Although the internationalists need crises to make sudden leaps in their agenda, steady, seemingly uncoordinated, pressure from hundreds of directions without any perceived real opposition can accomplish the same result. In the space above, we have provided only a few of the highlights in the ongoing battle for federal control of education.

Part V

The Executive Branch in the 21ˢᵗ Century

Chapter 14

CFR Dominance:
George W. Bush Administrations
(2001–2009)

Road to the White House

George W. Bush sought to follow in his father's footsteps, but lacking his father's intellect and drive, he required a lot of help. George was an average student at Phillips Academy in Andover, Massachusetts, the same prep school his father had attended. He likely got into Yale only because of his father's connections.

Academics was not George's strong suit and the young Bush gathered a reputation as a partying jock with an alcohol problem. With mediocre grades at Yale, George would be denied admission to the University of Texas Law School. In his senior year at Yale, George, like his father, was accepted into Yale's secret "Skull and Bones" society. George was given the code name "Temporary."

Following graduation from Yale in 1968, the young Bush joined the Texas Air National Guard and served his two years of active duty, leaving the Guard as a first lieutenant. George obtained an early release from the Guard to attend Harvard Business School, from which he earned an MBA in 1975. Returning to Texas George W. Bush followed his father's example and pursued a career in the oil business.

In 1978, George contested for an open seat in the House of Representatives and lost. During the campaign his father's strong Establishment connections had become an albatross the younger Bush could not overcome, despite his likeable personality.

After his defeat, George decided against another try while his father held national office. Instead, in 1988, he moved his family briefly to Washington, D.C. to work on his father's successful campaign for the presidency. When Bill Clinton made the elder Bush a one-term president, it opened the way for George W. to enter the 1994 Texas gubernatorial race. George won the governor's seat in his first try, against an incumbent governor, and was re-elected in

1998 by a whopping 69 percent of the popular vote, becoming the first Texas governor to win back-to-back terms.

In June 1999, while governor of Texas, George Bush declared his candidacy for president. Candidate Bush would cultivate the image of a "compassionate conservative" while relying heavily on the connections of his father to create a credible candidate and run the administration should he gain office. Indeed, it is difficult to think of any president who was more of a figurehead in his administration than George W. Bush.

The "Vulcans"

Just before Christmas of 1999, the *New York Times* drew attention to a team of "familiar foreign policy experts" who were helping George W. develop and articulate foreign policy positions for his campaign.[1] The *Times* described the group as "eight hawkish advisers with broad foreign policy experience under President Ronald Reagan or Mr. Bush's father, President George Bush."

The eight-person team was led by Condoleezza Rice, "a Russia specialist in President Bush's National Security Council, and Paul D. Wolfowitz, a senior Pentagon official in the Bush administration...." Rice would name the team, the "Vulcans."

The other six members of the team were:

- Richard L. Armitage, an assistant secretary of defense under Reagan-Bush;
- Robert D. Blackwill, a National Security Council specialist under Bush;
- Stephen J. Hadley, an assistant secretary of defense under Bush;
- Richard Perle, as assistant secretary of defense under Reagan-Bush;
- Dov S. Zakheim, a deputy under secretary of defense under Reagan-Bush;
- Robert B. Zoellick, under secretary of state under Bush.

The *Times* also identified George P. Shultz (Reagan's secretary of state) and Richard B. Cheney (President Bush's secretary of defense) as "two unofficial senior advisors."

The team of advisors and the sympathetic reporter all took pains to make it appear as though candidate Bush was still the leader, coming with "a set of broad foreign policy principles and priorities." The reporter nevertheless acknowledged: "Unlike his father or President Clinton, Mr. Bush is not likely to immerse himself in the arcana of policy, leaving more running room for his advisers."

Of the 10 names mentioned by the *Times*, all but Armitage were members of the CFR. And all but the 80-year old Shultz would take leadership positions in the new Bush administration (Hadley not until Bush's second term).

Candidate Bush was fortunate that the topic of the team's ties to the Establishment's Council on Foreign Relations was taboo for the press. And his Democratic opponents, Al Gore and Joe Lieberman, certainly were not going to make an issue of it, since Joe Lieberman was a CFR member.

Indeed, as vice president, Dick Cheney would joke about voter sensitivity to the issue at a February 15, 2002 meeting at the Council's headquarters. Cheney introduced his televised remarks with these words, drawing knowing chuckles from his "sophisticated" audience:

> It's good to be back at the Council on Foreign Relations. I've been a member for a long time, and was actually a director for some period of time. I never mentioned that when I was campaigning for reelection back home in Wyoming....

Although the elder Bush stayed in the background, reportedly to give his son independence, other reports claim that the father conferred daily with his son and other administration leaders.

CFR Staffing

When George W. Bush took office, he already had several members of his new team picked out. Notable appointments from the Pratt-House roster included:

- Colin L. Powell, as secretary of state.
- Condoleezza Rice, as national security advisor. (Rice would become secretary of state at the start of George Bush's second term.)

- John D. Negroponte, as U.S. representative to the United Nations.
- Robert B. Zoellick, as U.S. trade representative.
- John Robert Bolton, as under secretary of state for arms control and international security.
- Paula J. Dobriansky, as under secretary of state for global affairs.
- George J. Tenet for CIA director.
- Donald Rumsfeld, as secretary of defense.
- Paul D. Wolfowitz, as the deputy secretary of defense. (Note: Wolfowitz would later head up the internationalists' World Bank.)
- Peter W. Rodman, as assistant secretary of defense.
- Henry H. Shelton, as chairman of the Joint Chiefs of Staff.
- Anne O. Krueger, as a member of the Council of Economic Advisers.
- Kenneth W. Dam, as deputy secretary of the treasury.
- Elaine Chao, as secretary of labor.
- Christine Todd Whitman, as EPA administrator.
- I. Lewis "Scooter" Libby, as chief of staff for the vice president.
- Ann Veneman, as secretary of agriculture. After four years in this position, Veneman would become the fifth executive director of UNICEF.

And, of course, there was Vice President Dick Cheney. Several close observers reasoned that Cheney was the real power in the Bush White House.

Both outgoing Vice President Al Gore and incoming Vice President Dick Cheney shared spots as emeritus members of the Aspen Institute's Strategy Group. Perhaps, there was something else Cheney was not telling voters.

One Bush appointment particularly highlights George W.'s ties to the Establishment: Richard N. Haas was selected as the director of policy planning for the State Department. In that position, Haas would serve as a close adviser to Secretary of State Colin Powell. Since July 2003, Haas has been *president* of the Council on Foreign Relations.

And in May of 2004, President George W. Bush would continue the string of presidential rubber stamps for Alan Greenspan as chairman of the Fed. Greenspan, you may recall, was a director of the CFR from 1982 to 1988 and a Trilateralist.

Advancing Insider Objectives

The George W. Bush administration continued along the same Establishment course as did Bill Clinton's, although President Bush postured quite differently in order to appeal to a conservative core constituency. To preserve his "conservative" image, Bush would appear to slow down the Establishment's radical agenda in a few areas, such as the environment, but in several others, such as education, Bush actually picked up the pace.

• **Regionalism.** Right out of the starting blocks of his presidency, George Bush embraced the Insiders' regionalism strategy for undermining the sovereignty of nations, using the promise of greater prosperity through free trade as the bait. A scant three months after his inauguration, in April of 2001, President Bush attended the Quebec Summit of the Americas.

The national "representatives" at the Quebec Summit were pushing for a "Free Trade Area of the Americas" (FTAA), an expansion of NAFTA to include the entire hemisphere. Ostensibly, a Bill Clinton initiative, the real engine behind the FTAA was David Rockefeller (see Chapter 7).

President Bush was principally a figurehead in Quebec. Accompanying him were Secretary of State Colin Powell and U.S. Trade Representative Robert Zoellick — both CFR members. Addressing the conference in Quebec on April 21 Bush stated: "We know from NAFTA that open trade works.... The time has come to extend the benefits of free trade to all our peoples and to achieve a free trade agreement for the entire hemisphere."

Picking up the timeline established by his predecessor, President Bush pledged to work toward completing negotiations by 2005. That bit of optimism proved unwarranted, but the Bush administration did make significant advances toward that objective. In particular, it negotiated the Central American Free Trade Agreement and pushed CAFTA through Congress (see Chapter 7). The administration argued that CAFTA was a useful steppingstone to a hemispheric agreement.

Two months following the Quebec Summit, President Bush attended an EU-U.S. Summit in Goteborg Sweden, where he also supported the internationalist agenda. On June 14, 2001 he stated:

I strongly believe in NATO expansion, and I believe that the EU ought to expand, as well.... I don't view the European Union and its consolidation as a zero-sum game for the United States. I believe the stronger Europe is, the better it is off for America.... I am concerned about isolationism and protectionism, not only amongst some voices in Europe, but also in my own country.... And so I view a strong EU as good for the world....

Whoever had prepared President Bush's speech took the opportunity to whip a dead horse — the bogeyman of isolationism — an ongoing Insider campaign of intimidation to ensure that no force would dare challenge the internationalist agenda.

• **North American integration.** President Bush also took early steps to promote North American integration and increase U.S. aid to Mexico. On September 6, 2001, just five days before the terrorist attacks on the world trade towers, President Bush met with Mexican President Vicente Fox. At the conclusion of their meeting they announced the "Partnership for Prosperity." President Bush pledged his commitment to a more expansive immigration policy that would "match a willing [U.S.] employer with a willing [Mexican] employee."

Much to the consternation of many in his party, on January 4, 2004 President Bush proposed legislation that would provide "legal status, as temporary workers, to the millions of undocumented men and women now employed in the United States, and to those in foreign countries who seek to participate in the program and have been offered employment here."

Many Americans in areas hard hit by uncontrolled *illegal* immigration strongly opposed any further "amnesty," recognizing that past amnesties had fueled additional illegal immigration. The Bush administration would strongly insist that its proposal was not "amnesty," but you be the judge.

With heightened national security concerns following the September 11, 2001 terrorist attacks, an obvious step should have been to tighten security at our southern border. But that didn't fit the internationalist agenda.

Instead, the January/February 2004 issue of *Foreign Affairs* introduced the concept of a "continental security perimeter." In "North America's Second Decade," Robert A. Pastor (CFR) advocated "an alternative course" to enforcing our national borders, in which "security fears would serve as a catalyst for deeper integration." Progress along Pastor's course would require "true leadership, new cooperative institutions, and a redefinition of security that puts the United States, Mexico, and Canada inside a continental perimeter, working together as partners."

Subsequently, the Council on Foreign Relations would sponsor a three-nation "Independent Task Force on the Future of North America." Among the American members of the Task Force were Robert Pastor (CFR), Carla A. Hills (CFR director and later co-chair of CFR), James R. Jones (CFR), Gary C. Hufbauer (CFR and CFR VP 1997-98), and Jeffery J. Schott. Hufbauer and Schott had authored a 1994 report of the Institute for International Economics (a CFR-aligned think tank) that proposed a Western Hemisphere Free Trade Area (a precursor name to the FTAA) following the pattern of the European Union.

In May 2005, the CFR's Independent Task Force issued its report, "Building a North American Community," which included a proposal for a North American Security Perimeter. On June 9, Task Force co-chair Robert Pastor appeared before a subcommittee of the Senate Foreign Relations Committee to present the plan.

Following Pastor's testimony, CNN anchorman Lou Dobbs and CNN correspondent Christine Romans informed their viewers of the incredible scope of the game plan underway:

Romans: "The idea here is to make North America more like the European Union...."

Dobbs: "Americans must think that our political and academic elites have gone utterly mad at a time when three-and-a-half years, approaching four years after September 11, we still don't have border security. And this group of elites is talking about not defending our borders, finally, but rather creating new ones. It's astonishing."

A few months earlier, on March 23, 2005, President Bush held a special summit in Waco, Texas with Mexican President Vicente Fox and Canadian Prime Minister Paul Martin. At Baylor University, the three heads of state called for a "Security and Prosperity Partnership of North America." Cabinet officials for the three nations were given 90 days to form a variety of working groups to come up with concrete proposals for implementing the Partnership.

The cabinet ministers issued their joint report, which paralleled the CFR proposal, on June 27, 2005. One month later to the day, U.S. Assistant Secretary of State for Western Hemisphere Affairs Roger F. Noriega testified before a House subcommittee, revealing what had been transpiring without congressional oversight: "Thus far, we have identified over 300 initiatives spread over twenty trilateral [meaning U.S., Canada, and Mexico] working groups on which the three countries will collaborate."

• **The national debt.** On February 27, 2001, with only a month in office, President Bush addressed a joint session of Congress. His remarks made clear that, like his predecessors, he would not recognize the Constitution as the established authority over what the federal government could do.

"Government has a role, and an important one," said the president. "Our new governing vision says government should be active, but limited; engaged, but not overbearing. And my budget is based on that philosophy."

At the same time, President Bush stepped up his effort to sound like a determined conservative:

Many of you have talked about the need to pay down our national debt. I listened, and I agree. We owe it to our children and grandchildren to act now, and I hope you will join me to pay down $2 trillion in debt during the next 10 years. At the end of those 10 years, we will have paid down all the debt that is available to retire. That is more debt, repaid more quickly than has ever been repaid by any nation at any time in history.

However, in an earlier February 22nd press conference, Bush explained that his budget would only slow down the rate of growth of government: "This is a town where if you don't increase the budget by an expected number, it's considered a cut." Bush's budget proposal, entitled "A Blueprint for New Beginnings," called for a spending increase of 5.7 percent. [2]

The president's budget did *project* a $2 trillion pay-down over 10 years in that portion of the national debt *held by the public*. The projection for the gross national debt over the same period showed an increase of $1.5 trillion.

Bush did get Congress to pass a tax-cut, a fiscally responsible measure. But without reductions in federal spending there would be no reduction in the burden of government on the taxpayer as a consumer. Government deficits would be financed through monetary inflation, ultimately falling on the private sector.

• **Federal aid to education.** In his Fiscal 2002 budget proposal, President Bush called for expanding the budget authority of the unconstitutional Department of Education by a whopping 11.5 percent. (This increase followed an estimated 35.7 percent increase in 2001.) The Bush proposal, when enacted with "bipartisan" support from Ted Kennedy and George Miller, became known as the "No Child Left Behind Act of 2001."

At the signing of the Act on January 8 of 2002, President Bush would boast:

> [W]e're going to spend more money, more resources [for education], but they'll be directed at methods that work. Not feel-good methods, not sound-good methods, but methods that actually work.... We're going to spend more on our schools, and were going to spend it more wisely.

Joining President Bush at the signing ceremony was Senator Ted Kennedy. Bush would refer to the ultra-liberal as a "fabulous United States senator." Later in the day, in Kennedy's home state, President Bush acknowledged the senator's help in enacting the legislation: "[A]s a result of his hard work, we put together a good piece of legislation that has put Republicans and Democrats on the side of the schoolchildren in America."

A month later, President Bush submitted his budget for Fiscal 2003. The new budget asked for $56.5 billion for the Education

Department — a 12.7 percent increase.

• **Medicare expansion.** President Bush also contributed greatly to the expansion of federal entitlement programs that would threaten to break the bank a decade later. In his February 27, 2001 address to Congress, the newly elected president boasted:

> To meet the health care needs of all America's seniors, we double the Medicare budget over the next 10 years. My budget dedicates $238 billion to Medicare next year alone, enough to fund all current programs and to begin a new prescription drug benefit for low-income seniors....
>
> Many working Americans do not have health care coverage, so we will help them buy their own insurance with refundable tax credits. And to provide quality care in low-income neighborhoods, over the next five years we will double the number of people served at community health care centers.

A few months later, President Bush called for expanding Medicare's coverage:

> Second, all seniors today and tomorrow will be offered a range of new Medicare plans, including an improved and updated Government plan, as well as others offered by nongovernment insurance plans. All the Medicare plans must offer benefits at least as comprehensive as the Government plan. All will be regulated by the Federal Government, and all of them must offer prescription drug coverage.[3]

Amazing what a president can get away with when the Establishment media and attacks from the far Left bolster his reputation as a conservative!

• **"Saving the planet."** The Bush administration balked at signing the Kyoto protocol on global warming, terming it "a flawed treaty." A few similar announcements in opposition to the most radical demands of the environmental lobby and Bush would become a useful target of the Left and earn him points with his conservative constituency.

Indeed, Carol Browner, the EPA chief under Clinton, would refer to the Bush administration as the "worst environmental administration ever."[4]

However, the Bush administration was far from the enemy of the environmentalist agenda that President Bush's opponents painted. In his June 11, 2001 speech announcing his opposition to Kyoto, President Bush stated: "America's unwillingness to embrace a flawed treaty should not be read by our friends and allies as any abdication of responsibility. To the contrary, my administration is committed to a leadership role on the issue of climate change."

Thus, the President effectively accepted Al Gore's radical premise that the world was facing serious global warming due to the industrial release of carbon dioxide — a diabolical pretext for government regulation of industry. And President Bush supported the strategy of an international agreement to help drive the power grab:

> [C]limate change, with its potential to impact every corner of the world, is an issue that must be addressed by the world.... That is why I am today committing the United States of America to work within the United Nations framework and elsewhere to develop with our friends and allies and nations throughout the world an effective and science-based response to the issue of global warming.

Embracing the environmentalist agenda at home, in early 2002 President Bush proposed new "cap and trade" legislation (the "Clear Skies Initiative"), boasting: "This legislation will constitute the most significant step America has ever taken — has ever taken — to cut power plant emissions...."[5]

As a final example, on April 19, 2001 President Bush announced his intention to sign the UN's Persistent Organic Pollutants (POP) treaty, enthusiastically endorsed by the radical environmental lobby. In doing so, he proclaimed: "And now, a Republican administration will continue and complete the work of a Democratic administration. This is the way environmental policy should work."

Nonsense. The POP treaty would further restrict the use of 12 ostensibly dangerous chemicals, the so-called "Dirty Dozen." According to Bush, "this agreement addresses a global environmental problem. These chemicals respect no boundaries and can harm Americans even when released abroad." However, among the 12 are important pesticides, such as DDT, which had been responsible for virtually eliminating malaria.

Amazingly, even the Establishment's *New York Times* allowed a bit of sanity on the DDT ban to grace its editorial pages. In a column entitled "What the World Needs Now is DDT," editorial writer Tina Rosenberg argued:

> Yet, what really merits outrage about DDT is not that South Africa still uses it, as do about five other countries for routine malaria control and about ten more for emergencies. It is that dozens more do not. Malaria is a disease Westerners no longer have to think about. Independent malariologists believe it kills two million people a year, mainly children under 5 and 90 percent of them in Africa.... Yet DDT, the very insecticide that eradicated malaria in developed nations, has been essentially deactivated as a malaria-control tool today. [6]

When a full loaf of the Left's radical agenda was politically unattainable, the Bush administration worked to implement a half loaf. The anti-Bush attacks from the environmental lobby provided cover for the administration to implement strategic areas of the agenda, while preserving its conservative posture.

• **Homeland security.** Although the September 11th terrorist attacks caught the nation by surprise, the Council on Foreign Relations was ready with a list of solutions, which were embraced by the Bush administration.

As explained in Chapter 8, instead of restoring America's independent layers of security, the Bush administration reacted by concentrating authority in a new and potentially dangerous Department of Homeland Security.

The other significant internal reaction was congressional authorization for greatly expanded federal surveillance of the public, known as the Patriot Act of 2001, and for airport searches of traveling civilians. But border security remained as porous as ever.

To demonstrate its support for national security, Congress allowed the Patriot Act to be stampeded into law. The House passed the Patriot Act on October 24, the Senate the following day, and President Bush signed the measure into law on the 26th. Representative Ron Paul (R-Texas), only one of three Republicans in the House to vote against the Patriot Act, complained:

> It's my understanding the bill wasn't printed before the vote — at least I couldn't get it. They played all kinds of games, kept the House in session all night, and it was a very complicated bill. Maybe a handful of staffers actually read it, but the bill definitely was not available to members before the vote.[7]

In order to allay public concerns and win congressional support, the Patriot Act included sunset provisions so that the government powers would expire unless renewed by Congress. But Congress has regularly renewed the provisions.

• **UN Resolution 1373.** In its reaction to the 9/11 terrorist attacks, the Bush administration championed the authority of the terrorist-friendly United Nations.

On September 28, 2001, the UN Security Council adopted Resolution 1373. Resolution 1373 set requirements for member states to follow in combating terrorism, and it set up the "Counter-Terrorism Committee" (CTC) to "monitor implementation of this resolution." The United States and other UN members were now required to submit regular compliance reports to the CTC.

The first U.S. report, dated December 19, 2001, referred to the USA Patriot Act and several other Bush administration actions as compliance with UN demands in Resolution 1373. The CTC response to the U.S. report was to demand more information about U.S. domestic policies by June 15th. On its long list of inquiries were the following:

> What measures does the United States have to prevent terrorists [from] obtaining weapons in its territory, in particular small arms or light weapons? What is the United States

legislation concerning the acquisition and possession of such weapons?...

Are there agencies and procedures at the local level for monitoring sensitive activities, such as combat sports and shooting with light weapons, paramilitary training, the piloting of aircraft, biological laboratories, and the use of explosives for industrial purposes?

And, of course, the Bush administration complied with the request. In an earlier November 10th address to the UN General Assembly President Bush committed his support to 1373:

The most basic obligations in this new conflict have already been defined by the United Nations.... We have a responsibility to share intelligence and coordinate the efforts of law enforcement.... We have a responsibility to deny weapons to terrorists and to actively prevent private citizens from providing them.... [T]his struggle is a defining moment for the United Nations, itself. And the world needs its principled leadership.

Principled leadership? Within weeks following 9/11, the UN General Assembly voted overwhelmingly to give Syria a two-year seat on the Security Council. In 2002, the year following 9/11, the UN placed Qadaffi's Libya on its Human Rights Commission.

• **Global war on terror.** Of course, the U.S. response to the 9/11 attacks that garnered world attention was the launching of a global war on terror. The Bush administration ordered an immediate invasion of Afghanistan and an invasion of Iraq in 2003.

America thus began a no-win war on terrorism that would embroil our troops in the Middle East and enhance the authority of the UN. We call the war "no-win" for several reasons, including:

— The ultimate state sponsor of terrorism — the former Soviet Union (as shown in Chapter 8) — was left off the hook;

— The nest of terrorist regimes (and terrorist organizations), known as the United Nations, was given ultimate authority over the operation; and

— An ongoing terrorist threat serves internationalist plans to build the UN's authority through UN-approved or UN–conducted "peacekeeping" operations.

• **2005 (UN) World Summit**. In mid-September 2005, the United Nations convened a summit meeting of world leaders, a follow-up to the 2000 Millennium Summit. At the end of the summit, representatives of the 191 member states, including the U.S., signed the "World Summit Outcomes" document. The document stipulates:

> We endorse the creation of an initial operating capability for a standing police capacity to provide coherent, effective and responsible start-up capability for the policing component of the United Nations peacekeeping missions and to assist existing missions through the provision of advice and expertise.

The Outcomes document also appears to open the door for "independent" financing of a UN standing army or rapid reaction force. Specifically, the document commits the UN to establishing a Peacebuilding Commission that would invite representatives of the World Bank and International Monetary Fund to attend its meetings.

The CFR hand can be seen in the entire affair. On June 15, 2005, a few months before the summit, the U.S. Congressional Task Force on the United Nations released its report, "American Interests and UN Reform. The co-chairs of the Task Force, Newt Gingrich and George Mitchell, were both members of the CFR, as were many of the Task Force members and supporting experts.

The Task Force recommended that "member-states must substantially increase the availability of capable, designated forces, properly trained and equipped, for rapid deployment to [UN] peace operations...." [8] Not surprisingly, the UN Outcomes document mirrored this and many of the Task Force recommendations.

As an illustration of internationalist coordination, a year earlier the Bush administration had launched the Global Peace Operations Initiative to train 75,000 foreign military personnel in peacekeeping operations (see Chapter 6). That program would be carried forward by the Barak Obama administration.

Chapter 15

CFR Dominance:
Barak Obama Administration
(2009+)

Road to White House

Following graduation from Columbia University in 1983, Barak Obama went to work for the Business International Corporation (1 year) and then the New York Public Interest Research Group, "a student-directed research and advocacy organization." He subsequently moved to Chicago to take a job as the director of the Developing Communities Project.

Obama entered Harvard Law School in 1988, graduating *magna cum laude*. While at Harvard he served as president of the *Harvard Law Review*. Following law school, Obama returned to Chicago, where he worked concurrently as a civil rights attorney and as a professor at the University of Chicago Law School.

Obama served three terms in the Illinois Senate, from 1997 to 2004. In 2000, he tried unsuccessfully for a seat in the U.S. House of Representatives. Two years later he began preparing for a run at the U.S. Senate.

In 2004, the contest for a U.S. Senate seat from Illinois was wide open in both primaries. Obama started out as a decided underdog. That changed when environmental groups (such as the Sierra Club and the League of Conservation Voters) endorsed and invested in Obama. [1] With that boost, he was able to achieve a landslide victory in the Democratic primary and go on to win in the general election. Even Obama acknowledged that the "green" support was pivotal in his 2004 win.

A scant three years later, in February 2007, Barak Obama would launch his successful campaign for the White House — an incredibly rapid rise in the political world.

Obama's ties to the Left were obvious, his connections with the Establishment less so. However, his successful bid for the

Democratic presidential nomination made it clear that he had the Establishment's blessing and was willing to carry its ball.

The same can be said about Obama's selection of liberal Senator Joe Biden as his running mate. Biden won election to the U.S. Senate from Delaware in a come-from-behind narrow victory in 1972. Biden was just a couple weeks short of his thirtieth birthday (he would turn thirty before taking office, thus meeting the constitutional requirement). As chairman of the Senate Foreign Relations Committee Biden generally supported the internationalist agenda.

However, Barak Obama's Establishment ties became obvious with the selection of his presidential transition team, organized even before he was elected. The team was co-chaired by John Podesta, Bill Clinton's last chief of staff. Six of the 12 advisors on the 15-person transition team were members of the CFR:

- William M. Daley, son and brother of Chicago mayors, secretary of commerce under President Clinton, and later member of the Executive Committee of J.P. Morgan Chase & Co.;
- Christopher Edley, Obama's professor at Harvard Law School;
- Michael Froman, a classmate of Obama at Harvard;
- Janet Napolitano, governor of Arizona;
- Federico Peña, secretary of transportation and then energy under President Clinton; and
- Susan Rice, member of the Atlantic Council and assistant secretary of state for African affairs under President Clinton.

In choosing his national security team, President-elect Obama would also consult with Brent Scowcroft, who had chaired President George W. Bush's Foreign Intelligence Advisory Board from 2001 to 2005. [2]

CFR Staffing

Many conservatives, new to the dangers threatening our nation, have the mistaken idea that President Obama is his own man, pursuing his own radical agenda. And certainly, a number of his blatantly radical statements, actions, and ties have fostered that impression.

Obama is a radical to be sure, but in no way an "independent" radical. There is little president Obama has advocated or instituted that hasn't long been a part of the Establishment's agenda. And Obama has shown his complete subservience to that agenda and the Establishment forces behind it. That subservience is particularly evident in the choices he has made (or been handed) for staffing key posts in his administration.

President Obama campaigned on the slogan "Change We Can Believe In" and then "Change We Need." But filling his administration with CFR members and prior Clinton staffers was not change. Among his prominent Pratt-House appointees were:

- Timothy Geithner, president of the New York Federal Reserve Bank, as secretary of treasury. No outsider, Geithner attended the exclusive Bilderberg meeting in 2004.

- Peter Orszag, as director Office of Management and Budget. Orszag, a veteran of the Clinton White House, was invited to join the CFR in 2010.

- Former Harvard President Lawrence H. Summers, as director of the National Economic Council. (Summers served as secretary of treasury for two years under Bill Clinton.)

- Paul A. Volcker to chair the president's Economic Recovery Advisory Team. Volcker was chairman of the Board of the Federal Reserve from 1979 to 1987 and a multi-term director of the CFR.

- Robert M. Gates, as secretary of defense, a holdover from the George W. Bush administration. Gates had been a trusted CFR member in government going back to the Reagan years. In the Bush senior administration, Gates was the deputy national security advisor under Brent Scowcroft and before Bush's term was up succeeded William Webster as director of the CIA.

- Janet A. Napolitano, as secretary of homeland security.

- Eric K. Shinseki, as secretary of veteran affairs.

- Susan E. Rice, as U.S. ambassador to the United Nations. Rice served as assistant secretary of state for African Affairs during President Clinton's second term. She is also a Trilateralist, a Rhodes Scholar, a member of the Aspen Strategy Group (of which Cheney and Gore were emeritus members), and a senior fellow with the Brookings Institution.

- Thomas E. Donilon, as deputy national security advisor (promoted to national security advisor in October 2010). Donilon was also a Trilateralist.

- James B. Steinberg, as deputy secretary of state. Steinberg was also a Trilateralist, a senior fellow at Brookings, and a member of the Aspen Strategy Group. He was succeeded in July 2011 by William Joseph Burns (CFR).

- Kurt M. Campbell, as assistant secretary of state. Campbell was a director of the Aspen Strategy Group.

- Richard C. Holbrooke, as special representative to Afghanistan and Pakistan. A former Trilateralist, Holbrooke had held many positions in government, including U.S. representative to the United Nations under President Clinton.

- Anne-Marie Slaughter, as director of policy planning at the State Department. Slaughter had been a director of the CFR for six years, immediately prior to her selection. She now serves as a director at the Atlantic Council.

- Karen Mills to head up the Small Business Administration.

In 2011, as part of a midterm makeover of his economic team, President Obama would tap Gene Sperling (CFR) to head up his National Economic Council, replacing Lawrence Summers. This was the same job that Sperling had held during the last four years of the Clinton administration. Prior to the Obama restructuring, Sperling had been acting as a counselor to Treasury Secretary Geithner.

President Obama also went to the Atlantic Council to staff his administration, picking James L. Jones as his national security advisor. Jones resigned as chairman of the Atlantic Council to take on the new assignment.

Jones, a retired Marine Corps. general, had served as commandant of the Marine Corps. In November 2010, he gave up his post as national security advisor. The following year he would be accepted into the CFR.

Among the CFR members already mentioned and also serving on the Atlantic Council board were: Susan Rice, Retired General Eric Shinseki, Richard C. Holbrooke, and Anne-Marie Slaughter.

The CFR's 2011 *Annual Report* claimed that 529 of its members (12 percent) were employed in government.

Non-CFR Staffing from the Clinton Administration

Significant non-CFR appointees drawn from the Clinton administration include:

- Leon Panetta, as director of the CIA and later secretary of defense, replacing Gates. Panetta had been President Clinton's White House chief of staff (and earlier head of the Office of Management and Budget), following 16 years as a radical congressman from California.

- Carol Browner, EPA administrator during the eight years of the Clinton administration, as the White House coordinator of energy and climate policy, a new post — the so-called "energy czar." At the time of her appointment by President Obama, a little known part of her radical resume came to light. She had recently been a member of the Socialist International's Commission on a Sustainable World Society. [3] Browner resigned her "energy czar" post abruptly in January 2011, and her post was abolished.

- Hillary Clinton, as secretary of state (husband, Bill, is a CFR member).

- Eric H. Holder Jr., as attorney general.

- Shaun L.S. Donovan, as secretary of HUD.

• Rahm Emanuel, as White House chief of staff.

Fed Chairman Ben Bernanke

On August 25, 2009, President Obama announced that he was reappointing Ben Bernanke to a second four-year term as Chairman of the Federal Reserve. Nowhere is a president's subservience to the Establishment more solid than in his relationship to one of the Insiders' most important creations — the Federal Reserve. In commenting on the Bernanke reappointment, CNNMoney.com pointed to some revealing history:

> Over the past three decades, the country has had only three Fed chairmen. New presidents have tended to keep Fed chiefs in place regardless of political party to maintain continuity in monetary policy and confidence in markets. Paul Volcker was appointed by President Carter in 1979 and retained by Ronald Reagan. Alan Greenspan, a 1987 Reagan appointee, served under four presidents including President Clinton. Bernanke, 55, was appointed to the top job in 2006 by President George W. Bush, after serving as Bush's chair of the Council of Economic Advisors.[4]

One might expect this bi-partisan "cooperation" in the selection of Fed Chairmen to raise questions regarding "Wall Street" influence — particularly, in light of the Fed Chairman's massive authority and independence. According to Time.com: "The Fed chairman is often described as the second most powerful U.S. official; the main check on him is the first most powerful official's power not to reappoint him."[5]

Paul Volcker and Alan Greenspan were both CFR directors prior to their appointments as Fed Chairman, and Volcker became a director again when he turned over the Fed reins to Greenspan. But Bernanke was never a CFR member.

Is Bernanke an exception to the Establishment's control of the post? The Establishment media joined together in portraying Bernanke as independent of Wall Street. Time.com referred to Bernanke as "a financial overlord from Main Street rather than Wall Street."[6] And in announcing the reappointment, President Obama implied the same.[7]

However, it would be extremely naive to think that Bernanke could gain and hold his position without the blessing of the Insiders. Moreover, Bernanke has *some* ties in the public record. For example, when Bernanke received his Ph.D. in economics from MIT in 1979, his thesis adviser was Stanley Fischer.

Fischer had earned degrees in economics from the Fabian Socialist London School of Economics before receiving *his* Ph.D. at MIT. Fischer would later become a CFR member, a Trilateralist, and, in 1994, the first deputy managing director of the IMF.

Support for the internationalist UN (see below) and internationalist control of the Federal Reserve is not change.

Advancing Insider Objectives

Once in office, the president quickly embraced several radical steps ostensibly to deal with the economic crisis he had inherited. Those steps made the American people uneasy and led to a voter revolt in the midterm (2010) election, giving the Republicans control of the House.

We examine here several actions taken by President Obama, primarily during his first two years in office when his party held control of the House and Senate:

• **ObamaCare.** Following White House Chief of Staff Rahm Emanuel's maxim of "never let a serious crisis go to waste," President Obama seized the "opportunity" of an inherited recession to increase federal regulation of our nation's healthcare and health insurance industries.

The president's argument that the "reform" would provide urgently needed economic relief was pretty thin, as major portions of ObamaCare were not scheduled to take effect for several years, likely to allow adverse reaction to dissipate.

In a nationally televised address to Congress on September 9, 2009, President Obama delivered an eloquent plea to enact new "reform" legislation. His arguments followed a long-established pattern of clever socialist deception:

> More than four decades ago, this nation stood up for the principle that after a lifetime of hard work, our seniors should

not be left to struggle with a pile of medical bills in their later years. And that's how Medicare was born. And it remains a sacred trust that must be passed down from one generation to the next.

The president's audacious claim that the "nation stood up" for socialized medicine hides the revolutionary organization that had been working for decades to lay the groundwork for this federal seizure of power. The Socialist Party had endorsed a compulsory system as far back as 1904.

And within the federal bureaucracy several individuals had labored tirelessly to build support for this step. In 1968, President Johnson promoted one of the notables, Americans for Democratic Action member Wilbur J. Cohen, to Secretary of Health, Education, and Welfare.

Marjorie Shearon, a former consultant to Senator Robert A. Taft, wrote in her 1967 study of the drive for socialized medicine: "Cohen's crowning achievement of the Great Society — Medicare — is simply an import from nineteenth century Germany [Bismarck] — not new, not original." [8]

Indeed, Cohen was among those who prepared President Truman on how to overcome resistance to the program. In his November 1945 message to Congress, Truman emphasized: "I repeat — what I am recommending is not socialized medicine." [9]

Following Barak Obama's 2008 election victory, the *Wall Street Journal* recognized what was coming: "But like it or not, when our new government takes office in January, socialized medicine may well be on its way into America." [10]

Incredibly, in his September 2009 address to Congress, President Obama also stated:

If we do nothing to slow these skyrocketing costs, we will be spending more on Medicare and Medicaid than every other program combined. Put simply, our health care problem is our deficit problem, nothing else comes close....

Yet he proposed to finish the job that had got us in trouble. Unfortunately, *genuine* reform *is* needed, because government has created a system that is hugely expensive and detrimental to controlling costs.

The decades-old drive for government control of medicine has nothing to do with a misguided zeal to provide better healthcare for more Americans. The real objective of the sponsors, behind the deception, has always been about power — seizing an opportunity to make Americans dependent on the federal government for basic needs. As far back as 1970, Robert Welch saw through the deception:

> The main thrust of all the publicity now being let loose on the American people, in a deliberately distorted and biased disparagement of the medical profession and its services, is to convince the public that some kind of crisis exists. For the socialists learned long ago that they can get away with all kinds of schemes and legislation, and increases in the size and power of government, which the public would not otherwise accept, if these measures are inaugurated under the pretense that they are required by some emergency. [11]

• **Economic stimulus.** President Obama's first major action was to sign the American Recovery and Reinvestment Act in February 2009. Congressional and public acceptance of the $787 *billion* "economic stimulus bill" was accomplished through an atmosphere of urgency and crisis — a collapsing economy. Without a crisis, such an unprecedented government-spending spree on behalf of socialist revolution would have never flown.

Two primary spending areas were education and health care. The final stimulus bill contained a massive $90.9 billion *increase* in federal aid to education (on top of $68.6 billion annually). Although it was presented as a stand-alone investment, much of this "one-time" aid will undoubtedly raise the bar for future annual spending.

As we move down this road, it is well to keep in mind the ultimate goal of the Insiders with this program. Fabian Socialist and "esteemed" humanist philosopher Bertrand Russell explained the objective more than a half-century ago:

> When the technique has been perfected, every government that

has been in control of education for a generation will be able to control its subjects securely without the need of armies or policemen.[12]

The carrots and sticks in the "American Recovery and Reinvestment Act," will help the federal education establishment complete the power grab begun during the Eisenhower administration. Clearly the Obama administration is seeking to put the federal government in the driver's seat over all education. Consider these statements from a March 10, 2009 "White House Fact Sheet on Education:"

> Providing a high-quality education for all children is critical to America's economic future.... Progress toward this goal requires a race to the top to reform our nation's schools. It requires holding schools accountable.... It requires a national strategy to confront America's persistent dropout crisis, and strengthen transitions to college and career....
>
> With funding provided through the American Recovery and Reinvestment Act, the U.S. Department of Education will work with states to upgrade data systems to track student progress and measure the effectiveness of teachers.

Similarly, the socialist efforts to control health care were apparent in the stimulus bill. Much of the $147.7 billion for health care in the "stimulus bill" was designed to drive through revolutionary changes.

In a February 9th editorial, former New York Lieutenant Governor Betsy McCaughey sounded an alarm over several provisions "slipped in without discussion" into the pre-conference Senate version of the "stimulus bill":

> One new bureaucracy, the National Coordinator of Health Information Technology, will monitor treatments to make sure your doctor is doing what the federal government deems appropriate and cost effective. [13]

McCaughey's editorial hit a nerve. Seeking to downplay McCaughey's concerns, Linda Bergthold, "a working group leader in Hillary Clinton's Health Care Reform Task Force in 1993," retorted: "Does anyone care about the facts? They are simple. This so-called Federal Health IT Coordinator was actually established by President Bush in 2004. His office is not a new bureaucracy. It was a Republican idea." [14] Why are we not comforted?

• **More socialist revolution.** A chasm has opened up between the Founders' vision of the federal role and what the leaders of both political parties espouse today. The Obama administration's $3.83 trillion FY 2011 budget proposal sought to widen that chasm. On February 1, 2010, several departments held press conferences to unveil their portions of the budget. Others issued statements trumpeting their leadership.

At his department's press conference, Education Secretary Arne Duncan proudly announced:

The budget includes a 7.5 percent increase in discretionary spending for the Department of Education. It's one of the largest increases ever proposed.... [The president's budget] is investing heavily in education at every level from early childhood education to K to 12 reform to college access. It's a cradle to career agenda.

In decades past, the Agriculture Department drew fire from constitutionalists because of its price support policies and restrictions on farm production. However, the Department's mission has expanded greatly. Secretary Tom Vilsack's budget statement reflected the modern role:

The challenges facing rural communities for decades have grown more acute, which is why the Obama administration is committed to new approaches to strengthen rural America. Rural Americans earn less than their urban counterparts, and are more likely to live in poverty. More rural Americans are over the age of 65, they have completed fewer years of school, and more than half of America's rural communities are losing population.... This budget will assist rural communities create prosperity so they are self-sustaining, economically thriving, and growing in population.

In her opening remarks at the HHS press conference, Secretary Kathleen Sebelius boasted:

> We're investing new funds in what I consider to be the backbone of the American health care system, community health centers....
>
> On top of that, we have almost $1 billion in funding to strengthen and support our country's health care workforce. We're going to use the money to increase the capacity of nursing schools....

There is no limit to government's eagerness to "help":

> Often, [middle-class families are] also dealing with aging parents.... These [HHS] programs provide relief to family caregivers whether it's ... an adult day care center where they can drop a parent off for the day, or transportation to get the senior to the doctor or a store.

We could go on and on, with department after department. What we have here is an administration and Congress that refuse to uphold the Constitution. The result is a socialist monster that destroys our economic prosperity and lays the foundation for the extinction of liberty. The Constitution does not need to be amended — it simply needs to be enforced.

• **Green war on energy.** One way the Insiders hope to control Americans is to make them dependent on the federal government for the basic necessities — health care, housing, food, transportation, *and energy*. An obvious goal of the Establishment's green agenda is to induce energy scarcity leading to government rationing.

With our nation's immense natural resources and technological advances, Americans could have been enjoying plentiful, inexpensive supplies of energy for decades. But that happy prospect was frustrated by a well orchestrated anti-energy campaign, masked as seeking soft or "renewable" energy alternatives.

In the late sixties and early seventies, the anti-nuclear movement, in cooperation with revolutionaries in government, largely killed the use of this American technology on American soil. Oil from shale has been another stifled opportunity. Colorado is the Saudi Arabia of shale oil. [15] Yet for years this resource has been off limits to development. In 2005, columnist George Will (former CFR) astutely observed:

> One of the collectivists' tactics is to produce scarcities, particularly of what makes modern society modern — the energy requisite for social dynamism and individual autonomy.... Focusing on one energy source at a time, they stress the environmental hazards of finding, developing, transporting, manufacturing or using oil, natural gas, coal or nuclear power.[16]

In his 2009 *Green Hell* exposé, Steve Milloy provides a dose of reality regarding the promises that a modern society can be run anytime soon on the alternative sources being touted by the Obama administration. Milloy also points out the enormous expense in trying.

Moreover, Milloy argues that when push comes to shove green leaders will oppose even their "renewable" sources where these sources look like they might offer serious help, since the real objective is *no energy*.

As we have shown in Chapter 8, the green movement is financed and supported from the top. Just as the Obama administration was getting underway, Fareed Zakaria, former managing editor of the CFR's journal *Foreign Affairs*, gave us an Insider's answer to our economic woes, while supporting the president's green energy agenda:

> The key [to getting out of this mess] is we need new sources of productivity. The tech bubble, housing prices, and debt are all used up. We need a new fuel for the US economy and that fuel could be green energy.[17]

To provide authority for this view Zakaria quoted Joseph Stiglitz (CFR), former chairman of President Clinton's Council of Economic Advisers and former chief economist of the World Bank:

> We have to be thinking about the long run and begin to think

about it today and there is really only one answer I think. And it is the conversion to you might say a green economy, conversion addressing the problem of global warming. That is the one non-bubble solution that will help get us into sustained growth. [18]

Of course, Zakaria and Stiglitz take it for granted that government will have to promote this conversion. They want us to believe that requiring our industry to carry the enormous overhead of carbon-reduced production in order to fight the fiction of manmade global warming will somehow provide vitality to a struggling economy.

The Obama administration was well staffed with global-warming scaremongers to promote the green agenda. However, the radical plans of the Obama climate team ran into obstacles. In 2009, the political climate regarding climate change began to change. More and more members of the public were becoming aware that many experts were challenging the manmade global warming hysteria. [19]

And then on the eve of the December 2009 UN Climate Change Conference (the Copenhagen Summit), "Climategate" broke loose on the Internet. The *Nashua* [New Hampshire] *Telegraph* provided a good description of the scandal:

> Climategate exploded in the United Kingdom on Nov. 19. A whistleblower — it's unclear who — copied approximately 1,000 e-mail files and some 3,000 other documents from the servers in the Climate Research Unit at the University of East Anglia [which provided most of the global warming data used by the UN].... The e-mails show a clique of climatologists colluded to overstate man-made global warming. They manipulated evidence to achieve that end. In addition, they plotted to silence skeptics and peer-review publications holding skeptical views. [20]

• **The green war on the automobile.** Private transportation is another administration target. In his 1992 bestseller, *Earth in the Balance*, Vice President Al Gore wrote:

> [The automobile's] cumulative impact on the global environment is posing a mortal threat to the security of every nation that is more deadly than that of any military enemy we're

ever again likely to confront.[21]

On May 20, 2009, *The Washington Post* reported:

[T]he new fuel-efficiency and tailpipe-emissions standards unveiled yesterday at the White House will push automakers and motorists in a direction aimed at reducing U.S. oil dependence and the emissions of greenhouse gases, just part of the administration's program for remaking the ailing American car industry.[22]

Around the same time, General Motors announced that it would close 1,100 of its dealerships (about one in five) in late 2010. And Chrysler decided to eliminate a quarter of its dealerships.

• **2011 Libyan civil war.** Following in the footsteps of his predecessors, President Obama used the February 2011 Libyan uprising to enhance the authority of the United Nations over U.S. military operations. On March 19, AP reported:

President Barack Obama announced on Friday that he had given the go-ahead for U.S. forces to participate in operations designed to enforce the provisions of a U.N. Security Council resolution demanding that Ghadafi cease firing on civilians.... "Our consensus was strong and our resolve is clear," Obama said. "The people of Libya must be protected and in the absence of an immediate end to the violence against civilians our coalition is prepared to act and to act with urgency."[23]

As the violence escalated, another UN resolution authorized member states (as part of NATO) to enforce a no-fly zone over Libya, and Obama quickly involved U.S. forces — without prior congressional approval.

Congressional leaders began to grumble when the deadline imposed by the (unconstitutional) War Powers Resolution for seeking additional authority from Congress was exceeded. However, as *Congressional Quarterly* reported: "[E]very president since Nixon has said, essentially, 'you are not the boss of me, so just pay the bill' when it comes to the commander in chief's power to deploy the armed forces." [24] Particularly for UN "peacekeeping," we might add.

Muammar Gadhafi had ruled Libya since he led a military coup to overthrow King Idris I in 1969. In the intervening decades, Gadhafi's regime became one of the world's most brutal and oppressive. In addition, Libya became a Soviet-backed surrogate terrorist state and multiple terrorist groups were trained in Libya. So Gadhafi certainly deserves no sympathy.

However, those facts about Libya were widely known, and still the "international community" tolerated Gadhafi. In 2001, the United Nations even invited Libya to serve on its Human Rights Commission. But apparently in 2011, the UN decided that Gadhafi could be sacrificed. Meanwhile major regimes with a greater track record of genocide, such as Communist China, whose leaders had savaged Tibet, for example, sat in judgment as respected members of the UN Security Council.

Chapter 16

What Can and *Must* Be Done!

The picture we have painted so far will undoubtedly overwhelm many readers. And it should. But keep in mind that we have focused our attention on the poorly understood problem as a necessary prelude to discussing a solution.

So we have examined the strengths and successes of an organized Conspiracy, while ignoring America's layers of strength, weakened perhaps, but still in place. And we have put off until now a discussion of the Conspiracy's vulnerabilities.

A big mistake many individuals make, going back almost a half century, is to wake up one day and give up the next. Typically the individual had been trusting that nothing really bad could happen to America, until one day a friend finally persuades him to do some reading and he discovers the Conspiracy.

And then our example throws in the towel, without even making the effort to find what the opportunities are for stopping the Conspiracy. For almost 50 years, we have heard their excuse for not getting involved: "It's too late!"

It's Late, but Not *Too* Late!

At some point it could well become "too late." But we know it is not too late when the Conspiracy must still hide its true aims from the American people and employ elaborate pretexts and deceptions to advance its plans.

A primary objective of the Insiders, following established revolutionary principle, is to demoralize their much more numerous intended victims, so they will cease to resist. The individual who gives up hands the Conspiracy an unintended victory.

Actually, our situation should appear more overwhelming to those unfamiliar with the organized subversion described in this book. For what can one do when cultural and political subversion appear to be coming from every direction without any common thread?

But once one recognizes that a small, but powerful group is orchestrating the assault through deception, the prospect of stopping it becomes not easy, but more manageable.

We certainly don't mean to suggest that the task is anything but an uphill battle. But the *real battle* isn't where many initially think it is — with the Conspiracy. There is no question in the authors' minds that *a sizeable minority* of informed, committed Americans, organized under sound leadership, can stop the Conspiracy, undo its gains, and put America back on a path to new heights of greatness, honoring God, once again.

The much tougher challenge, as your authors see it, is to inform and organize that sizeable minority of modern American patriots who will voluntarily devote some of their time (and resources) to the task.

Let's examine both of these challenges — building a sizeable grassroots organization and using it to confront the Conspiracy — starting with the second one first.

Confronting the Conspiracy

As with any problem, half the solution lies in correctly identifying the problem. And that means recognizing that there is a Conspiracy, the extensiveness of its influence, its objectives, and its principal strategies and tactics — that is, its common deceptions.

Any realistic solution must be commensurate with the problem. And that's why so many efforts to address America's problems are completely unrealistic.

For example, pure political action that does not confront the Conspiracy's grip on our opinion-forming institutions, such as education and the media of communications, can't achieve its announced goals. Indeed, political candidates who attempt to sell themselves or their party as the answer to America's problems are deceiving themselves and their constituents.

The key to stopping the Conspiracy is to recognize its strengths and its weaknesses, as well as America's many layers of strength. The power of the Conspiracy stems from its ability to reward ladder-climbers. **A primary weakness is that its innermost core of committed followers is necessarily small.**

We have all heard the expression "divide and conquer." For a small group to gain dictatorial power over an entire population, it must be clever and immoral. It must confuse its intended victims as to its aims, divide and isolate them. In that way, any group that thinks of resisting is small and can be neutralized by pitting it against others.

The clever power seekers we face also work to discourage, impoverish, create dependency, intimidate, and ultimately disarm. However, as the Conspiracy advances, **it operates largely on bluff**, pretending to be the wave of the future and much stronger than it really is.

Another primary weakness is that **its agenda runs counter to the overwhelming desire of people to be free**. And so the Conspiracy's only immediate hope for implementing its agenda is through **deception. It cannot stand up to an aroused and informed public**. As the great British statesman Edmund Burke observed: "The people never give up their liberties but under some delusion."

And that points to **the primary path to stopping the Conspiracy — exposure.** The Conspiracy cannot prosper if its objectives, plans, and methods are exposed to the light of day. We don't mean that the innermost secrets of the Conspiracy, such as its membership list and individual culpabilities, have to be publicized. Ferreting out that information is a job for properly motivated investigative agencies.

Fortunately, enough of the Conspiracy's operations are already in the public record to stop the Conspiracy. Those operations just need to be explained to a much broader segment of the public — and acted upon.

Drawing on Our Layers of Strength
In embracing a solution, it is also vital to understand America's layers of strength and make use of them. It is a trap, for example, to ignore the bulwarks against tyranny in our constitutional system and attempt to foment militant rebellion and anarchy. Such unjustified and unwise action provides the Conspiracy with a useful pretext to crackdown on all of our liberties.

America has many layers of strength, which the Conspiracy has worked to erode. Among them are positive character traits such as: a spirit of self-reliance and adventure; a strong desire to help others and improve the world; responsibility; religious faith; and a sense of fair play. Important traditions include: free enterprise and the free market; widespread private gun ownership; home schooling and private education; an abundance of churches; the traditional family; and local police.

Two important layers of strength — our constitutional Republic and the American middle class — greatly support the power of public opinion:

• **Our constitutional Republic.** With our Constitution, the founding fathers provided for a continued separation of powers between federal, state, and local governments. And they further identified and separated the federal government's limited powers into three branches — executive, legislative, and judiciary — with numerous checks and balances to help prevent (but not guarantee against) usurpation of power by any one of the three.

Moreover, the Constitution provided the people with a primary route for controlling the federal government — our voice in and the power of the House of Representatives. This power is poorly recognized today. James Madison, often credited with being the "father of the Constitution," emphasized in Federalist No. 58 that a simple majority in the House alone has the power to bring government under control:

> The House of Representatives cannot only refuse, but they alone can propose the supplies requisite for the support of government. They, in a word, hold the purse — that powerful instrument ... [for reducing] ... all the overgrown prerogatives of the other branches of government. This power over the purse may, in fact, be regarded as the most complete and effectual weapon with which any constitution can arm the immediate representatives of the people, for obtaining a redress of every grievance, and for carrying into effect every just and salutary measure.

The reason the House hasn't exercised that authority in recent times is that no simple majority has, or can acquire on its own, the desire and backbone to do so. Such a majority would have to stand up to the Conspiracy's grip on the parties and withstand its dominating influence on public opinion.

Realistically, the necessary backbone must come from an

informed, engaged electorate following new leadership, provided through a new channel of communications.

• **America's middle class.** A strong middle class is one of the greatest bulwarks in any nation against government tyranny. Tyranny always tries to reduce the people into two classes — the many poor and struggling versus the privileged few at the top. A strong middle class is not dependent on government favor and has the independent means to resist the accumulation of unaccountable power in government.

Respected American novelist Taylor Caldwell argued:

> The middle class made the dream of liberty a possibility, set limits on the government, fought for its constitutions, removed much of governmental privilege and tyranny, demanded that rulers obey the just laws as closely as the people, and enforced a general civic morality. [1]

There are many more good people than bad, so numbers are on our side. Moreover, the Conspiracy still does not dominate word of mouth and cannot prevent organizing among the middle class.

Power of Public Opinion

Revolutionary strategists fully understand the power of public opinion, supported by a strong middle class, to block their schemes. That's why their strategy focuses so heavily on manipulating public opinion, deceiving public opinion, confusing public opinion, dumbing down the public, and weakening and controlling the middle class.

To neutralize and misrepresent public opinion, revolutionary tactics call for the orchestration of mass demonstrations, and the use of purportedly "independent" organizations to create "pressure from below" in support of legislation. Revolutionary organizers also claim their own non-governmental organizations (NGO's) represent the public and should have a voice in democracy.

In fact, the Conspiracy's penetration of government institutions, an important part of revolutionary strategy, can accomplish little without its complementing efforts to influence public opinion. In recognition of that fact, the Conspiracy has, in substance, pursued the strategy articulated by Italian Communist theoretician Antonio Gramsci and his followers.

Gramsci argued that in the developed Western democracies it was a mistake to "count solely on the power and material force that are given by government." [2] Instead, Gramsci insisted that for a revolution to be successful the supporting culture first had to be changed.

The altered culture would then prepare the people, intellectually and morally, to accept the revolution. In essence, the Gramscian battle cry became "capture the culture." Rudi Dutschke, one of Gramsci's disciples, described this strategy of culture war as conducting "the long march through the institutions." [3]

However, long before Gramsci's ideas gained authority in revolutionary circles, American Insiders and Fabian Socialists had begun to lay the groundwork for their revolution by capturing strategic positions for the molding of public opinion.

Although revolutionaries understand the power of public opinion, it is often a challenge to help budding patriots adequately appreciate this strategic force.

What Can't Work

For any relatively small force to prevail over time, it must stay focused on sound strategy. To maintain that focus in the freedom fight, leaders and serious activists need to recognize what won't and can't work and why. Here are several of the most tempting errors:

• **Fighting the battle on purely ideological grounds.** In 1967, Dr. James Lucier, who would serve for six years as minority staff director for the Senate Foreign Relations Committee, summarized an important lesson: "The first job of conspiracy is to convince the world that conspiracy does not exist."

A major player in that effort was the late William F. Buckley Jr. (CFR). Because of his position as the Establishment-anointed Mr. Conservative, Buckley was able to persuade many that it was folly to consider any notion of a conspiracy. As noted in the introduction, one tactic has been to make the conspiracy claim sound ridiculous through exaggeration and distortion or by highlighting the wild charges of "convenient" strawmen.

The desire to avoid appearing ridiculous is always strong. So even those who recognize that there *is* a Conspiracy are sometimes tempted to avoid presenting the evidence, arguing that perhaps "the public is not yet ready to be told such things."

However, we can't defeat a Conspiracy by cooperating in covering up its existence. Perhaps a parallel will help drive home the point: If a town is beset by arson, the problem won't be solved with campaigns and speeches about the need to strengthen and enforce building codes.

• **The quick fix.** One doesn't have to wait long to encounter new variations and proponents of "the quick fix," which squanders the resources and energies of Americans. The central error in the quick fix proposals is a failure to recognize the extent of our problem. The present Conspiracy has been working toward its goal, building its influence and putting programs in place, for well over a century. No single bill, lawsuit, or candidate can bring down the Conspiracy's house.

• **Depending on partisan politics to save us.** This is just one variation of the natural desire for a quick fix that doesn't disrupt our priorities too much. Unfortunately, many Americans are enamored with the idea of working to send a good guy to Washington and then relying on him to fight our battles for us. The weakness is that election "victories" alone leave the Conspiracy's ability to confuse and mislead intact.

As an example, in 2011 amidst deep public concern over federal spending, the media and the parties managed to cast the battle as one over spending caps to limit the *size* of government. But any real reform requires eliminating and phasing out entire *unconstitutional* programs and departments — an opportunity never discussed in the major media.

• **Corollary: Electing a new president**. This option is an out and out swindle. (See "The Great American Swindle" on the Freedom First Society website.[4]) As should be clear from the history presented here, the presidency has become an Establishment stronghold. Until Establishment control of the national media has been bypassed, no politician with a serious chance of being elected threatens that grip.

The Insiders undoubtedly delight in watching Americans expend their energy in the fruitless hope that they can bring about real change by selecting one of the Establishment-approved alternatives. The Establishment certainly encourages the illusion that the primary opportunity Americans have for setting the direction of their government is to choose between the presidential nominees of the two major parties every four years.

Instead, as intended by the framers of the Constitution (see above), the best opportunity Americans have for immediate *political* impact is to influence the House of Representatives. And "sending a good guy" to Washington or "dumping a bad" is only a small part of what needs to be done to get real results in the House. (See FFS Strategy, below.)

• **Viewing the battle as entirely in Washington.** Much of our problem does stem from bad legislation, dating back at least to 1913. And there is the threat of even worse to come. But major legislative reversals require sound strategy.

A good place to start is to realize what the enemies of freedom had to do to accomplish their legislative victories. They had to follow the Gramscian strategy of "the long walk through the institutions" in order to win public acceptance of their gains in Washington.

For perspective, keep in mind that only approximately 12 percent of the CFR's membership are government officials. The rest exercise considerable influence in advancing the international-socialist agenda through foundation funding, the media, education, the law, business, think thanks, and a myriad of other non-governmental organizations.

An effective organization confronting the Conspiracy may focus its *campaigns* on legislative results. But to challenge seriously the Conspiracy's influence in Washington, our desired organization must change the *local* political environment. And that means competing with the corrupted institutions that help form local public opinion.

In the long run, sound strategy must seek to change the balance of forces by cleaning up existing institutions or creating new ones not dominated by the Conspiracy's change-agents.

• **Opposing the Conspiracy as a lone soldier.** Many conservative individualists are non-joiners by inclination. And so we run into individuals who argue they can change the world merely by handing out literature without representing or endorsing any organization.

However, those who truly wish to be effective need to invest in building and working within an organization. The enemy is very well organized, indeed places great emphasis on organization. No one would think seriously of fighting a war as a lone soldier. Only organization that harnesses the natural strength of the vast majority of Americans whose liberties are at stake can win.[5]

The Primary Challenge

The opportunity for the right grassroots organization to stop and then rout the Conspiracy has been well established in campaigns of the past. The primary challenge is, and has always been, to build that organization *solidly* to sufficient size.

We will describe here a few of the principles, opportunities, and hurdles to overcome in that task. For a more thorough explanation, we urge the serious reader to obtain a copy of the authors' *Organize for Victory!*

• **Prepare to meet opportunity.** Experience teaches that "success occurs when opportunity meets preparation." However, being prepared to seize opportunities requires persistence. The present struggle to preserve freedom has been a long one. Yet great opportunities to reach and enlist our fellow citizens must come along as the Conspiracy works to consolidate its gains.

Right now appears to be one of those times. Large numbers of Americans are concerned because of a seriously depressed job market and an obvious radical in the White House. The challenge is to harness the strength of America's awakening middle class before it is weakened to the point of impotence.

Despite the Conspiracy's obvious momentum, there are sound reasons to believe that our opportunities are much greater than they appear on the surface. Although the Conspiracy seeks to create the illusion that its agenda is an unstoppable wave of the future, much of its strength is just that — illusion.

America has been more resilient than the Insiders who gathered in Paris at the Majestic Hotel in 1919 could ever have imagined. As the nation expanded west, an unfettered, free-market economy produced exploding opportunity and an unprecedented middle class.

• **Harness technology, wisely.** While advancing technology steadily offers improved convenience in communication and has increased the availability of information, it has not changed human nature.

Harnessing technology, such as the Internet, should be part of steadily upgrading tactics to work smarter, to communicate more easily among like-minded members and to find, persuade, enlist, and empower prospects with the informational tools to persuade others. But throwing out too wide a net without the ability to follow up may accomplish little.

What is needed are committed soldiers and leaders, not uninvolved observers. An important lesson is that busy people are much more likely to examine our message seriously enough to take action, when they are contacted repeatedly with personal attention from people they know and respect.

• **Help others avoid tangents and traps.** A good yardstick for judging any proposed action program is to ask: Will the proposed program lead to building organization focused on exposing the Conspiracy? For decades, inadequate or false leadership has led countless Americans astray — many more than it would take, if properly focused, to defeat the Conspiracy.

An important part of building a winning organization is to help concerned Americans avoid those traps and embrace a better program. A little booklet that assists in that effort is *Tangents and Traps* by Don Fotheringham (published by and available through Freedom First Society).[6]

• **Size alone won't do it.** Although numbers are essential for a successful bottom-up strategy, most large organizations are incapable of doing what needs to be done.

For an organization to be effective in this freedom fight, it must be built solidly. That means several things. For starters, the leaders, the members, and the organization's financial supporters must be committed to the right mission for the organization — building an organization to expose and rout the Conspiracy.

In addition, the organization must be willing and able to take the point — to take tough positions and occupy the high ground. When that is done, other organizations will follow at a slower pace in the leader's footsteps. An organization capable of taking the point must develop the right culture and an inspiring track record.

So the task is not just to enlist concerned citizens with the correct values. They must also be helped to an understanding of what needs to be done, or else they won't accept tough leadership, and they won't be tough themselves with their political representatives.

A further essential building step is involving members in active Chapters. Putting your name on a mailing list accomplishes only so much. The real impact is accomplished by individuals who link arms and commit to working together regularly.

FFS Strategy

The Freedom First Society offers leadership to Americans willing to commit some of their time to effective action in the freedom fight. In its broad outlines, FFS follows a strategy developed and honed decades earlier by Robert Welch.

The FFS strategy for restoring constitutional government is summarized in the statement: "Congress is the Key." In fact, our primary focus is on influencing the House of Representatives by changing the political climate in the congressional districts. Our target is to build and lead a significant organization of members and Chapters in at least a majority of congressional districts (218), who will work to influence public opinion in those districts while increasing their numbers.

How many members do we need in each district? Our rule of thumb, based on previous experience, is that 500 to 1,000 active members, less than 0.2 percent of the adult population, will do it. Of course, that number presupposes active members in effective Chapters pursuing the organization's concerted action campaigns.

A primary goal of this effort is to build a Congress that "Votes the Constitution!," paraphrasing one of our campaigns. A powerful motivator for most representatives is the prospect of reelection. While representatives may respond to destructive pressures from party leadership, experience shows that many will buck that leadership if confronted by informed constituent opinion molders who refuse to accept fluff and lame excuses in exchange for correct votes.

Furthermore, long experience shows that by changing the political climate elections pretty much take care of themselves. The election process is important, of course, but not the weak link in transforming Washington. Accordingly, FFS does not take part in partisan politics or support any candidates (members are, of course, free to do so as individuals).

While we would like to have committed statesmen occupying a majority of House seats, in fact it is not necessary "to throw all of the bums out" to accomplish real change. A few faces replaced by informed voters sends a signal to astute incumbents to change their stripes.

Astute incumbents have a wet finger that is very sensitive to political winds. And the best way to change the political winds is to build an informed electorate. Unless that is done, throwing a bum out just results in his replacement by another representative with a similar lack of backbone, who ends up following his corrupted party leadership.

Recommendations for Non-members

We offer several suggestions regarding immediate action for non-members who wish to make a contribution in the freedom fight:

• First, reread and study this book. For those who wish to read deeper regarding the problem, a list of recommended reading is provided at the end of this book. And for solution, please consider reading your authors' *Organize for Victory!*

• Recognize that knowledge alone will not save America, nor will listening to articulate talk-show hosts and admiring the influence of others. Becoming informed is only part of the answer. The Conspiracy could care less what even a sizeable minority of Americans know — unless they do something constructive with it. Numbers in support of principled action is the key to victory.

• When you are convinced that the authors are on the right track, we encourage you to join Freedom First Society (see www.freedomfirstsociety.org for a membership application and a list of founding principles) with the object of supporting an existing Chapter or building the nucleus for a Chapter.

Chapters are where the real action starts — for both recruiting and focused national concerted action campaigns. By enlisting those you influence into Chapters they can become centers of influence, thereby multiplying and continuing your impact. A growing number of active Chapters is what will put FFS on the map nationally and give FFS members credibility in Washington.

• To extend your influence and recruit others to constructive action in the freedom fight, obtain several copies of this book and begin lending them to relatives, friends, neighbors, and associates. Follow up on your lending to encourage actual reading and subsequent action.

• While leaders are always in great demand, recognize that by joining the right organization you don't need pre-existing influence to make a real difference. The primary requirements for a positive contribution are patriotism and character.

• To harness the power of organization, you need to follow good leaders. But always put your faith in principles you understand and champion, not in men.

It Must Not Happen Here!

Americans dare not be disarmed by the smiling faces of the internationalists. Their track record of perfidy in building their new world order is well established. They are responsible for the blood and Communist slavery of millions. Even worse should be expected if the internationalist conspirators are ever successful in consolidating unaccountable global power.

We have examined the Establishment's support for the Communist takeover of Russia and China as well as its contribution to the rise of Hitler. Friendly governments have been toppled in Nicaragua and Iran, only to be replaced by tyrannical regimes.

Although the internationalists pretend that their United Nations is the route to world peace and world law, it may be well to look at one of its early ventures still heralded by the UN and its internationalist supporters as a success. We are speaking of the UN's 1961 invasion and subjugation of Katanga.

In 1960, when Belgium withdrew from Africa and gave independence to the Congo, Moscow-backed Communist Patrice Lumumba gained control of the central government in Leopoldville. A reign of terror was unleashed on the hapless nation.

In response, one province, Katanga, under the leadership of the pro-Western Moise Tshombe seceded from the Congo and declared its independence. But the UN would have none of it and decided to topple the Tshombe government.

In the process, the UN showed the world its true face. The UN undertook airstrikes on Elizabethville, the capital of Katanga, followed by the invasion of UN forces, with the full support of the Leftist Establishment in the United States. 46 doctors in Elizabethville, the capital of Katanga, tried desperately to gain the attention of the Western governments to no avail. The following year they documented the horrible tragedy in *46 Angry Men*, revealing the murders, rapes, and other atrocities committed against civilians by UN "peacekeeping forces" gone wild.[7]

As another example, the unimaginable genocide visited on Rwanda in 1994 was facilitated by earlier UN action to disarm the Tutsi victims.[8] Odette Nyiramilimo, one of the survivors of the genocide charged:

Really, it was UNAMIR [the UN "peacekeeping" mission to Rwanda] that tricked us into staying. We saw all these blue helmets, and we ... thought even if Hutus start to attack us the three thousand men of UNAMIR should be enough.[9]

It is not difficult to project the lines if the internationalists are not stopped.

And the Conspiracy *will* succeed in consolidating unaccountable power unless more Americans wake up to the design and embrace a sound program of action. As in Jonathan Swift's tale of Gulliver in the land of the tiny Lilliputians, the Insiders continue to fasten snares on the sleeping American giant until one day it wakes up to find it cannot move.

The Choice Is Ours!

The answers to a few simple questions will determine our fate:

• Are there enough Americans with patriotism in their hearts, who are willing to take on the dreadful challenge that has been thrust upon us? That challenge, an uphill battle, is to preserve our precious inheritance of freedom for future generations. We believe the answer is yes, there are enough.

• But can we acquire the help to reach them? How much do those who understand what's happening today value the sacrifices and contributions of past generations and true leaders in the cause of freedom?

We are speaking of the men who declared and fought for our nation's independence (a seemingly uphill, almost impossible battle against the English empire at the time). We are also thinking of those tremendously unusual leaders who met in Philadelphia for five short months and sacrificed personal ambition to frame our Constitution in the long-term interest of our nation and its people. And many others.

• Are we willing to allow undeserving corrupt men to steal the inheritance entrusted to us for future generations? Are we really too busy or tied to personal interests and commitments to make the effort?

Or perhaps we can leave the challenge to someone else, while we go about our own business. That's really the choice each of us must make. We hope the readers of this book will decide that America is worth fighting for! Recognizing that there will never be a draft in this war.

Nevertheless, the war is just as real as if there were a draft. It is a war to decide whether we and our posterity will continue to enjoy the fruits of freedom. Moreover, the war won't go away if we choose to ignore it or stay on the sidelines, until it *is* too late.

Four-star Marine General Lewis W. Walt (1913–1989) served with distinction in three of our nation's wars (World War II, Korea, and

Vietnam) and received many decorations for valor in combat. After retiring from active duty, General Walt wrote:

> Neither monetary policy nor foreign policy nor military policy is fixed and unchangeable. Any or all can be changed simply by making a new decision.... The things we don't like — our military weakness, our constant edging toward a World Government, our inflationary economy, and our confused foreign policy — are all the products of decisions of specific individuals. [10]

General Walt understood where responsibility must be found for a nation to remain free — in the people themselves:

> I think that the future of our country boils down to this simple proposition: either we as individual Americans will assume the responsibilities of citizenship or our nation, as the land of the free, will be destroyed. [11]

In 1961, Robert Welch delivered another inspiring call to action:

> Whether the drama of the Twentieth Century winds up as an unrelieved and horrible tragedy, or whether despite all of the suffering throughout its earlier acts the play closes with a happy ending, is still to be decided by the cast of characters — no matter what the nefarious playwrights behind the scenes have planned.
>
> Most important among these players on the worldwide stage are still the American people.... Beyond any question we have the chance to change the course of history — to change it infinitely for the better at one of the darkest crises of all of man's centuries upon this earth.
>
> To fulfill that great promise we must moderately lament the sorrows and mistakes which brought us where we are.... But our epic undertaking is to prevent the even worse sorrows that otherwise are to come.
>
> To that ennobling and energizing purpose we are called upon to give the best that is in us. We are fighting, against terrific odds, for the greatest stakes in history — universal human freedom against universal slavery — and we intend to win. [12]

Yes, the stakes are huge. And we, too, intend to win. But we can't do it with only a handful of patriots. Our hope for victory depends upon pulling thousands and tens of thousands of responsible men and women of character into this fight. Freedom or global slavery — the choice is ours!

Notes

Introduction

1. Dan Smoot, *The Invisible Government*, Americanist Library edition (Boston: Western Islands, 1965). [First edition published in 1962 by the Dan Smoot Report, Inc.]
2. Ibid., p. 30.
3. *Congressional Record*, February 23, 1954. Quoted in Phoebe and Kent Courtney, *America's Unelected Rulers: The Council on Foreign Relations* (New Orleans: Conservative Society of America, 1962), pp. 1, 2.

Chapter 1
The CFR's War *on* U.S. Independence

1. Philip Kerr, "From Empire to Commonwealth," *Foreign Affairs*, December 1922, pp. 97–98.
2. *American Public Opinion and Postwar Security Commitments* (New York: CFR, 1944), quoted in Alan Stang, *The Actor* (Belmont, Mass.: Western Islands, 1968), p. 35.
3. Joseph Kraft, "School For Statesmen," *Harper's*, July 1958, p. 64.
4. *Christian Science Monitor*, September 1, 1961, p. 9.
5. J. Anthony Lukas, "The Council on Foreign Relations: Is It a Club? Seminar? Presidium? Invisible Government?," *New York Times Magazine*, November 21, 1971, pp. 125–26.
6. Alan Brinkley, "Minister Without Portfolio," *Harper's*, February 1983. (Quoted in Drummey, below.)
7. James J. Drummey, "The Council on Foreign Relations," *The New American*, April 7, 1986.
8. Chester Ward and Phyllis Schlafly, *Kissinger on the Couch* (New Rochelle, N.Y.: Arlington House, 1975), p. 150.
9. Ibid., p. 146.
10. Ibid., pp. 150, 151.
11. Ibid., p. 151.
12. Michael Hirsh, "The Death of a Founding Myth," Special Davos (International) Edition of *Newsweek*, December 2002–February 2002, p. 18.
13. Professor Arnold Toynbee in a June 10, 1931 speech before the Institute for the Study of International Affairs in Copenhagen.
14. Ibid.
15. R.J. Rummel, *Death by Government* (New Brunswick, N.J.: Transaction Publishers, 1994), p. 9 in 2008 paperback.

Chapter 2
The Great Federal Reserve Deception

1. Carroll Quigley, *Tragedy and Hope: A History of the World In Our Time* (New York: Macmillan, 1966), p. 950.
2. Ibid., p. 130.
3. Ibid., p. 51.
4. Ibid., p. 52.
5. Stephen Birmingham, *Our Crowd* (New York: Dell, 1967). Compare with Clement Eaton, *History Of The Southern Confederacy* (New York: The Macmillan Company, 1954).
6. Quigley, p. 325.
7. Ibid., p. 324.
8. Congressman Wright Patman's newsletter to constituents, June 6, 1968.
9. *The Writings Of Thomas Jefferson*, Vol. X (New York: G.P. Putnam & Sons, 1899), p. 31.
10. Gustavus Myers, *History Of The Great American Fortunes* (New York: Random House, 1936), p. 556n. See also, Gary Allen, "Conspiratorial Origins of the Federal Reserve," *American Opinion*, March 1970.
11. Frederick Lewis Allen, *The Great Pierpont Morgan* (New York: Bantam, 1956), p. 8.
12. Quigley, p. 952.
13. Ibid., pp. 530, 531.
14. Ibid., p. 945.
15. Frederick Lewis Allen, "Morgan The Great," *Life* magazine, April 25, 1949.
16. Ferdinand Lundberg, *America's 60 Families* (New York: The Vanguard Press, 1938), p. 69.
17. Frank Vanderlip, "Farm Boy To Financier," *Saturday Evening Post*, February 9, 1935, p. 25.
18. Ibid., p. 70.
19. *Congressional Record*, June 13, 1911.
20. Lundberg, pp. 110–112.
21. Ibid., p. 114.
22. Ibid., pp. 115–116.
23. Ibid., pp. 109, 113.
24. Gabriel Kolko, *The Triumph of Conservatism: A Reinterpretation of American History, 1900-1916* (New York: The Free Press, 1963), p. 217.
25. Ibid., pp. 205, 211.
26. Ibid., p. 186.
27. Vanderlip, p. 72.
28. Gary Allen, "Conspiratorial Origins of the Federal Reserve," *American Opinion*, March 1970.
29. Congressional Record, December 22, 1913.
30. Senator Henry Cabot Lodge Sr. remarks on December 17, 1913, Congressional Record, June 10, 1932.
31. William P. Hoar, "Life in the 'Brier Patch,'" *The New American*, September 16, 1996.

32. Kolko, p. 247. Also, George Sylvester Viereck, *The Strangest Friendship In History: Woodrow Wilson and Colonel House* (New York: Liveright, 1932), p. 37.
33. Lundberg, p. 122.
34. Kolko, pp. 251–252.
35. CNNMoney.com, "Bernanke's $1 trillion hangover," July 6, 2009.
36. Oswald Spengler, *Decline of the West, Vol. II: Perspectives of World-History* (New York: Alfred A. Knopf, 1979), p. 401.
37. Richard R. Byrd, 1910, quoted in Allen, "Tax or Trim: Why We Need Tax Reform Immediately," *American Opinion*, January 1975.
38. *U.S. News & World Report*, February 16, 1970.
39. Cordell Hull, *The Memoirs of Cordell Hull*, Vol. I (New York: MacMillan, 1948), p. 76.

Chapter 3
The "First Try" at "World Order"

1. The other three Texas governors aided by House were: Charles A. Culberson (1894), Joseph D. Sayers (1898), and S. W. T. Lanham (1902).
2. George Sylvester Viereck, *The Strangest Friendship In History: Woodrow Wilson and Colonel House* (New York: Liveright, 1932).
3. Charles Seymour (ed.), *The Intimate Papers of Colonel House*, Vol. I, *Behind The Political Curtain: 1912 – 1915* (Boston: Houghton Mifflin, 1926), p. 114.
4. Thomas Sugrue and Edmund W. Starling, *Starling of the White House: The story of the man whose Secret Service detail guarded five presidents from Woodrow Wilson to Franklin D. Roosevelt* (New York: Simon and Schuster, 1946), p. 41.
5. Edward Mandell House, *Philip Dru: Administrator: A Story of Tomorrow – 1920–1935* (New York: B. W. Huebsch, 1912), Chapter VI, p. 35 in RWU Press edition, 1998.
6. Seymour, pp. 152–159.
7. Thomas W. Phelps, *Wall Street Journal*, July 1937, quoted by Westbrook Pegler, "U.S. Fascism Spawned in 1912," *Los Angeles Examiner*, August 26, 1954, p. I-25.
8. Gary Allen, "The C.F.R. Conspiracy to Rule the World," *American Opinion*, April 1969.
9. Westbrook Pegler, "U.S. Fascism Spawned in 1912," *Los Angeles Examiner*, August 26, 1954, 1-25.
10. Ferdinand Lundberg, *America's 60 Families* (New York: Vanguard Press, 1937), p. 141.
11. Colin Simpson, *The Lusitania* (Boston: Little, Brown and Company, 1972), pp. 127–130.
12. Ibid., p. 131. Refers to Joseph Kenworthy and George Young, *The Freedom of the Seas* (London: Hutchinson & Co., 1927), p. 211.
13. Simpson, p. 130.
14. Ibid., p. 194.
15. Ibid., pp. 203, 204.

16. Ibid., pp. 264, 265.
17. Ibid., pp. 5, 267, 278 (fn. 19).
18. Ibid., p. 157.
19. William H. McIlhany II, *The Tax-Exempt Foundations* (Westport, Connecticut: Arlington House, 1980), pp. 60, 61.
20. Ibid., p. 61.
21. Jennings C. Wise, *Woodrow Wilson: Disciple of Revolution* (New York: Paisley Press, 1938), quoted in William P. Hoar, "World War I," *American Opinion*, January 1976.
22. Antony C. Sutton, *Wall Street and FDR* (New Rochelle, N.Y.: Arlington House, 1975), pp. 88, 89.
23. Curtis B. Dall, *F.D.R. My Exploited Father-in-Law* (Tulsa: Christian Crusade Publications, 1968), p. 71.
24. Warren P. Mass, "The People's Choice," *The New American*, October 26, 1987.
25. Ibid.
26. Carroll Quigley, *Tragedy and Hope: A History of the World In Our Time* (New York: Macmillan, 1966), p. 952.
27. Gary Allen with Larry Abraham, *None Dare Call It Conspiracy* (Rossmoor, Calif.: Concord Press, 1971), pp. 71, 72.
28. Sutton, *Wall Street and the Bolshevik Revolution* (New Rochelle, N.Y.: Arlington House, 1974), pp. 82, 83.
29. Ibid., p. 25.
30. Allen, p. 68.
31. James J. Drummey, "The Bolshevik Revolution," *The New American*, October 26, 1987.
32. R.J. Rummel, *Death by Government* (New Brunswick, N.J.: Transaction Publishers, 1994), p. 82 in 2008 paperback.
33. Max Eastman, "The Character and Fate of Leon Trotsky," *Foreign Affairs*, January 1941, p. 332.
34. *Congressional Record*, June 15, 1933.
35. Quigley, p. 308.
36. *New York American*, quoted in Don Bell, "Who Are Our Rulers?" *American Mercury*, September 1960.
37. Sutton, *Wall Street and the Rise of Hitler* (Seal Beach, Calif.: '76 Press, 1976), p. 35.
38. Ibid., p. 109.
39. Ibid., p. 31.

Chapter 4
Resetting the Stage for Revolution

1. William P. Hoar, "Reflection on the Great Depression," *American Opinion*, June 1979. Quotes Hoover in Herbert Hoover, *The Memoirs Of Herbert Hoover: The Great Depression 1929-1941* (New York, Macmillan, 1952).
2. Curtis B. Dall, *FDR: My Exploited Father-In-Law*, 2nd edition (Christian Crusade Publications, 1968), p. 49.

3. Gary Allen, "The Anti-Economics of Boom and Bust," *American Opinion*, April 1970.

4. Rose L. Martin, *Fabian Freeway: High Road to Socialism in the U.S.A. 1884–1966* (Boston: Western Islands, 1966), p. 262.

5. Dall, p. 185.

6. Gary Handy, "The Purpose Is Destruction," *JBS Bulletin*, February 1980.

7. The Ickes diary was published posthumously in three volumes as: *The Secret Diary of Harold L. Ickes* (New York: Simon & Shuster, 1953–54). However, Simon & Shuster omitted the revealing passage, which had appeared earlier in a magazine. The discrepancy is discussed by Westbrook Pegler, "Fair Enough," *The Billings Gazette*, December 11, 1953 (King Features Syndicate). The sanitized Simon & Shuster version of the events for July 16, 1935 appears on pp. 399–402 in volume I. In a "Publisher's Note" in that volume, Simon & Shuster promised to deposit the complete diary manuscript with the Library of Congress.

8. "Report of the Special Committee on Tax-Exempt Foundations," Government Printing Office, December 15, 1954, cited in Dan Smoot, *The Invisible Government*, Americanist Library edition (Boston: Western Islands, 1965), pp. 133–34. [First edition published in 1962 by the Dan Smoot Report, Inc.]

9. "Report, Special House Committee to Investigate Tax-Exempt Foundations," 1954, pp. 176–77, quoted in John Stormer, *None Dare Call It Treason* (Florissant, Missouri: Liberty Bell Press, 1964), p. 210.

10. John Toland, *Infamy: Pearl Harbor and Its Aftermath* (New York: Berkley Books, 1983); and John Howland Snow, *The Case of Tyler Kent* (New Canaan, Conn.: The Long House, 1946).

11. Winston S. Churchill, *The Second World War, volume III: The Grand Alliance* (Boston: Houghton Mifflin, 1950), p. 21.

12. William Stevenson, *A Man Called Intrepid* (New York: Balantine Books edition, 1976), p. 170. [Note: William Stephenson quoted not same as author Stevenson.]

13. See, for example: Charles Callan Tansill, *Back Door to War, The Roosevelt Foreign Policy, 1933–1941* (Chicago: Henry Regnery, 1952).

14. Stimson diary for October 16, 1941 quoted in Toland, p. 273.

15. Stimson diary for November 25, 1941 quoted in Robert A. Theobald, *The Final Secret of Pearl Harbor* (Old Greenwich, Conn.: Devin-Adair, 1954), p. 76.

16. George Racey Jordan, *From Major Jordan's Diaries* (New York: Harcourt, Brace, 1952).

Chapter 5
The "Second Try" at "World Order"

1. G. Edward Griffin, *The Fearful Master: A Second Look at the United Nations* (Belmont, Mass.: Western Islands, 1964), p. 87.

2. *The Review Of The News*, May 31, 1972, p. 60.

3. "Conferences: Chief Clerk," *Time*, April 16, 1945.

4. "Activities of U.S. Citizens Employed by the UN," Hearings, Senate Committee on the Judiciary, 1952.

5. Gary Allen, "Stop the Bank Gang," *American Opinion*, February 1979, p. 12.

Chapter 6
The "Third Try" at "World Order"

1. U.S. Senator Robert Taft, quoted by Representative James B. Utt, *Congressional Record House*, January 15, 1962.
2. "Excerpts from Clinton's Speech on Foreign Policy Leadership," *New York Times*, August 14, 1992.
3. *New York Times* editorials: "The New World Army," March 6, 1992; "The Unsung New World Army," May 11, 1992; "Help the U.N. Arm for Peace," November 27, 1992. Also: Paul Lewis, "U.N. Chief Asks for Armed Force to Serve as a Permanent Deterrent," *New York Times*, June 19, 1992.
4. Senator Trent Lott, *Congressional Record*, October 5, 1993, p. S13043.
5. President Clinton's Millennium Summit Address, September 6, 2000.
6. Frank A. Capell, *The Review Of The News*, August 21, 1974.
7. Harland Cleveland, *The Third Try at World Order: U.S. Policy for an Interdependent World* (New York, Aspen Institute for Humanistic Studies, 1977), p. 3.
8. Ibid., pp. 8, 9.
9. Richard Cobden quoted in Robert Welch, *The Blue Book of The John Birch Society* (Belmont, Mass.: Western Islands, 1959), p. 150.
10. Michelle Nichols and Catherine Bremer. "Hotel maid to testify, IMF chief pressured to quit," Reuters, May 18, 2011.
11. "The Testimony of the Honorable William J. (sic) Middendorf II On The United Nations Convention on the Law of the Sea Before The Senate Armed Services Committee," April 8, 2004," http://armed-services.senate.gov/statemnt/2004/April/Middendorf.pdf
12. 1970s speech recounted in Robert Muller, *New Genesis: Shaping a Global Spirituality* (Garden City, New York: Doubleday, 1984), pp. 27–28.
13. Ibid., pp. 29–30.
14. Harlan Cleveland, "The United Nations: Its Future is its Funding," *Futures*, March 1995, reprinted in Harlan Cleveland, Hazel Henderson, Inge Kaul, editors, *The United Nations: Policy and Financing Alternatives: Innovative Proposals by Visionary Leaders* (Washington, D.C.: The Global Commission to Fund the United Nations, 1996), p. 109.
15. Ibid., p. 110.
16. Ibid., p. 111.

Chapter 7
Progressive Regionalization

1. The 1995 State of the World Forum sponsored by the Gorbachev Foundation was held at the Fairmont Hotel in San Francisco. Brzezinski's September 28 audiotaped remarks were published in "Global Gorby," *The New American*, October 30, 1995.

2. Laurence H. Shoup and William Minter, *Imperial Brain Trust: The Council on Foreign Relations and United States Foreign Policy* (New York: Author's Choice Press, 1977), p. 35.
3. "Marshall's True Legacy," *The New American*, August 4, 1997.
4. Hilaire du Berrier, "A Union in Disunity," *The New American*, May 26, 1997, quoting Evangeline (Mrs. David K. E.) Bruce. See also, Nelson D. Lankford, *The Last American Aristocrat: The Biography of Ambassador David K.E. Bruce*, 1898–1977 (New York: Little, Brown and Co., 1996), p. 6.
5. Antony C. Sutton and Patrick M. Wood, *Trilaterals Over Washington*, Vol. II (Scottsdale, Arizona: The August Corporation, 1981), p. 112.
6. Ambrose Evans-Pritchard, "Euro-federalists financed by US spy chiefs," *The Telegraph*, September 19, 2000.
7. Ernst H. van der Beugel, *From Marshall Aid to Atlantic Partnership: European Integration as a Concern of American Foreign Policy* (Amsterdam, London, New York: Elsevier Publishing Co., 1966), p. 323.
8. Michael J. Hogan, *The Marshall Plan: America, Britain, and the reconstruction of Western Europe, 1947–1952* (Cambridge University Press, 1987). Professor Hogan identified "four agencies [that] played an important role in shaping and promoting the ERP [European Recovery (Marshall) Plan]." The four were the Council on Foreign Relations (CFR), the Business Advisory Council (BAC), the Committee for Economic Development (CED), and the National Planning Association (NPA) (pp. 97, 98). "The result," wrote Hogan, "was something like a coordinated campaign mounted by an interlocking directorate of public and private figures. Of the nineteen people on the executive board of the Marshall Plan Committee, eight were members of the CFR and two of these were also members of the BAC, CED, or NPA" (p. 98).
9. See, for example, Lord Bruce of Donington, *International Currency Review*, Vol. 23, No. 3, Summer 1996, p. 21.
10. Peregrine Worsthorne, "When Democracy Betrays the Peoples," London's *Sunday Telegraph*, August 4, 1991.
11. Christopher Booker and Richard North, *The Great Deception: A Secret History of the European Union* (London, New York: Continuum, 2003), pp. 430, 431.
12. Christopher Booker, "Britain and Europe: The Culture of Deceit," speech to the Bruges Group [a UK-based think tank], October 4, 2001.
13. *European Movement and the Council of Europe* with forewords by Winston S. Churchill and Paul-Henri Spaak, published on behalf of the European Movement (London, New York: Hutchinson & Co, 1958), p. 48. For Monnet's hand, see the *HduB Reports*, April 1972, p. 2. Also, "United States of Europe," *The New American*, April 10, 1989.
14. Roger Cohen, "A European Identity: Nation-State Losing Ground," *New York Times*, January 14, 2000.
15. "European Court ruling bans corporal punishment of UK children," *The Guardian*, Wednesday, September 23, 1998.
16. Philip Shishkin, "Tough Tactics: European Regulators Spark Controversy With 'Dawn Raids,'" *Wall Street Journal*, March 1, 2002.
17. Booker, "Britain and Europe."

18. Editorial, "Mr. Gingrich's False Alarm on Trade," *New York Times*, May 8, 1994.
19. David Rockefeller, "A Hemisphere in the Balance," *Wall Street Journal*, October 1, 1993.
20. M. Delal Baer, "North American Free Trade, *Foreign Affairs*, Fall 1991. Baer (CFR) was director and senior fellow of the Mexico Project at the Center for Strategic and International Studies, a CFR-aligned think tank in Washington, DC.
21. "The World Trade Organization," Hearing Before the Committee on Ways and Means, House of Representatives, 103rd Congress, 2nd Session, June 10, 1994, Serial 103-86, p. 131.
22. "Insider Report," *The New American*, January 23, 1995.
23. "Insider Report," *The New American*, February 6, 1995. Also, Steven Greenhouse, "Trade Talks in Miami: Momentum Isn't There," *New York Times*, December 1, 1994.
24. Anthony DePalma, "Talks Tie Trade In the Americas To Democracy," *New York Times*, April 23, 2001.
25. "President Announces Step to Expand Trade & Create Jobs," Remarks by the President to the World Affairs Council National Conferenceand Organization of American States,Washington, D.C., January 16, 2002, http://georgewbush-whitehouse.archives.gov/news/releases/2002/01/20020116-13.html
26. Jonathan Weisman, "Administration Trying to Build CAFTA Majority Vote by Vote; Clash in House With Democrats Takes on Added Status," *Washington Post*, July 21, 2005.
27. Edmund L. Andrews, "How Cafta Passed House by 2 Votes," *New York Times*, July 29, 2005.
28. Adam Liptak, "Review of U.S. Rulings by Nafta Tribunals Stirs Worries," *New York Times*, April 18, 2004.

Chapter 8
Post-Cold War Pretexts

1. Lincoln P. Bloomfield, Study Memorandum No. 7, *A World Effectively Controlled By the United Nations*, Institute for Defense Analyses (State Department contract No. SCC 28270, February 24, 1961), delivered March 10, 1962, Chapter III: Assumptions.
2. Ibid., Chapter III and Chapter V: Principal Problems in Achieving a World Order.
3. Gladwin Hill, "'Environmental Crisis' May Eclipse Vietnam as College Issue," *New York Times*, November 30, 1969.
4. "The Greatest Sham on Earth," *The New American*, March 26, 1990.
5. Norman Cousins, abstracts from two addresses delivered on Earth Day, April 22, 1970 published as "Managing the Planet," in *Earth Day — The Beginning* (New York: Arno Press & The New York Times, 1970), p. 242.
6. "Ruining America to Build China," *The New American*, November 29, 2004.
7. Gary Allen, "Swindle, Treason, and Dodge," *American Opinion*, November 1969.

8. Steve Milloy, *Green Hell: How Environmentalists Plan to Control Your Life and What You Can Do to Stop Them* (Washington, D.C.: Regnery, 2009), p. 4.
9. Ibid.
10. "Behind the Environmental Lobby," *The New American*, April 4, 2005.
11. Gerald O. Barney, editor, *The Unfinished Agenda: The Citizen's Policy Guide to Environmental Issues: A Task Force Report Sponsored by the Rockefeller Brothers Fund* (New York: Thomas Y. Crowell Co., 1977), p. 155.
12. Laurence Rockefeller, "The Case for a Simpler Life-Style," *Reader's Digest*, February 1976.
13. Barney, editor, pp. 15, 66.
14. Amory Lovins, "Energy Strategy: The Road Not Taken," *Foreign Affairs*, October 1976.
15. See, for example, statement of Barbara Link, president of the National Environmental Education and Training Foundation, meeting of the Environmental Grantmakers Association in 1992, Session 17: "Environmental Education K-12," as reported in. "Behind the Environmental Lobby," *The New American*, April 4, 2005.
16. The Report of United Nations World Commission on Environment and Development (also known as the Brundtland Report) was published as *Our Common Future* (New York: Oxford University Press, 1987).
17. "The Greatest Sham on Earth," *The New American*, March 26, 1990.
18. George F. Kennan, "This is No Time for Talk of German Reunification," *Washington Post*, November 12, 1989.
19. Gorbachev speech, "The River of Time and the Necessity of Action," Fulton, Missouri, May 6, 1992.
20. Eric Harrison, "Gorbachev Backs World Government," *Los Angeles Times*, May 7, 1992.
21. Maurice Strong, foreword to Julian Burger, *Gaia Atlas of First Peoples: A Future for the Indigenous World* (New York: Anchor [DoubleDay], 1990).
22. William K. Stevens, "Lessons of Rio: A New Prominence and an Effective Blandness," *New York Times*, June 14, 1992.
23. Dixy Lee Ray, *Environmental Overkill: Whatever Happened to Common Sense?* (Washington, D.C.: Regnery Gateway, 1993), p. 10.
24. Ibid., p. 205.
25. Arnold Kunzli and Karl Marx, *Eine Psychographie* (Wien, Frankfurt, Zurich: Europe Verlag, 1966), pp. 703, 712, 715, quoted in Ray S. Cline and Yonah Alexander, *Terrorism: The Soviet Connection* (New York: Taylor & Francis, 1984), p. 9.
26. Claire Sterling, *The Terror Network: The Secret War of International Terrorism* (New York: Holt, Rinehart and Winston and Reader's Digest Press, 1981), p 14. Sterling takes quote from Stefan Possony and Frances Bouchey, *International Terrorism — The Communist Connection* (Washington: American Council for World Freedom, 1978), p. 47.
27. Ibid., pp. 249–50.
28. Ibid., p. 286.
29. James J. Drummey, "The Terror Conspiracy," *The New American*, February 27, 1989.

30. Sterling, p. 286.
31. Drummey.
32. Donald H. Rumsfeld, "A New Kind of War," *New York Times*, September 27, 2001.
33. The National Lawyers Guild was cited as "the foremost legal bulwark of the Communist Party, its front organizations, and controlled unions" by the House Committee on Un-American Activities in *Guide to Subversive Organizations and Publications* (Washington D.C.: U.S. Government Printing Office, 1950), p. 121.

Chapter 9
CFR Dominance:
Truman, Eisenhower & Kennedy/Johnson Administrations

1. Carroll Quigley, *Tragedy and Hope: A History of the World In Our Time* (New York: Macmillan, 1966), pp. 1247–48.]
2. Ibid., p. 1248.
3. Walter Isaacson and Evan Thomas, *The Wise Men: Six Friends and the World They Made* (New York: Simon and Schuster, 1986), p. 22.
4. Ibid., pp. 100–101.
5. Ibid., p. 20.
6. M. Stanton Evans, *The Politics of Surrender* (New York: Devin-Adair, 1966), p. 340.
7. Isaacson and Thomas, p. 21.
8. Arthur M. Schlesinger Jr., *A Thousand Days: John F. Kennedy in the White House* (Boston: Houghton Mifflin, 1965), p. 128.
9. Freda Utley, *The China Story* (Chicago: Regnery, 1951), p. 13.
10. Senator Joseph R. McCarthy, *America's Retreat From Victory: The Story of Joseph Catlett Marshall* (New York, Devin-Adair, 1951), p. 90.
11. Rep. John F. Kennedy speech at Salem, Massachusetts, January 30, 1949, quoted in James MacGregor Burns, *John Kennedy: A Political Profile* (New York: Harcourt, Brace & World, 1961), p. 80.
12. "Institute of Pacific Relations," Report of the (Senate) Committee on the Judiciary, Eighty-Second Congress, Second Session, Hearings held July 25, 1951 — June 20, 1952 by the Internal Security Subcommittee (Washington, D.C.: U.S. Government Printing Office, 1952: ordered to be printed: July 2 [legislative day June 27]), p. 223, quoted in William P. Hoar, "Guilty as Charged," *The New American*, January 11, 1993.
13. Quigley, pp. 946, 947.
14. Ibid., p. 954.
15. R.J. Rummel, *Death by Government* (New Brunswick, N.J.: Transaction Publishers, 1994), pp. 98, 99 in 2008 paperback.
16. David Rockefeller, "From A China Traveler," *New York Times*, August 10, 1973.
17. Robert Welch, Jr., *The Life of John Birch: In the Story of One American Boy, the Ordeal of His Age* (Chicago: Henry Regnery, 1954), p. 80.

18. Charles A. Willoughby and John Chamberlain, *MacArthur, 1941–1951* (New York: McGraw-Hill, 1954), p. 402.

19. Douglas MacArthur, *Reminiscences* (New York: McGraw-Hill, 1964), p. 375.

20. Mark W. Clark, *From the Danube to the Yalu* (New York: Harper & Bros., 1954), p. 315.

21. Adlai E. Stevenson, "Korea in Perspective," *Foreign Affairs*, April 1952, p. 360.

22. Oswaldo Aranha, "Regional Systems and the Future of U.N.," *Foreign Affairs*, April 1948, p. 420.

23. See, for example, Roberta Ducci, "The World Order in the Sixties," *Foreign Affairs*, April 1964, pp. 389–90.

24. Welch, *The Politician: A look at the political forces that propelled Dwight David Eisenhower into the Presidency* (Appleton, Wis.: Robert Welch University Press, 2002).

25. Rosalie M. Gordon, *Nine Men Against America: The Supreme Court and Its Attack on American Liberties* (New York: Devin-Adair, 1958), pp. 73-74. Summarizes Frank Hanighen in *Human Events*, January 6, 1958.

26. Ibid., pp. 97–100

27. Rose L. Martin, *Fabian Freeway: High Road to Socialism in the U.S.A. 1884–1966* (Boston: Western Islands, 1966), p. 402.

28. Welch, *The Politician*, p. 109. See also: "21 in House Back GOP's Ideas," *Los Angeles Times*, July 4, 1950, p. 11.

29. Ibid. (Welch).

30. Ibid. and quoting Biddle from J. C. Phillips, *Borger* (Texas) *News-Herald*, *circa* October 1954.

31. Martin, p. 402.

32. For further information on Republican Advance, see George F. Hobart, "Liberal Republicans Look To '64," *National Review*, September 25, 1962, pages 227–229; Remarks of Senator Pat McCarran, *Congressional Record*, Eighty-Third Congress, Second Session, page 14337; and, J. C. Phillips, *Borger* (Texas) *News-Herald*, *circa* October 1954.

33. Welch, *The Politician*, pp. 7, 8.

34. Ibid., p. 36.

35. Dwight D. Eisenhower, *Crusade In Europe* (Garden City: Permabooks, 1952 [originally published by Doubleday in 1948]), pp. 437–440.

36. See, for example, Julius Epstein, *Operation Keelhaul* (Old Greenwich, Conn.: Devin-Adair, 1973) and Nicholas Bethell, *The Last Secret* (New York: Basic Books, 1974).

37. Stephen E. Ambrose, *Eisenhower* (New York: Simon and Schuster, 1983), Vol. I, p. 437.

38. John Foster Dulles, *War or Peace* (New York: Macmillan, 1950), p. 40, quoted by Robert W. Lee, *The United Nations Conspiracy* (Belmont, Mass.: Western Islands, 1981), p. 141.

39. "American Malvern," *Time* magazine, March 16, 1942.

40. Ibid.

41. Christian Herter, *Toward an Atlantic Community*, a Council on Foreign Relations Policy Book (New York: Harper & Row, 1963), e.g., pp. 58, 59.

42. Eric Pace, "C. Douglas Dillon Dies at 93; Was in Kennedy Cabinet," *New York Times*, January 12, 2003.

43. Representative Michael A. Feighan, *Congressional Record*, August 31, 1960, p. 17407. Also see Vol. 106, p. 18785.

44. "Protest Over Berlin," *New York Times*, August 16, 1961.

45. *New York Times*, February 24, 1957, p. 34.

46. Earl E.T. Smith, *New York Times*, September 26, 1979, p. A24. See also Smith, *The Fourth Floor* (New York: Random House, 1962), pp. 169–74.

47. *Harvard Times-Republican*, April 18, 1957. *The Harvard Times-Republican* was a newspaper published by the Harvard College Republican Club. Also quoted in the *Congressional Record*, April 17, 1958, p. A-3080.

48. Gary Allen, "The Radicals Are After Your Children," *American Opinion*, May 1971.

49. John B. Medaris, *Countdown for Decision* (New York: Putnam, 1960), pp. 120, 155.

50. Rene A. Wormser, *Foundations: Their Power and Influence* (New York: Devin-Adair, 1958), p. 349.

51. Ambrose, Vol. 2, p. 57.

52. J. Anthony Lukas, "The Council on Foreign Relations: Is It a Club? Seminar? Presidium? Invisible Government?" *New York Times Magazine*, November 21, 1971, p. 123.

53. W.H. Lawrence, "McCarthy Hearing Off a Week as Eisenhower Bars Report: President Orders Aides Not to Disclose Details of Top-Level Meeting," *New York Times*, May 18, 1954, p. 1.

54. Schlesinger, Arthur M. Jr., *A Thousand Days: John F. Kennedy in the White House* (Boston: Houghton Mifflin, 1965), p. 590.

55. Ibid., p. 8.

56. Edward R. Annis, M.D., *Code Blue: Health Care in Crisis* (Washington, D.C.: Regnery Gateway, 1993), p. 48.

57. Clifton Brock, *Americans for Democratic Action* (Washington: Public Affairs Press, 1962), p. 18. Quoted in Annis, p. 48.

58. Annis, p. 49.

59. Walter Isaacson and Evan Thomas, *The Wise Men: Six Friends and the World They Made* (New York: Simon and Schuster, 1986), pp. 21, 591–593.

60. Ted Sorensen, *Counselor: A Life at the Edge of History* (New York: Harper, 2008), p. 232.

61. Allen, "Insiders of the Great Conspiracy," *American Opinion*, September 1982.

62. Walt Rostow, *The United States in the World Arena* (New York: Harper & Brothers, 1960), p. 549.

63. Lukas, p. 126.

64. David Halberstam, *The Best and the Brightest* (New York: Random House, 1972), p. 60.

65. *The Pentagon Papers* as published by *The New York Times* (New York: Bantam Books, 1971), p. 158. See also General Maxwell D. Taylor, *Swords and Plowshares* (New York: W.W. Norton, 1972), p. 401.

66. *The Politician*, p. 274.

67. "FTAA: Welcome Mat for Terrorists," *The New American*, December 19, 2003.
68. Robert W. Lee, "How *American Opinion* Magazine Has Been on Target," *American Opinion*, March 1984.
69. William P. Hoar, "A Retrospective on Lyndon Baines Johnson," *American Opinion*, April 1982.
70. Robert A. Caro, *The Years of Lyndon Johnson (Vol. II): The Means of Ascent* (New York: Vintage Books, 1991), p. xxix.
71. Hoar.
72. Jamie McIntyre CNN Military Affairs Correspondent and Jim Barnett CNN Producer, "The story behind LBJ's Silver Star: Merits of late president's wartime record still debated," Copyright 2003 Cable News Network LP, LLLP.
73. J. Evetts Haley, *A Texan Looks at Lyndon: A Study in Illegitimate Power* (Canyon, Texas: Palo Duro Press, 1964), p. 42.
74. Caro, *The Years of Lyndon Johnson (Vol. I): The Path to Power* (New York: Alfred A. Knopf, 1982). p. xix.
75. Eric F. Goldman, *The Tragedy Of Lyndon Johnson* (New York: Knopf, 1969), p. 83.
76. See Estes vs. Texas, 381 U.S. 532 (1965).
77. Caro, *Atlantic Monthly*, October 1981 (excerpt from forthcoming *The Years of Lyndon Johnson (Vol. I): The Path to Power*).
78. James Perloff, *The Shadows of Power: The Council on Foreign Relations and the American Decline* (Belmont, Mass.: Western Islands, 1988), p. 131.
79. Hans Sennholz, "Great Society: The Everything Deal," *American Opinion*, February 1965.
80. Sennholz, "Great Society: After Us the Deluge," *American Opinion*, April 1966.
81. The *Arizona Republic* quoted in ibid.
82. William Kling, "Thomas Hails Johnson, Raps Goldwater," *Chicago Tribune*, May 30, 1964.
83. Admiral Chester Ward, "McNamara: Burnham Dared Call It Reason," *American Opinion*, May 1967. Also, Gary Allen, "The Unelected: How Do We Move Left From Here," *American Opinion*, June 1968.
84. *U.S. News & World Report*, October 10, 1966.
85. Ward.
86. Declassified rules of engagement, *Congressional Record*, March 6, 14, and 18, 1985.
87. Emerson's remarks paraphrased by Dr. Pham Kim Vinh in "Heroes of Vietnam," *The New American*, February 24, 1986. Also, published in *Human Events*, May 18, 1985. See also R.D. "Patrick" Mahoney, "The Tragedy of Southeast Asia," *The New American*, February 1, 1988.
88. Chesly Manly, "U.S.-Red Bloc Links Questioned," *Chicago Tribune*, December 26, 1966, quoting dispatch from Stettin, Poland, in the Oct. 1 issue of *Die Pomersche Zeitung* of Hamburg.
89. Wallis W. Wood, "While Brave Men Die," *American Opinion*, June 1967.

Chapter 10
CFR Dominance:
Nixon, Ford & Carter Administrations

1.   Edith Kermit Roosevelt, "Elite Clique Hold Power in U.S.," *Indianapolis News*, 12-23-61.
2.   J. Robert Moskin, "Advise and Dissent," *Town & Country*, March 1987, p. 156. See also: Gary Allen, *Richard Nixon: The Man Behind the Mask* (Boston, Mass: Western Islands, 1971); Allen, *Nixon's Palace Guard* (Boston, Mass: Western Islands, 1971); and Allen, *Kissinger: The Secret Side of the Secretary of State* (Seal Beach, Calif.: '76 Press, 1976).
3.   Roscoe and Geoffrey Drummond, "President Proves Himself To Be A Liberal-In-Action ..." *Indianapolis News*, January 22, 1969, p. 17.
4.   John Kenneth Galbraith, "Richard Nixon and the Great Socialist Revival," *New York* magazine, September 21, 1970.
5.   James Reston, "Uniquack on the Nixon Budget," *New York Times*, 1-31-1971.
6.   *Battle Line*, February 1970, quoted in Gary Allen, *Richard Nixon: The Man Behind the Mask* (Belmont, Mass.: Western Islands, 1971), p. 1.
7.   William Safire, "To Pay Paul," *New York Times*, May 16, 1983.
8.   Kirk Kidwell, "American POWs Still Languish in Southeast Asia," *The New American*, February 2, 1987. See also: Alan Stang, "Code: Why Reparations Are Unthinkable," *American Opinion*, June 1973.
9.   "The Review of the News," *JBS Bulletin*, September 1982. Also: Gary Allen, "Trade Trap," *American Opinion*, November 1980; and Allen, "Ten Years Later Many Americans Are Calling it Conspiracy (Part II)," *American Opinion*, April 1983. See also "Suppressed Testimony of Antony C. Sutton," *The Review of the News*, circa September 1982.
10. Antony C. Sutton, *Western Technology and Soviet Economic Development 1917 to 1930* (Volume I) (Stanford University, Stanford, Calif.: Hoover Institution Press, 1968); Sutton, *Western Technology and Soviet Economic Development 1930 to 1945* (Second volume of a three-volume series) (Stanford University, Stanford, Calif.: Hoover Institution Press, 1971); Sutton, *Western Technology and Soviet Economic Development 1945 to 1965* (Third volume of a three-volume series) (Stanford University, Stanford, Calif.: Hoover Institution Press, 1973).
11. Sutton, *National Suicide: Military Aid to the Soviet Union* (New Rochelle, New York: Arlington House, 1973), p. 253.
12. Ibid., p. 258.
13. Senator William Armstrong (R-Colo.), "Technology Transfer: Selling the Soviets the Rope," speech to U.S. Senate, *Congressional Record*, April 13, 1982, pp. S3386-89.
14. Ibid.
15. Gerald Ford televised remarks following Nixon resignation speech, August 8, 1974 (ABC News video available on web at http://abcnews.go.com/Archives/video/aug-1974-ford-president-10549853).
16. The National Lawyers Guild was cited as "the foremost legal bulwark of the Communist Party, its front organizations, and controlled unions" by the House

Committee on Un-American Activities in *Guide to Subversive Organizations and Publications* (Washington D.C.: U.S. Government Printing Office, 1950), p. 121.

17. Victor Lasky, *Jimmy Carter: The Man and the Myth* (New York: Richard Marek, 1979), pp. 159–160.

18. Barry M. Goldwater, *With No Apologies* (New York: William Morrow, 1979), p. 286.

19. Zbigniew Brzezinski, "America and Europe," *Foreign Affairs*, October 1970, p. 29.

20. Brzezinski, *Between Two Ages: America's Role in the Technotronic Era* (New York: Viking, 1970), p. 308.

21. Ibid., p. 72.

22. Goldwater, pp. 284-85.

23. Kenneth Reich, "Carter Urges Stronger U.S. Ties to Other Democracies," *Los Angeles Times*, June 24, 1976, Part I, p. 12.

24. Gore Vidal, *Imperial America: Reflections on the United States of Amnesia* (New York: Nation Books, 2004), p. 104.

25. Jimmy Carter speech in Boston on February 17, 1976 quoted in Robert C. Turner, *I'll Never Lie to You: Jimmy Carter in his Own Words* (New York: Ballantine Books, 1976), p. 48.

26. Lasky, p. 161; Walter Isaacson and Evan Thomas, *The Wise Men* (New York: Simon and Schuster, 1986), p. 726.

27. Brzezinski, *Power and Principle: Memoirs of the National Security Adviser*, 1977–1981 (New York: Farrar, Straus, Giroux, 1983), p. 289.

28. Gary Allen, "The Background and Record of Jimmy Carter," *American Opinion*, October 1980.

29. John Rees, "The Disastrous Foreign Policy of Jimmy Carter," *American Opinion*, May 1980.

30. "The Transition: Vance and Lance: The Selection Begins," *Time*, December 13, 1976.

31. Transcripts of taped conversations with Carter officials were published in *Nicaragua Betrayed*, written by motion picture producer Jack Cox based on extensive interviews of Somoza (Belmont, Mass.: Western Islands, 1980).

32. "Introduction to the Palace Guard," *The New American*, February 22, 1993.

33. Somoza, p. 401.

34. "The Panama Canal Giveaway," *The New American*, June 21, 1999.

35. Jane H. Ingraham, "Panama Canal Giveaway: The Final Countdown," *The New American*, May 15, 1995.

36. Jimmy Carter, *Keeping Faith: Memoirs of a President* (New York: Bantam Books, 1982), p. 173.

37. Ibid., Chapter 1, fn. 19, p. 178.

38. "The Battle, Blow by Blow," *Time*, October 18, 1976, pp. 17, 18.

39. Dan Smoot, "On The Created Energy Crisis," *The Review of the News*, November 28, 1973. Also see Gary Allen, *Tax Target: Washington* (Seal Beach, Calif.: '76 Press, 1978), Chapter 9.

40. Edward Cowan, "ENERGY CHIEF WARNS COMFORT WILL DROP AND PRICES WILL RISE; 65-DEGREE HOMES FORECAST: O'Leary Says

Policy Will Include Change in Driving Habits; Rise in Gasoline Cost Is Hinted," *New York Times*, February 14, 1977.

41. Alan Stang, "The Carter Energy Act," *American Opinion*, October 1977.

42. Robert Young, "U.S. slips to No. 3 in production of oil," *Chicago Tribune*, March 25, 1979, p. 16.

43. "What Baby DOE Will Cost," *Wall Street Journal*, June 1, 1977, p. 16.

44. William Z. Foster, *Toward Soviet America: The Book the Communists Tried to Destroy* (originally published in 1932), foreword by Francis E. Walter.

Chapter 11
CFR Dominance:
Reagan, Bush, & Clinton Administrations

1. Gary Allen, "Conservatives are dubious about the Christmas Waltz: Ronald Reagan," *American Opinion*, December 1982.

2. Alan Stang, "Schweiker at Welfare," *American Opinion*, February 1981.

3. Tom Wicker, "Razzle Dazzlin' 'em," *New York Times*, July 27, 1976.

4. Stang.

5. James Perloff, *The Shadows of Power: The Council on Foreign Relations and the American Decline* (Boston: Western Islands, 1988), p. 168.

6. Antony C. Sutton, *The Best Enemy Money Can Buy* (Billings, Montana: Liberty House Press, 1986), p. 25.

7. Allen, "Regan at Treasury," *American Opinion*, February 1981. Also see: Hedrick Smith, "Staunch Conservatives Opposed Choice of Regan for the Treasury," *New York Times*, December 13, 1980.

8. Allen, "The Republican Convention and Ronald Reagan," *American Opinion*, September 1980.

9. Presidential Determination No. 82-19, August 30, 1982.

10. Lester Thurow, *Newsweek*, January 23, 1984, p. 49.

11. David Nelson Rowe, *The Carter China Policy: Results and Prospects* (1980), p. 10.

12. Robert W. Lee, "The Candidacy of George Bush" *The New American*, January 18, 1988.

13. UN Security Council transcript, January 31, 1992.

14. Presidential announcement, June 22, 1989.

15. *Monitor's* editorial board, "It's bipartisan: Barack Obama and George H.W. Bush agree on community service," *Christian Science Monitor*, October 16, 2009.

16. Ibid.

17. Bob Davis, "White House, Reversing Policy under Pressure, Begins to Pick High-Tech Winners and Losers," *Wall Street Journal*, May 13, 1991.

18. President Bush and bipartisan budget committee announced agreement in a televised ceremony at the White House Rose Garden on September 30, 1990. Note: President Bush defended the agreement on national television on October 2, 1990. See also: "The Budget Battle; Countdown to Crisis: Reaching a 1991 Budget Agreement," *New York Times*, October 9, 1990.

19. "A New Domestic Order — the President's Budget," *The New American*, April 23, 1991.

20. Jeffrey H. Birnbaum, "Clinton Received a Vietnam Draft Deferment for an ROTC Program That He Never Joined," *Wall Street Journal*, February 6, 1992.

21. Mr. Clinton's letter to Colonel Eugene Holmes, *Congressional Record*, July 30, 1992, pp. H7051–52.

22. Affidavit by Colonel Eugene Holmes, *Congressional Record*, September 17, 1992, p. H8720.

23. Father Richard McSorley, *Peace Eyes* (Washington, D.C.: Center for Peace Studies, Georgetown University, 1978).

24. Floyd G. Brown, *"Slick Willie": Why America Cannot Trust Bill Clinton* (Annapolis, Maryland: Annapolis-Washington Book Publishers, 1992).

25. Martin Carnoy and Derek Shearer, *Economic Democracy: The Challenge of the 1980s* (White Plains, N.Y.: M. E. Sharpe, 1980).

26. S. Steven Powell, Ph.D., *Covert Cadre: Inside the Institute for Policy Studies*, (Ottawa, Illinois: Green Hill Publishers, Inc., 1987), p. 200.

27. Edward Timperlake and William C. Triplett II, *Year of the Rat: How Bill Clinton Compromised U.S. Security for Chinese Cash* (Washington, DC: Regnery Publishing, 1998).

28. Ibid., p. 2.

29. Ibid., p. 43.

30. Warren Christopher remarks at December 28, 1993 news conference in Los Angeles. See U.S. Department of State Dispatch, Volume 5, Number 1, January 3, 1994 (Bureau of Public Affairs); also Marc Lacey, "Talbott Selected for No. 2 Post at State Dept," *Los Angeles Times*, December 29, 1998.

31. Al Gore, *Earth in the Balance: Ecology and the Human Spirit* (New York: Houghton Mifflin, 1992), pp. 305–360.

32. Gwen Ifill, "Clinton Recruits 3 Presidents to Promote Trade Pact," *New York Times*, September 14, 1993. (Nixon and Reagan indicated their support for the pact, but could not attend Washington ceremony.) Re letter of NAFTA endorsement from five presidents to each representative see: Douglas Jehl, "The Free Trade Accord: The Overview; Scramble in the Capital for Today's Trade Pact Vote," *New York Times*, November 17, 1993.

33. Adam Clymer, "Clinton's Health Plan; Hillary Clinton Raises Tough Questions of Life, Death and Medicine," *New York Times*, October 1, 1993.

34. Michael R. Gordon, "U.S. Opposes Move to Rapidly Expand NATO Membership," *New York Times*, January 2, 1994. Also: "95/05/19 Fact Sheet: NATO Partnership for Peace," U.S. Department of State (Bureau of Public Affairs).

35. Francine Kiefer, "Clintonian 'tyranny' rankles Hill," *Christian Science Monitor*, November 9, 1999.

Chapter 12
Organized Subversion at Home

1. William H. McIlhany, II, *The Tax-Exempt Foundations* (Westport, Conn., Arlington House, 1980), p. 61.

2. Ibid.
3. Ibid., p. 62, drawing on C. Harley Gratten, "The Historians Cut Loose," *American Mercury* (August, 1927), reprinted in Harry Elmer Barnes, *In Quest of Truth and Justice, De-Bunking the War Guilt Myth* (New York: Arno Press & the *New York Times*, 1972), pp. 142–64 (originally, Chicago: National Historical Society, 1928).
4. Charles Beard, "Who's to Write the History of the War?" *Saturday Evening Post*, October 4, 1947, p. 172.
5. Harry Elmer Barnes, ed., *Perpetual War for Perpetual Peace* (Caldwell, Idaho: Caxton, 1953), pp. 15, 16, 18.
6. Carroll Quigley, *Tragedy and Hope: A History of the World In Our Time* (New York: Macmillan, 1966), p. 937.
7. *Congressional Record*, February 9, 1917, Volume 54, pp. 2947–48.
8. Gary Allen, "The Media: A Look at Establishment Newspapers," *American Opinion*, September 1970.
9. Herman H. Dinsmore, All *the News That Fits: A Critical Analysis of the News and Editorial Content of The New York Times* (New Rochelle, NY: Arlington House, 1969).
10. Dinsmore, *The Bleeding of America* (Belmont, Mass.: Western Islands, 1974).
11. Schlesinger, Arthur M. Jr., *A Thousand Days: John F. Kennedy in the White House* (Boston: Houghton Mifflin, 1965), p. 128.
12. Sydney H. Schanberg, "Communist Rule Is at Least Uncertain; Napalm is Not; Indochina Without Americans: For Most, a Better Life," *New York Times*, April 13, 1975.
13. Peter Brimelow, *Alien Nation: Common Sense About America's Immigration Disaster*, Harper Perennial edition (New York: Harper Collins, 1996), afterword, p. 293.
14. Robert L. Bartley, "Open Nafta Borders? Why Not?" *Wall Street Journal*, July 2, 2001.
15. Allen, "A Look at Establishment Newspapers," *American Opinion*, September 1970.
16. William Safire, "Citizen of the World," *New York Times*, May 16, 1985.
17. Franklin Foer, *The New Republic*, May 8, 2000.
18. *Newsweek* quoted in "Out-FOXing Conservatives," *The New American*, June 18, 2001. See also, David M. Alpern "What Makes Rupert Run?" *Newsweek*, March 12, 1984.
19. "Behind the Bias," *The New American*, February 10, 2003.

Chapter 13
Mobilizing the Attack Forces

1. Fifteenth Report, California Senate Fact-finding Subcommittee on Un-American Activities, 1970.
2. Rose L. Martin, *Fabian Freeway: High Road to Socialism in the U.S.A. 1884–1966* (Boston: Western Islands, 1966), p. 3 and *The General Election and After*, Fabian Research Series, No. 102 (London, The Fabian Society, 1946).

3. Ibid., p. 110. Quoting from: *The New Britain: The Labour Party's Manifesto for the 1964 General Election* (London: The Labour Party, Transport House, 1964), p. 22.
4. Official Socialist International website (socialistinternational.org), "About Us."
5. Martin, p. 374. Quoting from *The World Today: The Socialist International Perspective* (London: A Socialist International Publication, no date), p. 11.
6. Martin, p. 343.
7. Ibid., p. 4.
8. Ibid., p. 322. Letter reproduced in Kingsley Martin, *Harold Laski: A Biographical Memoir* (New York: The Viking Press, Inc., 1953) on page opposite 135.
9. Carroll Quigley, *Tragedy and Hope: A History of the World In Our Time* (New York: Macmillan, 1966), p. 938.
10. Ibid.
11. Ibid., p. 939.
12. Gary Allen, "Foundations: Swindle, Treason, and Dodge," *American Opinion*, November 1969. See also: Frank Hughes, *Prejudice And The Press*, (New York: Devin-Adair Company, 1950).
13. Walter Lippmann, *A Preface to Politics* (New York, London: M. Kennerley, 1913), p. 307.
14. Graham Wallas, *The Great Society: A Psychological Analysis* (Lincoln, Nebraska: University of Nebraska Press, 1914).
15. Martin, p. 423.
16. Samuel L. Blumenfeld, "Lippmann: Portrait of the Pundit as a Young Man," *American Opinion*, March 1965. Also, William P. Hoar, "The Treaty: Versailles and the League of Nations," *American Opinion*, February 1976.
17. Martin, p. 169.
18. Ibid., p. 172.
19. Mina Weisenberg, *The L.I.D., Fifty Years of Democratic Education, 1905 – 1955* (New York: League for Industrial Democracy).
20. Edward R. Annis, M.D., *Code Blue: Health Care in Crisis* (Washington, D.C.: Regnery Gateway, 1993), pp. 25, 26.
21. Ibid., p. 26.
22. Alan Stang, "Hubert Humphrey and the Battle of Chicago," *American Opinion*, October 1968.
23. Annis, pp. 32, 33.
24. Ibid., pp. 31, 32. See also: Milton and Rose Friedman, *Free to Choose*, Appendix A. "Socialist Platform of 1928" (New York: Avon Books, 1979), p. 229.
25. Francis X. Gannon, *Biographical Dictionary of the Left*, Vol. I. (Boston: Western Islands Publishers, 1969), p. 495.
26. Annis, p. 64.
27. Ibid., p. 69.
28. Ibid., p. 75.
29. Martin, p. 446.
30. Ibid., p. 146. Martin quoted material from: *Forty Years of Education* (New York: League for Industrial Democracy, 1945), pp. 46–47.

31. Martin, p.446, and quoting Lippmann from *LA Times*, May 8, 1966.
32. Samuel L. Blumenfeld, *N.E.A.: Trojan Horse in American Education* (Boise, Idaho: The Paradigm Co., 1984), pp. 61, 62.
33. Ibid., p. 135.
34. Blumenfeld, "Down the Slippery Slope," *The New American*, August 8, 1994.
35. Ibid. See also: Conclusions and Recommendations of the Commission, Report of the Commission on the Social Studies (New York: Charles Scribner's Sons, 1934).
36. Harold Laski, quoted in William P. Hoar, *Architects of Conspiracy: An Intriguing History* (Boston: Western Islands, 1984), p. 72.
37. René A. Wormser, *Foundations, Their Power and Influence* (New York: Devin-Adair, 1958), pp. 142–143.

Chapter 14
CFR Dominance: George W. Bush Administrations

1. Eric Schmitt, "A Cadre of Familiar Foreign Policy Experts Is Putting Its Imprint on Bush," *New York Times*, December 23, 1999.
2. The detailed budget for Fiscal 2002, which Bush submitted in April 2001, called for federal outlays of $1,961 billion in 2002 as compared to $1,856 billion in 2001.
3. George W. Bush, Rose Garden at the White House, July 12, 2001. See *Public Papers of the Presidents of the United States, George W. Bush, 2001, Book 2, July 1 to December 31, 2001* (Washington D.C.: Office of the Federal Register), p. 841.
4. Matthew L. Wald, "Carol M. Browner," *New York Times*, November 26, 2008.
5. President Bush proposed his "Clear Skies Initiative" on February 14, 2002. Introduced in House and Senate on February 27, 2003 as the "Clear Skies Act of 2003."
6. Tina Rosenberg, "What the World Needs Now is DDT," *New York Times*, April 11, 2004.
7. Kelly Patricia O'Meara, "Police State," *Insight on the News*, December 3, 2001.
8. "American Interests and UN Reform: Report of the Task Force on the United Nations" (Washington, D.C.: United States Institute of Peace, 2005), p. 97.

Chapter 15
CFR Dominance: Barak Obama Administration

1. Steve Milloy, *Green Hell: How Environmentalists Plan to Control Your Life and What You Can Do to Stop Them* (Washington, D.C.: Regnery, 2009), pp. 195, 196.
2. NBC's Adrea Mitchell, "Obama Reaches Out to Bush 41 Veteran Scowcroft for Advice," HuffingtonPost.com, November 20, 2008.
3. Stephen Dinan, "Obama's climate czar has socialist ties," *The Washington Times*, January 12, 2009.

4. Jennifer Liberto, "Obama taps Bernanke for second term," CNNMoney.com, August 25, 2009.
5. Michael Grunwald "Why Obama Reappointed Bernanke to the Fed," Time.com, August 25, 2009.
6. Ibid.
7. Liberto.
8. Marjorie Shearon, *Wilbur J. Cohen: The Pursuit of Power, a Bureaucratic Biography* (Washington, D.C.: Gray Printing Co., 1967), p. 6.
9. Ibid., p. 91.
10. Pete Du Pont, "A Worrying Prognosis," *Wall Street Journal*, November 25, 2008.
11. Robert Welch, June 1970 *JBS Bulletin*.
12. Bertrand Russell, *The Impact of Science on Society* (New York: Simon and Schuster, 1953), pp. 29, 30.
13. Betsy McCaughey, "Ruin Your Health With the Obama Stimulus Plan," Bloomberg.com, February 9, 2009.
14. Linda Bergthold, "The Stimulus Bill Will Destroy American Health Care," *Huffington Post*, February 12, 2009.
15. Milloy, p. 37.
16. George F. Will, "Our Fake Drilling Debate," *Washington Post*, December 15, 2005, quoted in Milloy, p. 47.
17. Fareed Zakaria, "[Obama's] Financial plan is good, but not perfect," CNN.com, February 20, 2009.
18. Ibid.
19. For example, Dr. Arthur Robinson, editor of the *Access to Energy* newsletter, organized the Oregon Petition Project protesting the myth of catastrophic man-made global warming. As of 2008, the petition had been signed by over 31,000 American scientists, including more than 9,000 with PhDs! In particular, Frederick Seitz, former president of the U.S. National Academy of Sciences, endorsed the petition. Also, see Lawrence Solomon, *The Deniers: The World Renowned Scientists Who Stood Up Against Global Warming Hysteria, Political Persecution, and Fraud**And those who are too fearful to do so* (Minneapolis, Minn.: Richard Vigilante books, 2008).
20. Joe Konopka, "Climategate puts all global-warming research under a cloud," *Nashua* [New Hampshire] *Telegraph*, December 13, 2009.
21. Al Gore, *Earth in the Balance: Ecology and the Human Spirit* (New York: Houghton Mifflin, 1992)), pp. 325, 326.
22. Steven Mulson, "New Auto Standards vs. Old U.S. Preferences: Mileage Rules to Add to Price, Shrink Engines," *Washington Post*, May 20, 2009.
23. Robert Burns, US begins assault against Libyan air defenses," Yahoo' News (AP), March 19, 2001.
24. *Congressional Quarterly Daily Briefing*, June 15, 2001.

Chapter 16
What Can and *Must* Be Done!

1. Taylor Caldwell, "The Middle Class Must Not Die," *The Review of the*

News, May 29, 1974.

2. Antonio Gramsci, *Prison Notebooks*, Volume I (New York: Columbia University Press, 1992), p. 137.

3. Richard Grenier, *Capturing the Culture* (Washington, D.C.: Ethics and Public Policy Center, 1991), p. xiv.

4. Tom Gow, "The Great American Swindle," (Colorado Springs, Colo.: Freedom First Society, August 2007) posted at http://www.freedomfirstsociety.org/home/index.php/its-a-conspiracy/51-the-great-american-swindle.html

5. See "The Lone Soldier" in Don Fotheringham's *Tangents and Traps: How to Avoid Detours and Dead-ends on the Road to Freedom* (Colorado Springs, Colo.: Freedom First Society, 2010) and your authors' *Organize for Victory!* (Colorado Springs, Colo.: Freedom First Society, 2008).

6. Fotheringham.

7. The 46 Civilian Doctors of Elisabethville, *46 Angry Men* (Belmont, Mass.: American Opinion, 1962), originally published by Dr. T. Vleurinck, 96 Avenue de Broqueville, Bruxelles 15, 1962. See also: Philippa Schuyler, *Who Killed the Congo?* (New York: Devin-Adair, 1962).

8. "Report of the Independent Inquiry Into the Actions of the United Nations During the 1994 Genocide in Rwanda," December 15, 1999, paragraph 2 under II. Description of Key Events, Arusha Peace Agreement. Report posted at www.org/News/ossg/Rwanda_report.htm on 3/17/01.

9. Philip Gourevitch, "we wish to inform you that tomorrow we will be killed with our families" (New York: Picador, 1998), p. 102.

10. General Lewis Walt quoted in "They Paused to Remark," *American Opinion*, September 1979.

11. Walt quoted in "They Paused to Remark," *American Opinion*, September 1981.

12. Robert Welch, *JBS Bulletin*, March 1961.

Recommended Reading

A revisionist history of what has got America in trouble is a big story. In even the preceding lengthy summary, we have necessarily had to ignore many lines of importance and give a condensed treatment to others.

For those who wish to reinforce their understanding of this history and fill in some of the gaps, we include this short starter list of recommended reading. Most of these classics are available inexpensively through the online used-book market.

Annis, Edward R., M.D. *Code Blue: Health Care in Crisis.* Washington, D.C.: Regnery Gateway, 1993.

Blumenfeld, Samuel L. *Is Public Education Necessary?* Idaho: The Paradigm Co., 1981.

— *N.E.A.: Trojan Horse in American Education.* Boise, Idaho: The Paradigm Co., 1984.

Booker, Christopher and Richard North. *The Great Deception: A Secret History of the European Union.* London, New York: Continuum, 2003.

Hoar, William P. *Architects of Conspiracy: An Intriguing History.* Boston: Western Islands, 1984.

Jordan, George Racey. *From Major Jordan's Diaries.* New York: Harcourt, Brace, 1952.

Lane, Arthur Bliss. *I Saw Poland Betrayed: An American Ambassador Reports to the American People.* Americanist Library Edition. Boston: Western Islands, 1965.

Martin, Rose L. *Fabian Freeway: High Road to Socialism in the U.S.A. 1884–1966.* Boston: Western Islands, 1966.

McIlhany, William H., II. *The Tax-Exempt Foundations.* Westport, Conn.: Arlington House, 1980.

Milloy, Steve. *Green Hell: How Environmentalists Plan to Control Your Life and What You Can Do to Stop Them.* Washington, D.C.: Regnery, 2009.

Powell, S. Steven, Ph.D. *Covert Cadre: Inside the Institute for Policy Studies*. Ottawa, Illinois: Green Hill Publishers, Inc., 1987. Note: Heavy reading, but an impressive reference.

Ray, Dixy Lee, Ph.D. *Environmental Overkill: Whatever Happened to Common Sense?* Washington, D.C.: Regnery Gateway, 1993.

Shearon, Marjorie. *Wilbur J. Cohen: The Pursuit of Power, a Bureaucratic Biography*. Washington, D.C.: Gray Printing Co., 1967.

Simpson, Colin. *The Lusitania*. Boston: Little, Brown and Company, 1972.

Somoza, Anastasio as told to Jack Cox. *Nicaragua Betrayed*. Belmont, Mass.: Western Islands, 1980.

Sutton, Antony C. *The Best Enemy Money Can Buy*. Billings, Montana: Liberty House Press, 1986.

Welch, Robert. *Again, May God Forgive Us!* Belmont, Mass.: Belmont Publishing Co., 1971.

— *The Politician: A look at the political forces that propelled Dwight David Eisenhower into the Presidency*. Appleton, Wis.: Robert Welch University Press, 2002.